6 0 2 : Form of Futility

by Harding McRae

© 2015 Harding McRae Press

Print Edition
ISBN 978-0-9858494-4-3

e-Book Edition
ISBN 978-0-9858494-5-0

Please visit:
www.HardingMcRae.com

Other works by Harding McRae:
In The Beginning...
Always/Never

This novel is based on actual persons, places, and events.
Some character names have been changed to protect the identities of the innocent, the guilty, and the incarcerated.

Other names, characters, places, and incidents are either products of the author's imagination or are used fictitiously; any resemblance to real persons, living or dead, is unintentional and coincidental. Trademarks are the property of their respective owners.

All rights reserved, including the right to reproduce this book
or portions thereof in any form whatsoever.
No portion of this book may be stored in an electronic retrieval system
or distributed electronically without the express permission of the author.

Table of Contents

Acknowledgments ... v
Foreword ... vi
Chapter 1: *In My Heart of Hearts* ... 1
Chapter 2: *"He Descended into Hell...."* ... 14
Chapter 3: *Reception and the Road to Redemption* ... 26
Chapter 4: *And In the Fourth Month, He Arose from the Dead* ... 46
Chapter 5: *Drugs, Sex, and Rock 'n Roll* ... 66
Chapter 6: *R. E. S. P. E. C. T.—Find Out What It Means to Me* ... 86
Chapter 7: *Medical Misadventures, Dental Decay* ... 101
Chapter 8: *Bondage and Discipline* ... 115
Chapter 9: *Infection Detection and Other Farces* ... 129
Chapter 10: *Armed Babysitters with Attitude* ... 141
Chapter 11: *Philosophy, Spirituality and Robert* ... 158
Chapter 12: *Day by Day* ... 172
Chapter 13: *The Enemy Within* ... 184
Chapter 14: *It's the Little Things...* ... 199
Chapter 15: *Choices. Choices?* ... 213
Chapter 16: *Outrageous Outrages* ... 229
Chapter 17: *Indignities and Other Ramblings* ... 243
Chapter 18: *Back to the Future?* ... 255
Harding's Photo Album ... 269

Acknowledgments

When one writes a book anonymously, doing so makes acknowledgments difficult. It's fair to ask why I am doing so anonymously. There were, and are, threats against me and my family, even against some of my friends. I am cautious and hesitant about putting them at any risk. It is a crazy world we live in. Throughout my prison time, my family—my wife, father, brothers and sisters, in-laws, and many other extended family members—sustained me.

I am also blessed with incredible friends. They wrote letters and cards, subscribed to magazines and newspapers on my behalf, and visited. Over sixty friends applied for and received visitation permission to trek to the prison facility where I was housed. The trip was at least an hour drive, at a minimum, for most.

My wonderful editor, friend, and confidant, Max, is a rock. He and his wife, Martha, accompanied me spiritually throughout my ordeal.

There are also many fine Correctional Officers and staff. To mention them by name would not benefit their health or mine. There are many who aren't so fine that I'd like to mention by name, but will be charitable instead. Inmates provided me with stories to tell and lessons to relate. They also taught me how to survive in an environment I never dreamed I might one day encounter.

My final counsel is to avoid stereotypes when talking about prison and prisoners; the reality is that little difference exists between the two groups assembled on either side of the thin green line.

Foreword

> *What a piece of work is man!*
> *How noble in reason! How infinite in faculties!*
> *In form and moving, how express and admirable!*
> *In action how like an angel! In apprehension, how like a god!*
> *The beauty of the world! The paragon of animals!*
> *And yet, to me, what is this quintessence of dust?*
>
> —Hamlet,
> William Shakespeare

I'm not sure you're a member of the target audience for *602: Form of Futility*. More accurately, I'm not sure you're ready to tackle this institutional insanity our society has created. But if you are ready to hear about it, will you be ready to do anything in response? I hope you will, but I'm not sure. Quite frankly, I doubt it. Most will simply want to put their heads in the sand and ignore what is one of the most cancerous series of problems *our* society has created. Is this *really* what *we* had in mind?

If you're looking for another *"I was wronged, I got sent to prison"* book, that isn't my purpose. Most of those books are educational at some level, but not uplifting or inspirational. To be that—uplifting or inspirational—is my purpose. *What a piece of work is man!* A man can survive many crises he might predict would cause him to crumble. He might consider suicide or other escapist options. One can be bitter about the hand dealt, even lash out against family and friends . . . and anyone else who just happens to be in the vicinity. There is so much of that in today's world. For a time, I fell down that endless shaft into the abyss of despair and depression. There simply is more to life than that. Before being uplifted, many times we must hit rock bottom. Consider the alternative.

I survived. That is the personal element of this story. I genuinely believed at the outset I would not. Had I not been placed in custody the day of my conviction, I'm not sure I would be here to tell the story. This is a tale of positivism and the value of faith and hope. I believed in God before, but I don't think He'd shown Himself to me prior to prison. He definitely got my attention. I would not have survived without Him and my beliefs have been deepened. Nevertheless, it is not this book's purpose to proselytize. I believe each human being must come to those beliefs in their own personal way.

We humans are fragile. We make mistakes, we make excuses, and we make up stories—anything to avoid responsibility. It falls to an outside, independent agent to assess responsibility. Being human as well, that agent is subject to the same fragility-making mistakes, too, and, when taken as a whole, is called society. Where individual humans are capable of sympathy and other emotions—or not—society at large is not so proficient.

Societal issues are the fabric of this book. Yes, I'm a convicted felon. Society will never forget that and it isn't interested in hearing the details, only the headline. **Guilty!** Throw him away and forget about it. That's not as easy as it sounds. In part, this book is about my personal saga. However, it is also about the larger questions of responsibility, morality, and, frankly, the utter mess our judicial and penal systems have become. That also isn't someone else's responsibility—it's yours, it's mine . . . it's *ours*. Each of us must take ownership of part of it—of each inmate's actions and consequences.

In spite of society's label, I'm different from your average inmate, though I must admit there is no "average" inmate. There is, however, a typical one: poorly educated, with poor communication skills, and other poor skills in general—especially people skills. He isn't necessarily lazy, just unskilled. In fact, there are some darned smart inmates. Unfortunately, many of those who are smart don't know where or how to channel that intelligence. Instead, they join gangs or delve into substance abuse. From a human frailty standpoint, they are not unique; they are subject to the same temptations and weaknesses as any other human. But the way inmates deal with those inducements and the boredom is what separates them from the general public. Yet, I remind you, most will soon *be part of the general public* again. Almost all get out at some point. Wouldn't you like to keep them from going back? Or preventing them from even going there in the first place? The reality is this: most are salvageable.

It is their stories I will use as examples to illustrate the frustrations—systemic, general, and personal. I intend the stories to highlight the issues, but the issues are larger than the stories. Don't even think for a moment that they don't affect you. Are you a taxpayer, a citizen, a homeowner, a business owner? How about a parent, grandparent, or sibling? Trust me, it affects you.

I'll call this style of book, non-fictional fiction. That is, fiction based on reality. Similar to the narrator's introduction to the old TV series, *Dragnet*, the story you are about to read is true, but the names have been changed to protect the *guilty*. Several characters are an amalgam of real people—inmates, correctional officers and staff. This is also *my* story, although not in its entirety. I will not allow this episode to be the defining moment of my life. This "fiction" nevertheless will forever remain a small portion of my life. The rest of my life awaits another book. As Saul Bellows said, "Fiction is the higher autobiography."

So if you're looking for salaciousness, you may find a bit. If it's drama—well—maybe some of that also. Neither are my prime purpose. I hope to celebrate the joy of life, in spite of setbacks that are inevitable in anyone's. I encourage you to realize there is always hope. Humankind can be cruel and cruelly marvelous. How it works out for you depends on whether you choose to make lemonade out of the lemons.

"If you're going to make a statement, don't mumble."

Harding McRae

JANUARY, 2015

This book is dedicated to the four F's.

Chapter 1: *In My Heart of Hearts*

"I remember the day I died."

"Huh?"

"Play a card, old man," Pitr scolded. "Dead people don't play cards. You're playing Hearts with us right now. Not well, but you get it, don't ya?"

"It was November 3, 2009." I threw the ten of Hearts on the table.

"Trump hasn't been broken. You can't lead Hearts," this from a third player at our mixed table of four.

"Did no Pitr *tich jew* no thing?" This from our number two player, *Face*. I couldn't help noticing the perturbed look on his face—the pimpled, scarred countenance of a youngster much too young to be incarcerated and much too young to be talking this way to his "elders."

"That's when I died."

"Pitr, tell your bunkie he's not dead. Just a lousy card player. You can't lead Hearts and you know it," chimed the fourth player. "We're not falling for the same trick you tried on us four years ago."

"You tell him, *Stinky*," the slight-in-stature Pitr Peterovich spewed forth.

"Here we go again. The *I remember back in 2009* story," Stinky groaned.

Yeah, I remembered. Back to the first time—that first meeting of my card-playing group—four years ago. Card-playing therapy group really.

Stinky, Pitr, Face and I started playing Hearts whenever we found a spare moment. I didn't know them then—I don't really know them much better four years later. This first time we played, however, remains etched in my mind. At the time, I had no idea that I would survive four years in here. Looking back, in many ways the time actually passed quickly. I played trump in that first game of Hearts—just like today's game—when trump hadn't been broken. I was trying to play dumb then, to suck them into a trap. *Today* they didn't go for it; Face commenting about Pitr not teaching me anything proves it.

Teach me they did. They all did. My four years was a graduate course in criminology taught by the best instructors in our state. It was also a class in life. They'd heard my stories and I'd heard theirs for four years now. Who are these guys?

Once upon a time, four years ago…

"I remember the day I died."
They all stared at me.
"What is he talking about? Play cards."
"It was November 3, 2009." I threw the ten of Hearts on the table.
"You can't lead trump," this from Pitr Peterovich. Oh, it's pronounced *Pītr*, as in pie, like you eat, and tōr, as in I tore him a new, well . . . *Pitr*.
"You guys asked me to play," I replied timidly. At the time, I had only been here about three months.
"You said you knew how to play," Pitr countered.
"It was November 3, 2009," I repeated, tapping on the ten of Hearts.
"Yeah," Pitr exhaled. "You mentioned that already."

He was so named by his illegal-alien parents on the occasion of his birth in these United States of America, their attempt to give "a better shot at success" to their newborn son—he, a U.S. citizen by virtue of his birth in the State of Jefferson, part of this glorious country of ours. But it seems they had a few problems launching young Pitr on the road to success.

They *meant* to name him Peter, but didn't know how to spell it. Hence, Pitr, this in spite of the fact they chose Peterovich as a last name. Peterovich, pronounced like "Peter" and "ovich." Of course the "long I" in Pitr came later. Once his parents beamed down upon their newborn, the name Peter came immediately to their minds. Since *"i"* is pronounced like the English *"e"* in Spanish, they spelled it, *Pitr*. How they arrived at *Peterovich* remains unknown—maybe a Russian relative from the distant past, who knows? You'd think that since his last name had "Peter" in it, they could figure out his first name.

There were lots of things they couldn't figure out. That's how Jose and Maria Contreras, two Mexican immigrants from Sonora came upon the idea of naming their son Pitr Peterovich. Funny, but Pitr Peterovich's voice had no discernible Hispanic accent. If you closed your eyes, you could actually almost make out a Brooklyn-type accent. What he did have was a chip on his shoulder—who wouldn't with a name like Pitr.

"That's when I died."

"But you're not dead. We're trying to teach you to play Hearts, remember?"

"It was 3:37 p.m. In the afternoon."

"What the hell is he saying now?" "No, it's not 3:37 in the afternoon," Pitr remarked, in a condescending tone. "Can't you tell time?"

"You all need to listen better," I heaved a loud sigh. This is one of my more frustrating observations—no one listens. Not just in here, but everywhere. I think people hear what they want to hear, or what they hope to hear, even what they expect to hear, but not what they *actually* hear. No, we're not a country of listeners. That would interfere with concentrating on ourselves. We are too busy talking to listen. "I know how to tell time," sighing again. "What I said was *'It was 3:37 p.m. In the afternoon.'* Didn't you hear me say that?"

"You didn't say that," Pitr informed me.

"Yes, I did. But you didn't hear that, did you?" I noted.

"That's not what you said," Pitr snapped.

"So you know what I said better than I do?"

"Yes. Are you calling me a liar? 'Cuz homey, that would be disrespecting me," Pitr was agitated again.

"Let me get this straight. I'm disrespecting you because you know what I said and I don't know what I said? Is that what you're saying?" I leaned back where normally there would be a chair backrest, but not in here. A wooden backrest might be converted into a weapon.

"Are you disrespecting me?" A more disturbed Pitr bent forward.

"So now we're discussing whether I disrespected you, not what I said?"

"*Jes*. Dis is what he be talkin' 'bout," Face interjected.

"You're agreeing with him, Face?"

"He *es mi hermano*, my brother," A proud Face pushed out his chest as Pitr sat taller in his chair with a slight smile on his face.

"Let me try to understand," knowing full well what was going on. I simply enjoyed messing with their heads and forcing them into positions that were ridiculous—and dangerous to my health if I wasn't careful. "Face, you agree with Pitr because he is your brother?"

"*Jes.*"

"Not because he's right, because you know he's wrong."

"*Jes*… no. I don't know," A confused Face frowned. "*Jew* mixes up *mi* words. *Jew* does that to me. *Jew* disresp . . ."

"I'm sorry. I know. I disrespected you." Respect—a key prison concept. Except what is termed "respect" really isn't. **Respect—To feel or show deferential regard for; to avoid violation of or interference with; to relate or refer concern.** That's how the dictionary defines it. The prison definition is much simpler; it is defined in the negative—like much else in here. To disrespect means the other party didn't do or say what you wanted them to do or say—maybe just didn't like it is all. Clean, straightforward, easy, trouble-free. Well, not exactly. Respect in here, or the lack of it, creates more problems than it solves. It is complicated, tangled and far from being trouble-free. Very "me"-centric. Like many other things in prison.

That was the first time I'd ever really talked to the three Hearts players from my dorm. Part of my introduction to prison life—what's important and what isn't. A completely new set of rules, sort of rules, and non-rules that now governed my life. They would play a significant role in my education—and not just card games—real games. We met about four years ago—or was it an eon?

In the game today, I was growing bored. In a moment of silence, I took the break in the action to close my eyes and think back about the last four years. Soon this nonsense would be over—over for me at least, but not for those trapped in a system that's been broken far too long. With little chance for alteration—at least not without some serious external help—the "system" seems doomed.

Oh, what I'd learned in those four years. I came here thinking I knew a lot—and I did . . . about *my* world. But I knew nothing at all about this world, this *prison* world. What I thought I believed had changed. What I thought had changed as well. What was important, wasn't—what wasn't, was. It was an upside-down world for me, or was it?

Toby Keith summed it up—"I wish somehow I didn't know now, what I didn't know then."

At sixty-four years of age, I thought I couldn't grow anymore, that I couldn't learn any "new tricks," that I couldn't change my mind. Wrong. *So very wrong*. Age is not just chronological. It is a state of mind and your mind has to be ready, willing and able. Age is also situational. As we age, we get comfortable in our station in life and seem genuinely shocked when that circumstance changes. I felt more sure after these four years about what was right and wrong, good and bad, moral and immoral, ethical and unethical. Life seemed more black-and-white in here, not colored by shades of gray. Life isn't colored in primary tones, it *is* painted in shades of gray, tints of light and dark, veils of truth and deceit, hints of hope and despair, and particles of suffering and delight. I *had* learned much in these four years. *How would they color me?* Sang The Byrds in the 1960s, *"I was so much older then, I'm younger than that now."*

In that first game four years ago, Face counseled me matter-of-factly, "*Jew* still has no pick up the ten of *Corazon*. I thought *jew* say *jew* know how to play Hearts."

"I do," grinning. "I know the rules. I wouldn't want to disrespect you. I'm playing the ten of Hearts."

"But that means *jew* only . . ."

"I know what it means," smiling coyly.

"OK, Pitr. *Jew* has better beat the ten."

"What happened to the idea of no table talk?" I mocked.

Just let me out. "*Jew* got a *problema, jew* 602 it," Face stared back, moving into the table, but looking at Pitr. Face was a greasy and oily, large *Paisa* from somewhere in Mexico I'd never heard of. Based on his demeanor and bathing habits, it was not a place I intended to visit. The derivation of his nickname is obvious to anyone even glancing at his acne-scarred facade. Nicknames are a strange handle. How, why, and what they mean are a history unto themselves. Some nicknames are obvious, like *Face* because of his acne. Others, not so much, like *Pretzel* or *Tweazey*. Some commanded acknowledgment, like *Criminal* or *Dead*. They, and others like them, also communicated, "I know I'm in prison and probably will be forever. Don't mess with me." Others required some explanation, like *Rabbit* or *Tudgy*. I understood *Peanut* and *Bad Boy*, but not so much *Izzy* or *Jingle*. These were prison credentials, street references, and just plain laughable monikers. My problem was trying to recall all the nicknames. I found it easier to remember real names rather than nicknames, even though nicknames were supposed to be easier. Not for me. To me, everyone was Mr. Jones or Mr. Smith.

"Yeah. *Jew* go a-head and 6-0-2 it," Pitr slowly echoed, as he tossed the three of Hearts onto my ten, mimicking Face's accent. "Don't you see what he's doing?"

"That's *jew* highest? Are *jew* disrespecting *tú hermano*?" Face flushed red as he threw the eight of Hearts onto the pile. "*Muy mal*. It's up to *jew*, Stinky. Take him out."

"Not me," shaking his head. Stinky, our number four player, was a fat, White man of about fifty. He continued, "I got nothing," laying down the Queen of Spades to the increasing sound of a crowd in the hall outside our game room.

This day, four years later, the yard was coming back in from our two-hour exercise period—today from one-thirty until three-thirty in the afternoon. Our foursome skipped yard, choosing the comfort of our less-than-luxurious game room instead. Now passing before us was a mixed bag of mixed race, mixed age, mixed language, mixed-up specimens of men in various shades of health and disrepair, some disrepair from today's yard, more from years of substance abuse and life's abuse in general. The sounds and smells blended into a "perfume" impossible to ignore. It didn't evoke the scents of Chanel No.5 or White Diamonds, let alone horse tack, but it did scream.

This dissonance of noise, smells and dirt is what kept me in a perpetual state of sleep deprivation twenty-four hours a day. Shouts of "shower number two" and "save me a throne" wafted through the hall adjacent to our day room. Interruptions were as common as air in prison and seventy or so men jockeying for position in an old, dilapidated bathroom of six showers and six "thrones" was a tough distraction on a good day.

Looking out the door into the hallway brought several flights of impressions to mind. Facial hair and what it says about a man. I smiled while speculating as to their various meanings. There were beards, mustaches, pseudo well-coiffed hair and scruffy alike. Some were making a statement; some were saying they just didn't give a damn. Some were clean-shaven, others sported several days' growth. My favorites were the unusual—the fully-shaved head except for the top-of-the-head, thin pony-tail hanging halfway down the back, the Fu Manchu mustache, but only on one side of the face and the four-day beard growths accompanying perfectly combed hair, even after an hour or two in the sun. There is no pogonophobia here—no fear of facial hair.

Then there are the "tats"—tattoos on every inch of a body, including the face. *Yeah, that'll help you get a job on the outside.* Nothing says, "Hire me," like a dagger tattoo in your eye. Is it coming out or going in? Many an inmate came to prison with tattoos and acquired more while here. Others started their artistry in here. Whether from boredom or defiance, there is incredible art—and incredible artists as well. Still, I don't get defiling your body with tattoos. OK, one here or there to mark a significant event—like D-Day, or your wife. Wait, no on the wife after being in here. Listening to inmate's phone conversations convinced me they change their women like light bulbs—perhaps more often—so tattoos of a wife's name might require a change down the road.

Trying to change or remove a tattoo was an even larger problem—when you figured out your "true love" wasn't. Coming to prison has a way of throwing cold water on a relationship. Tattooed names gave way to tattoos of your "significant other's" lips placed strategically on your neck in pinkish-red. Of course, if your current squeeze knows what her lip-print looks like—and those on your neck aren't hers—you're in big trouble. Maybe it's a generational thing, but I've never understood tattoos. For some a sign of defiance, for others a sign of hopelessness.

And shaved body hair. I simply didn't understand the concept. Maybe it's another generational thing, or cultural or ethnic, but since when do men shave their body hair? Not occasionally, but carefully, frequently and diligently . . . every day in the shower. Not just arms, legs, but underarms, pubic hair, and scrotum. Personally, the notion of bringing a razor anywhere near my "privates" makes me queasy. Not so, the younger generation—this, all without benefit of shaving cream or gel.

Inmate clothes are another marvel. Several inmates earned quite a bit of income sewing, altering and enhancing our state-mandated uniforms, or "blues." *Blues* are blue denim pants, lighter blue shirts, styled after scrub suits from hospitals, both with **PRISONER** stenciled in large, yellow block letters—like no one knew who we were. You could wear other clothes in the dorm, but to meals, a.k.a. "chow," or basically any activity outside the dorm, state blues are required. The state also saw fit to provide undergarments: boxers, T-shirts and socks, all "white," or so I'm told they were at one time, but now various shades of gray, and all in disrepair and suffering from obvious neglect. In its infinite wisdom, the state believes only three of each item is necessary to maintain adequate hygiene in the system. Nothing helps maintain order in a dormitory of eighty men more than the group having a limited supply of clean undies. Clean, that is, if they even return from the laundry.

Laundry is sent out weekly for washing. When laundry doesn't come back, those three pair of *chones* suddenly become one pair for the entire week. That's why most did their own laundry instead of sending it out—in a small plastic bucket. Of course, in typical state fashion, we weren't allowed to have the small plastic buckets—weapons again. So with some regularity, a Correctional Officer, or "CO," would sweep through the dorm collecting buckets. Then on the next shift, inmates familiar with the CO on duty would beg for them back. And so the cycle went. A seasoned CO knew sending out laundry was like pouring water down a hole. Some were sympathetic—most weren't.

Still, all respected the concept of a clean dorm, especially when the warden expected it and inspected. It was the CO's butt in a sling if the dorm wasn't clean. Then again, his butt wasn't there for long without ours being right there with it. So each dorm had at least one CO who was grounded in reality—and gave the buckets back—along with other "luxuries" that kept the place half-way civil.

Yeah, a guy could make a good prison living repairing and maintaining the wardrobes of his colleagues—or even doing their laundry.

"Two soups" bought you a minimal repair, "four soups," even better.

There's no money in prison, but that didn't prevent commerce and capitalism. The standard currency is "soups." Soups are the packaged dry noodles and powdered flavoring sold at the canteen where we were allowed to shop once a month. Such a privilege we're given. Every dorm transaction is measured in terms of soups, with two soups being a common unit of barter. Each soup can be purchased for about twenty-five cents, if, and it's a big *if*, you have money on the books. If your family or friends, acquaintances or debtors, deposits funds in your account, after a month of holding it for clearance purposes, the prison allows inmates to draw against their accounts—with a small fee for the privilege, deducted first, of course, for the state. On one's appointed day, the line outside the canteen forms as each dorm is called by the CO in charge of the canteen. The COs were our benevolent jailers, supervisors, confidantes, guards, and keepers. Also known as the *jura*, *placa* and various other slurs and slangs, these in

Spanish, but with full equivalency in many other languages.

Like the game four years ago, today Face, and Pitr drew me back from the sensory repugnance at our doorway that first game.

"*Jew* play di Queen? Queen *es* thirteen points. Whose side are *jew* on?" Face sprayed spit as he shouted to the table guests.

"I ain't getting stuck with it," Stinky retorted with equal quantities of oral lather. "All you two ever want to do is complain about shit and file your damn 602s. I'll play any damn card I want—unless you'd like to take it to the bathroom?"

"*Jew* want some . . ." Face pushed against the table as he stood, preparing for war.

"Sit down," I broke in, sighing with exasperation. I was much more secure when it came to "counseling" my fellow prisoners four years in. "It's a card game. We're trying to pass time and not die in the heat on the yard. Remember?" It was a hot, humid, typical August day in the desert where our prison accommodations left nothing in doubt about where we were—muggy, smelly, musty, and sweaty, with an air of fungus hanging over everything. I shuddered anytime I thought about the medical conditions the atmosphere here created and quickly put those contemplations out of my consciousness. "Besides, I'm already dead. Remember? *It was November 3, 2009.*" Apparently, no one remembered from my beginnings.

"Here we go again," Pitr frowned. I guess I was wrong about their remembering.

"*It was 3:37 pm. In the afternoon.*"

"You're damned-sure alive and trying to shoot the moon again aren't you?" Stinky had a flair for the apparent.

"*¿Luna?*" Face shot back. "*¿Otra vez?* I trying to tell *jew. Pero*, no. *Jew* play the Queen. *Jew piss* of puke . . ."

"I remind you again," interrupting while picking of the trick of three Hearts and the Queen of Spades. "We're here to pass time in the shade. Oh, and there's no such thing as a piece of puke. Puke is a liquid, Face." I focused on the cards I held, knowing there really wasn't a need for it. This hand was a slam-dunk. Playing Hearts with these guys would pass time—in spite of the poor competition. I decided to draw out the tension a little further, leading back with the nine of Hearts. "Even a dead man can beat you guys."

"*Ay, chinga tú…*"

"English, my friend. For us peasants," I reminded Face. The hall noise grew louder as more inmates streamed back into the dorm, an eighty-six man dormitory always filled to capacity—built in the late 1920s, with little but superficial repairs since and certainly no major improvements. At least the showers were hot—except half of one winter when the water main was broken.

"Turn on the fan somebody. You guys stink," Stinky shouted at no one in particular.

I reflected on the irony of that request and the requester. "Hearts, gentlemen, is a game of skill, not luck," sweeping up the nine of Hearts-led trick, accumulating two more Hearts and one discard.

"ESCORT!!" Came the shout from the hall. We all knew what that meant.

"*Be y cojete tú solo . . .*" Face muttered, turning to face the wall. Stinky, Pitr, and I turned to the wall almost in tandem motion.

"FACE THE WALL!" With that, three COs hurried by, two grasping the arms of a handcuffed inmate and the third trailing behind with his few possessions. The dorm was graveyard quiet.

Stinky spit against the wall. The three of us stared at each other as we had the same thought. Who? Who were they taking out this time?

Pitr glanced over his shoulder at the precise moment the escorted inmate passed by, an example of timing learned over many years of observing similar occurrences. "Jaime," he whispered.

I daydreamed while we played today, thinking back to my first few days of this nightmare, to my panicked, schizophrenic emotions. I remember trying to sort them out using my street-smart algorithms, failing miserably. That first afternoon, recalling that first day four years later, *that . . . was the day I died*. It *was* at 3:37 p.m. It *was* on November 3, 2009. *That day,* as I was led from the courtroom in handcuffs placed over my three-piece suit, my lovely wife crying in disbelief, along with one or two hundred of my friends, *that day* I was numb. I never envisioned this happening to me. I never envisioned being able to survive it either.

But I did survive. With only a few more weeks to go until my release in early 2014, I was able reflect on what it all meant. What personal lessons—lessons for family and friends—what societal lessons?

Family and friends. Thank God for family and friends.

Yes, I thank God—thank Him first and foremost for giving me the strength to get through those first few hours and days, thank Him for the blessing of so many wonderful family and friends who stuck with me and thank Him for life itself. Now I could begin to look back and make some sense of the nonsensical. Even from this, there were positive lessons to learn—and negative ones, but I choose to emphasize the positive. To take from both instruction pools in the right quantities, and at the right times, had been, and would continue to be, my challenge. From this insanity, I would soon be returning to the sanity of freedom, but not to the same world.

It had taken a while, but it finally had dawned on me. God intended this for me as a wake-up call and a chance to start over. From this hallucination would come enlightenment, if I didn't blow it. From two worlds—my past and my present, the positive and the negative, the good and the bad—would spring the chimera created by God—the new me. Could I remember the life-lessons? Could I retain the memories and master them?

I died on November 3, 2009 at 3:37 p.m., in a Los Diablos courtroom. But I am to be reborn into a world now infinitely less threatening, one I want to embrace. That created a small problem—wanting to caress it today, now, this moment. Not in a few weeks—*now!* Grasp it and never let it go. *Now!* Born into a world I understood better than in the past and one I did not understand well at all in the future, but one I was excited to engage and explore. I was no longer afraid of life. Before, I went through the motions, not appreciating the real importance of family and friends and the insignificance of worldly possessions. I want to hug them all—every family member and friend—and not turn them loose. Now. Today. This minute. *Now!*

Don't get me wrong. I enjoy a good meal, a great conversation and a challenge at work. I simply don't want to be consumed by them again. How to guard against this is my new duty. Walking sentry over my obsessive tendency to jump head and heart into projects to the detriment of what and who is important. That is to be my unceasing gauntlet to step gingerly through each minute of each day. I am reborn!

After a few minutes, the dorm gradually returned to its normal activity level, although more subdued. Everyone was thinking about Jaime. Why? What was up with his removal? During those first few months I barely knew enough to ask the questions.

In today's game, I knew my level of boredom had been reached. Move on. Now, today, this minute—no time to waste. Let's get on it. I laid down the remaining cards in my hand, all the top Hearts from the Ace through the Jack, plus a few smaller stragglers. "That, my friends," even though they weren't, "is how you Moon." No one seems to have learned from my four years of playing. No one seems to learn in prison—another big problem.

That first game, the other three gamesters threw in their cards with various forms of cursing and other verbal abuses, in at least two languages, some of which I understood. That time was my first Moon with these new compatriots.

"I quit," Stinky declared.

"Good. You suck, too," Pitr countered. "You don't have to quit anyway. The son-of-a-bitch went out with that Moon. He beat us fair and square."

Fair and square? What a strange saying for our setting. I think not. I know there is *nothing* fair or square about prison—not in the State of Jefferson, or any other state. Not in this country or another, on this planet or elsewhere in God's multi-verse. Nothing fair or square about the justice system, or *injustice* system, as it is. Nothing fair or equitable, fair or blind, fair or balanced, fair or impartial, fair or immediate, fair or respectful. Nothing rehabilitative, only punitive, nothing corrective, only vindictive, nothing well considered, only cruel and unusual. No, now I have lived in a system of inequities, biases, and injustices—heavy-handed, unreasonable, irrational, and perverse, bureaucratically routine, wicked by its indifference, evil in its construction, and insipient in its enforcement. Banal, pointless, and wearisome, vengeful, unforgiving and malicious, hackneyed, anonymous, and instituted in private, away from the public eye or consciousness.

And which of "them" cares anyway? No, it is a system warped and distorted, flawed and twisted, abusive and misguided, a desecration of our values and a fatal flaw in our imperfect union. A training ground for domestic terrorists, of a sort. At once misconstrued, misconceived and misunderstood. That is where I live now.

But I survived! When I am reborn, would I remember it? Learn from it? Be able to change it?

Almost everyone in here will eventually get out—paroled, probated, pardoned—or, for a few unfortunate souls, deceased. Sooner or later, each and everyone would be back trying to endure in a world specifically structured to oppose their every move. Rather than breeding better criminals, shouldn't there be a higher purpose behind incarceration? Rather than providing a habitat for substance abuse, isn't there a more clean and sober approach that advances society's interests? Rather than a domain of immorality, isn't there a moral reason to not give up on humanity's discards? Rather than a province of depravity and decadence, isn't there a public benefit derived from rehabilitation, restoration and salvage? Doesn't the benefit of positivism outweigh the costs to society? There is a societal ambivalence towards prisons and prisoners. Historically, there has been since humankind's beginnings. It is a pendulum that swings back-and-forth between vengeance and salvation, punishment and rehabilitation, sadistic cruelty and restoration. There must be a better way.

Not without aligning the incentives of all the actors, including the state, the public and the individual. How do I really feel, in my heart of hearts?

Chapter 2: "He Descended into Hell...."

The LORD is my shepherd; I shall not want

"Stand up! Hands behind your back," the bailiff ordered, as two heavy hands rested on each of my shoulders and "helped" me up from my chair. As soon as I stood, I heard the rapid *click-click-click-click* of handcuffs ratcheting down on each wrist. I couldn't feel a thing—I was dead.

It was 3:37 p.m. on a clear Tuesday afternoon. Two sheriff's deputies led me from the courtroom through a locked door about ten feet from where I had been sitting at the defense table. The handcuffs were primarily for the public humiliation, certainly not for security. The minute I cleared the door, the handcuffs were removed and one of the deputies smiled ever-so-slightly in my direction. I thought it was a friendly gesture. I was wrong.

"Boy, are they gonna have fun with you," now grinning widely as he spoke. "Over here for fingerprints."

I barely heard him. Like a zombie—the living dead—I shuffled over to where he was standing. As I got there, he grabbed my left hand and rolled each of my fingertips across the Live Scan apparatus, then scanned all the fingers of each hand together on the imaging glass. Oh boy, the fingerprint system's gone high tech. After completing fingerprinting, he asked me about twenty minutes' worth of questions, most of which I'd answered at least ten times before for some other *apparatchik* of the state. I predicted this wouldn't be the last *Gestapo* interview. *It was November 3, 2009.* I was dead.

Over the next three or four hours—who knows how long it really was—I was shuffled around to various deputy sheriffs in the bowels of the courthouse, each with their own mundane task of insuring I was properly ensconced into the county jail system—another bureaucracy of ill-repute. Sometime after dark, I was cuffed to another inmate and loaded into a van capable of carrying twenty or so, but loaded from our local courthouse with only three others besides me en route to the Los Diablos County Jail. On arrival downtown, jailers herded us "cattle" into a room large enough to accommodate about one hundred, but currently holding closer to two hundred. The smell, the sweat, and the fear permeated. Corralled through a small door, we were sent one at a time into another large room. All I could think of was the Nazi gas chambers—each of us innocently, passively moving from one place to another, as if being led to slaughter, until we came to the last room. My thoughts of gas chambers were immediately reinforced—as we stepped into a large shower area where our clothes were taken from us and placed in another ubiquitous plastic bag. *Man, do I want the concession for plastic bags in the penal system.* I also hoped I'd see my clothes again someday.

After this mandatory shower—mandatory for all—we walked naked through another line until an over-bored, over-paid deputy threw a bundle of clothes at each of us as hard as he could, deriving great pleasure out of his minor sadism. Next came a "medical interview" lasting about three minutes. All they really wanted to know was what medications I was taking. I'm not sure why they even go to the trouble, because when it was time to take my medications, a nurse came around and handed me completely different meds. I tried to ask what they were, but was brushed off with, "just take them," as she stood there until I did. A few weeks later, I was told they were generic substitutions—although I was already taking generics.

It was well after midnight when I was shown an empty cell with a thin, two-inch pad resembling a mattress—no sheet, no blanket, no nothing. The only something was another sack lunch. One of the few consistencies in the jail was a sack lunch at every stop and no matter the time of day. I soon loathed these brown-paper traps and their contents. You eat when you want or when you can. After the same sparse offerings, in the few hours I'd been in the system, I was already tired of the God-awful peanut butter and the sugar-free jelly pack, tendered with at least one-day-old bread (more than likely one-week-old). I will never again knock anyone who "brown bags" it. None of the culinary delicacies mattered—I hadn't eaten in more than twelve hours. All I wanted to do was lay my burden down. Maybe this was a dream—a nightmare for sure—but maybe still a dream. No. I slid down into the depths of a world infamous structure called Los Diablos County jail, and I had the shakes and high blood pressure to prove it. I had descended into Hell.

After a few hours, I guess—there are no clocks anywhere—aroused by the noise outside my cell, I fell into another line heading for breakfast. At least it wasn't in a brown bag. After finishing in the ten minutes allowed, I was herded into another line, this one for morning medications. Before being given my blood pressure meds, they did take my blood pressure. It was sky high. A somewhat sympathetic woman in a lab coat asked me to sit on a bench nearby and started to talk soothingly about my BP. Not only did she mention that is was high, but she commented that I seemed tightly wound up and about to explode.

YA THINK? Let's see, I'm scared half to death, don't know where I am or what's happening next, and she thinks I'm "a little tense." She offered, and then insisted, I take the Ativan® she had brought to calm me down. After first resisting, I relented. Why not? What could it hurt? I was dead anyway.

That first full day was a series of seemingly endless lines of more humdrum questions and forms, punctuated by brief interludes for taking my blood pressure. It remaining elevated, but improved. On the second night—my second day and night in the county jail—around 8 p.m., I was transferred to the lowest level in the oldest part of the jail, into a dank, smelly dark cell—my fear was that I was descending further into hell. Housed with three current occupants—this was the happiest time I spent in the county jail. These three had been in the same cell for about six weeks and were smart, experienced and pleasant—not at all scary.

As tired as I was, that night we stayed up late into the early hours of the morning talking, telling stories, and laughing—something dead people didn't often do. Besides putting me at ease, these three were each raconteurs—one a professional actor with nonstop narratives about every subject but jail. They also assured me I would be safe with them and that I would likely stay in this cell for the duration of my time in the jail system before being transferred to the state. How long that might be was an open question because I was awaiting formal sentencing. The lawyers—my favorite people of late—had asked for a delay in sentencing. Whose side were they on?

So of course, after staying up at least until three in the morning, around seven later that morning I was mustered out of my bunk and told I would be transferred later that morning to "SuperMax." I was instantly anxious again in spite of the assurances of my three compadres. Around two that afternoon, I was strip-searched, shackled, and stranded—almost sounds like a rock group, huh?—then loaded on a bus for a forty-five minute trip, to a hub jail in the suburbs. After three days, I descended unto "SuperMax"—truly one scary-ass place.

On arrival there, I was unshackled, strip-searched, and stranded—a different rock group—handed new jail clothes, and placed in the ubiquitous holding cell for an hour or so. Eventually, they called my name and number, placed me in another line, and marched me towards the large dorm-cells of "SuperMax."

I learned that in the county jail, one walks with his shoulder on the wall and when a deputy or non-inmate passes, we inmates must stop and face the wall until they pass. Knowing when they've passed can be dicey, since they don't announce it and you're not supposed to look. If you're caught looking it isn't pretty. How one learns the shoulder lesson is by being loudly singled out by a deputy and screamed at until they sense you've had enough. Knowing when to turn around was an early lesson in the *Catch-22*s of the penal system.

Divided by floors and separated into modules on each floor, "SuperMax" is a series of areas (nursing stations in my former life) with dorm-cells (patient rooms) around a hub. The dorm-cells are positioned around a central station, about six to a hub. Each dorm-cell holds about one hundred or so, depending on how crowded they want to make it. Bunks can be three-tiered, but are the same overall height as the two-tiered ones. The middle guy in a three-stacker had better not be claustrophobic. Kind of gives new meaning to a double-double, huh?

I hadn't paid much attention to race in the last day or so—I was dead; dead people don't pay attention to anything—and my previous three cellmates did not care. That was about to change as my name was called. I entered the large dorm (where every available square foot of real estate was filled with bunks), and was greeted by stares from about one hundred or so pairs of eyes. Half the dorm was Black, the other half Hispanic. It seems I was the only White guy in the dorm. Quickly, a large gentleman with a shaved head and tattoos on the back of his cranium extended his hand to me and informed me I was "assigned" to the Hispanics, a.k.a. the "South-Siders." He put his arm around my shoulder and told me they would take care of me. I wasn't sure what that meant, but it sounded better than I initially envisioned.

New rules were first addressed. *Macho*, my "South Sider" leader, pointed out the obvious, which I hadn't noticed. There were ten or twelve tables in the front of the dorm and six to eight inmates sitting at each table. There was an invisible dividing line separating the Blacks from the Hispanics. I was told not to cross the line, even though I couldn't see an actual line. It's alright to talk to them, I was told, but no eating with them or playing games or getting too friendly. We "all"—all us "South-Siders"—lined up for chow together, sat together, and, I soon learned, paid a "tax" together. A little something for "the boys upstairs" I was advised. I didn't want to know exactly what or who that was. I faithfully and happily paid my dues of soap, shampoo, or whatever, and began sleeping better at night. That first week in "SuperMax" is mostly a haze.

The routines here were much the same as downtown—medical, chow, clothes exchange, body counts, and lights out. Soon fear was replaced with boredom. There's absolutely nothing to do here. For an obsessive-compulsive personality like me, that was maddening. The only reading material available was not my "style." I'm not a big crime novel fan. After a couple of weeks or so, stuff that fit "my style"—books and magazines—started arriving, courtesy of my wife and family. *Thank God.*

About a week into my stay, one of the deputies singled me out, "You," pointing to me. "Come here," he beckoned. "You don't look right."

"What, sir?"

"You don't fit the profile," he continued. "Tell me who you are."

"Well, I'm . . ."

"Now I remember. You're the guy on TV," the deputy laughed. "Roll it up!"

"Huh?"

"Roll it up. Get your stuff and come with me."

I wasn't sure exactly what roll it up meant but several of my "South-Sider" buddies did and were already packing my few possessions into a plastic bag. With passing pats on the back from my "homies," I pulled my bag over my shoulder and limped through the cell gate, met by the deputy.

"In here," pointing to the next dorm over. "This is for trustees. You'll like it better in here. Find Mr. Nguyen. He'll take care of you."

In no time, a pleasant, fifty-something Vietnamese man standing tall at five feet seven inches smiled and quietly directed me to an empty bunk. "Put your things here," pointing to a small bin under my bunk.

"What's a trustee dorm?"

"We serve the food and other things," Mr. Nguyen responded, smiling again. "You will be fine."

For the first time in "SuperMax," I think I took an unlabored breath and exhaled. I could feel tension drain out of me. I had been running on fear, adrenaline, dread, apprehension, anxiety, unease and alarm. Suddenly I was a puddle of emotion, crying as I sat on the bunk. I fell back and into a fetal position. Mr. Nguyen quietly stood up and left me alone. He knew. He'd been there.

It was late afternoon when I melted. I slept until the next morning, even through the 9 p.m. count. I guess the deputies knew, too. Or Mr. Nguyen told them—I never knew which. I felt better, although still numb. That dead sensation would last for several more months. The first image I saw was Mr. Nguyen, smiling as my eyes opened. I sat up as he sat down next to me.

"Today you will watch," Mr. Nguyen began. "Ask me questions, but not until we are back here. No questions while we are working. Just watch." During the breakfast meal, at lunch when we handed out brown bag lunches, and at dinner, Mr. Nguyen's crew labored to quickly serve the dorms in our section of "SuperMax" with a minimum of talking and even less wasted effort. Observing Mr. Nguyen, the master *maestro*, orchestrate the meals with nary a word was fascinating. I discovered the deputies chose wisely when they placed him in charge of the meal trustees. That night, after my day of observation, he sat down on my bunk and we talked—some about the trustee work, mostly about each other. I sensed he would be my shoulder to cry on while I was here.

Mr. Nguyen had been in the county jail system for about a year awaiting trial on some kind of fraud or embezzlement charge. He had arrived at the international airport with his wife and children on a pleasure trip to visit his ailing father in Orange County, California when FBI agents came on board the plane and handcuffed and arrested him in front of his family, and just as quickly escorted him away. He wasn't allowed to talk to anyone for three days—so much for humane treatment of a foreign national, huh? Mr. Nguyen was the founder and owner of a computer hardware business in Taiwan, shipping a lot of product to the U.S. via South Korea. According to him, the motherboards and RAM memory chips were switched in South Korea while in transit to inferior products—without his knowledge. According to the FBI, he knew, and was the reason they asked for bail of over a million dollars—"you have money. Look at all you made from switching chips," they accused—whatever happened to innocent until proved guilty? Oh yeah, I forgot about the "justice" system—hence, why he was stranded in the county jail for more than a year. Were it me, I would be a mental wreck. Mr. Nguyen was at peace.

I've never known anyone who could turn off the world the way Mr. Nguyen did. Trustee dorms are never quiet—since we were responsible for tasks twenty-four hours a day, someone was always awake—awake and noisy. Mr. Nguyen would simply lie down on his bunk, close his eyes, and fall asleep immediately. Or so I thought. He was actually praying first and sleeping later.

He was an atheist most of his life, especially as a younger man in Vietnam. His father had been a four-star general in the South Vietnamese army under President Ngo Dinh Diem before Diem was assassinated in 1963. Later, his father was head of intelligence. Educated in France and the U.S., the younger Mr. Nguyen was quite the playboy, by his own account. After the fall to the communist north, he found his way to Taiwan, penniless and with little hope. He embraced Roman Catholicism and found his peace. Over time, he also found his father again, now a broken man-of-a-former-general, in California. In Taiwan, young Mr. Nguyen rebounded successfully in business and made annual trips to visit his father and mother. He told me of many deep conversations with his mother and father about life and their past. On his mother's deathbed, she made him promise to discuss religion with his father. After a time, his father embraced Catholicism, too. His father had been on the last helicopter leaving the U.S. embassy in Saigon on April 30, 1975—quite a change for a hardened military veteran.

Mr. Nguyen became my mentor, my crutch, and my therapist. There were others in our dorm, each with a unique, sad story. There was a successful international dentist—here for making "terrorist threats" against his ex-wife's lawyer (you know how I feel about lawyers). An electrician who was sleeping one night when a burglar broke into his house, he pulled a gun and shot at the guy, who staggered outside, wounded and collapsed. The perpetrator lived and filed a civil suit against him for assault with a deadly weapon; the D.A. filed on him criminally. There were also a number of righteous cases—alleged murders, assaults, and the like. Mr. Nguyen's case was also inspiring and uplifting. He had managed to retain his faith and hope through it all. But how could I?

All inmates are jailed together for the most part. I'd heard there was a special section somewhere for VIPs—those at high-risk for being assaulted or worse—the

O. J. Simpson types. About seven weeks into my ten-week stay in the county jail system, I was summoned to a small room occupied by two stern-looking deputies. I was bewildered. They asked my name and had me show them my ID bracelet.

"Yeah, it's him," one muttered to the other.

"Huh? What?"

"Uh, we've been sent to talk to you about you being in fear for your safety. You're a high-risk inmate because of your case and previous occupation."

"Oh?"

"Have you been threatened? Do you feel at risk?"

"Gee, I don't know," suppressing my hostility. "I've been here for seven weeks so far without incident." I was torn between whether to be thankful they finally made it to see me, or outraged because of how long it had taken to this point in time. "Why? Is there something you know that you're not telling me?"

"No," one casually replied. "We offer protection to all high-profile subjects."

"I think I'm OK." I felt absolutely no sense of security in their offer. Talk about being a bit late. I guess they were too busy taking care of the other high-profilers. Yeah, that must be it.

"Well, if you change your mind, give us a call."

Yeah, like there are phones everywhere I can just pick up, not to mention I'd be injured by then. "Thanks, deputies," no sense in closing the option. "I think I'll keep things the way they are." Besides, I was already dead.

Over the next eight weeks, I passed the time working on Mr. Nguyen's team, worrying about tomorrow, being comforted and consoled by him. Gradually, a routine set in. Work breakfast and lunch (or lunch and dinner), come to the dorm, read, write, sleep (or try to sleep). After my first month, I was allowed weekly store visits and every-other-weekend visits from my wife, family, and friends—any who could make the forty-five minute trip north. Although dead, I lived for those visits. The rest of the time Mr. Nguyen was there to offer advice or a shoulder. He was my rock.

The routine was broken by short-notice trips back to court. These were always stressful, nerve-wracking, all-day trips, often for a mere ten or fifteen minute appearance—frequently without my uttering a single word. These sojourns began with a three-thirty wake-up call, the strip-and-shackle dance step, followed by the forty-five minute trip to the main jail downtown and the standard-issue holding cell—

provisioned, as always, with those "nutritious" brown bag lunches.

After waiting in a crammed holding cell for what seemed like forever, when your name and number were called, you queued up and were loaded into a van heading off to the local courthouse *du jour* where, upon arrival, you were once again unshackled and strip-searched, and placed in a holding cell until your case was called. After the appearance, I made the reverse trip back to "SuperMax." It was an all day affair, typically arriving back about ten at night. I can't imagine being in custody for a real trial. That trip would be daily for the duration of the trial. If sleep deprivation didn't get you, the trial surely would.

Every inmate in "SuperMax" wears *blues*, that is, standard issue dark blue denims and lighter blue top. That's because there aren't any "outliers" incarcerated there—or so goes the party line. In the main jail, there are inmates dressed in a cornucopia of colors. Each color means something different, which makes for easy identification by the custody staff. It also helps to identify the wearer to other inmates—*as a target*.

For instance, a "high-power" inmate—a gang leader, if he is known to the authorities, for example—is clothed in orange. There are "high-risk" prisoners sporting red—these guys were the real ones to be feared. However, the folks I really avoided were the ones wearing yellow tops and green bottoms—the psychiatric inmates. These compatriots can spit a mile and are generally unpredictable.

When you're transferred to the main jail while in transit to a courthouse, you pass by and through a ton of different holding cells, each of which is supposed to be segregated by color. A screw-up in placement can cause a riot—literally. Even walking by the yellow/green boys is scary. Other favorites are brown for hospital inmates, green or green and white for trustees, white for special trustees like cooks, and baby-blue for homosexuals. I never figured out what color they assigned to our transgender and transsexual fellow humans.

The last trip to court was for my sentencing. The trip was the same—the stress and the after effects significantly different. Mine was a high profile case, and had triggered many newspaper articles, local television news segments, even one on *Inside Edition,* and a few others on some national news programs. I had been instructed by my lawyers not to comment to any reporters, so the stories were always one-sided. That was fine with the news folks since, as one producer told us, "Getting his side would ruin a good story."

On sentencing day, before entering the courtroom, the bailiff told me, "There's more news out there than for the triple murder case we had last year." *Great*, I thought. For the record, no one died or came anywhere close to death in my case.

The courtroom itself was packed to the rafters with news media and spectators, and over a hundred more were in the hallway. Most of those were my friends and family—God bless all of them. In the front of the courtroom, in the jury box (how ironic), there banks of television and still cameras. I suffered through watching family members and friends plead with the judge for leniency, a most painful and humbling experience. I also addressed the court and the public—not to plead for leniency, but for sanity between my neighbors and the bicycle club that got me into my mess in the first place. It was kind of a Rodney King, *"Can't we all just get along?"* speech that fell on deaf ears for the most part.

The judge had the last word, admitting in open court that he had not read any of the 183 letters of support from family and friends—including letters from one ex-governor, two sitting federal judges, and various other lawyers, doctors, neighbors, and colleagues—and sentenced me without delay to state prison for five years. Actually, it was for two years, but because there were two victims, an additional three-year *enhancement* was added, this along with two "strikes" and an eighty-five percent requirement. I soon learned that meant I would serve eighty-five percent, not one hundred percent, a small consolation. With the final click-clacks of the cameras, I was summarily escorted out of the courtroom to the comfort and quiet of the back halls.

When the circus was over and I was safely transported back to the comfort of my jail cell-dorm around ten o'clock that night, I entered just as the nightly local news was on TV—showing *me*. One of the female deputies handed me a piece of cake—not normal inmate cake—but a great chocolate frosting cake, and she actually gave me a brief, non-regulation, hug. That was the highlight of my otherwise dismal day.

In "SuperMax," there were pulses of activity to break up the monotony—laundry exchanges once a week, occasional recreational outside time, mail, and telephone times. Mail was actually delivered five days a week, usually in the afternoon, albeit many days late. Nevertheless, mail was still a highlight. Telephones were at a premium. There were only four in my cell-dorm and the jockeying for each phone was intense.

Each call was restricted to ten minutes or so and was recorded, with an interrupting announcement informing both parties to the call of the recording—quite annoying in its repetition. But these calls were another highlight just the same.

One of our favorite distractions was a visit to ODR—Officer's Dining Room—where the deputies ate their meals. County jail didn't exactly have take-out service, so the powers-that-be pick the best-of-the-best trustee cooks to prepare meals for the jailers and deputies. If we trustees did something well or out of the ordinary, or if the deputies were just in a good mood, we trustees might get to go with them and retrieve a few food items—the best county jail chow I had during my stay. On one occasion, we were even allowed scraps from an outside fast food joint. I felt like a homeless person or an extra on a movie set getting the leftovers. Either way, it was a humbling, glorious experience.

One day, about four weeks into my stay, I was called to "the bars"—official visitors talked to you through the heavy-metal, floor-to-ceiling bars—to meet a guy of about sixty who asked for me by name. Nobody asks for you by name in jail—everyone asks for an inmate by number only. He had me escorted out from behind bars into a small room, then pulled up a chair and sat close to me. I had no clue as to who this man was.

Leaning in, he asked, "So, how are you doing?"

"I'm uh," hesitating, I fumbled for an answer, "I'm uh, I guess I'm OK."

"Not from what your friends tell me."

"Huh?"

"I'm sure you remember Steve and Norma, right?"

"Of course. My old high school friends from Tulsa," I nodded.

"They asked me to talk to you and give you this," he handed me a Bible. "It's a *CR Bible—Celebrate Recovery*. I'm guessing you know it. I run a version of *CR* in the jails here. I'm Mark. I know your pain. You see, I was an inmate here before. I'm a layman jail chaplain now. You will be fine, some tough times ahead for sure, but you'll make it," putting his hand on my knee and gently squeezing.

I couldn't help it—I broke down and cried like a baby. Here was a man who had been in my shoes and made it. Over the next, thirty minutes or so, we talked about our mutual experiences and commonalities. He was someone who had been in my shoes and survived. He knew the feelings of hopelessness and despair, the emptiness and aloneness. He knew the darkness without light—the opaqueness of not knowing what the future brings, not knowing about tomorrow. As reassuring as he tried to be, however, I simply couldn't see tomorrow, let alone next year, even less likely another four-and-a-half years from now. *I was still dead.*

Mark rose and patted me on the back, "Read this," pointing to the *CR Bible*. "You'll find the answers you need. Strength. Guidance. Faith and hope." Smiling widely, he handed me another small book. "This one is optional, your choice. It's all there," touching the miniature *Holy Bible*. "I'll stop by and see you every so often," ushering me back to the dorm.

As I slipped back into the dorm, I experienced a newfound sense of calm. Not hope yet, but I certainly became more tranquil, and it seemed that there was less turmoil—at least for the moment. I flopped down on the bunk. The next stage of my education was about to begin. I could feel the changes starting already. I picked up one of the two books Mark gave me and began to read.

Read from the beginning.

Read from page one, first chapter, first line.

"In the beginning, God . . . ."

I'd discovered the Bible again.

I recalled a Psalm: *"Yea, though I walk through the valley of the shadow of death, I will fear no evil . . . ."*

But was I capable of that strength?

Chapter 3: Reception and the Road to Redemption

*He maketh me to lie down in green pastures;
he leadeth me beside the still waters*

"I hate those bastards in Iraq," my just-arrived new cellmate announced. He was white and stared at the map I'd taped to the wall. "Where'd ya get the tape, *O.G.*?" He dropped his plastic bag of possessions onto the floor, continuing to stare at the map. "Are you on the top bunk or bottom?"

I was starved for companionship after six days alone in my cell in the state "Reception" prison called Jasco, my home since being transferred from the Los Diablos County jail a few weeks into January of 2010. Everything was new to me. I was way out of my element . . . and I was dead! The last two months before transfer here was a blur. What happened to me, my family, my friends, it was all a blur . . . because I was dead.

"O.G.?" I was puzzled.

"You," answered my blond, White nineteen year-old, thin-as-a-rail associate.

"Huh?"

"O.G. *Original Gangster*," he shrugged, in typical teenage-stupid fashion.

"I'm no gangster, original or otherwise."

"Huh?"

"What are you saying?" I grimaced, more from another example of something I didn't know.

"Original gangster. That's what old guys are called in prison," the kid matter-of-factly spoke without looking at me. He was still staring at the map, scanning it from top to bottom, left to right.

"Oh. Well, my name is . . ."

"Don't care," the kid cut me off. "You're O.G. to me," scrutinizing the map.

"I'm on the bottom bunk," staking my territory. "Are you trying to find something specific?"

"Yeah, I guess," the kid quietly answered. "Iraq."

"Well, first find the Middle East," I advised, noting he was looking at the western hemisphere. "Look to your right," as he turned his eyes to the left.

Standing up, I realized he had no clue. "You said you hated those bastards in Iraq. . . "

"No I didn't," the kid again cut me off.

"Yes, you . . . Never mind," thus began my education. I've heard it said that a teacher only needs to stay one lesson ahead of the students. That didn't seem to be a big problem for me. I thought he knew nothing. Little did I realize, but the kid would also be my professor—and I know he didn't realize that. The subject was *Prison 101*.

I thought prison was like the "real world"—*my* world.

Wrong!

Prison has its own set of rules, culture, and hierarchy. Who can talk to whom? Where can you sit . . . with whom can you share food . . . and with whom can you play games? TV days divide by race, and what happens if you don't honor that? Which toilets are for number one and which for number two, even though the toilets are exactly the same? Ten-to-ten, even though no one pays much attention to it—not until you violate it. Tenting, count time, and shadowing. "Paper check"—what the hell was that? Calling out, "Walking!"—what the hell does that mean? What's a "shot caller?" Slang and its meaning, and "spreads."

I had been transported to another planet—Planet Prison—and I stood out like I had green horns and antennae. Still, I was starved for companionship.

"Can you find the U.S.?"

"Hell, yes!" the kid snapped, searching through the Asian continent.

I decided the better part of valor was to point, thrusting my left index finger and landing on North America, "Here," tapping several times for emphasis.

"Hey," the kid raised his voice. "No pointing in prison."

"Why?"

"'Cuz you're telling on someone. Snitching"

"But I'm pointing to a place on the map," I protested.

"No pointing in prison," the kid commanded. Clearly, context means nothing.

How best to identify a place on a map? Lesson number one, or was it fifteen?

"This map, the kid wrinkled his forehead. "It's different from the ones I've seen before."

"Yeah, I know," I lightly shook my head. "That's the problem. Yeah, that's it. Each map is different."

"The tape, O.G. Where'd ya get the tape? I can use some," picking up his bag and throwing his possessions on the lower bunk.

I was scared to ask why he wanted the tape. "I could help you with geography. You know, where things are on the map," moving his bag to the upper bunk.

"Cool. I'm planning on getting my G.E.D.," the kid replied, looking directly into my eyes as he moved his stuff back to the lower bunk.

"I'm sorry. I thought I told you. I'm on the lower bunk. How far did you get in school?"

"I'm not sure. The Youth Authority busted me for pot when I was thirteen," the kid was thinking hard. "You *were* on the lower, O.G. I need it. What grade was I in then?"

"I don't . . . Never mind." I didn't know whether to make a stand on the bed issue or not. "We can start on reading. Do you like to read?"

"Yes," he gushed. "Crime novels, gangster and spy stuff. Anything with a lot of sex, guns, and killing."

"Great," I sighed. "Why do you *need* the lower bunk?"

"And torture," the kid added. "Got anymore of that tape?" He was unpacking his few clothes and toiletries and making the lower rack. "It doesn't matter. It's OK. I'll take the lower bunk."

"But I . . ."

"O.G.," laying his head against the back wall as he flopped down. "You can step on the bottom of my bunk to get up to the top." His advice had an air of finality. "When do we get a shower?"

"Thank goodness you asked," I replied. "I've been trying to get an answer since I got here."

"You mean you haven't showered since you got here?"

"Yeah."

"No wonder it stinks in here," the kid turned up his nose. "Did you *602* the bastards?"

"Huh? What?"

"Never mind," the kid closed his eyes.

I struggled up to the upper bunk, leaned back and closed my eyes. At least this one talks, I thought. I guess that's a good thing. I'd been in the state prison system for nine or ten days.

A dead man doesn't need to count the days.

The trek started when I was placed into another holding cell packed with other inmates for the remainder of the night. The two-hour bus ride had taken about sixteen hours, arriving at Jasco around 8 a.m., after being up all night in a holding cell at the county jail, awaiting transportation here. Efficiency was not a penal strong point. I guess it has something to do with them not giving a damn. Still, as a taxpayer, I *was* still a taxpayer, I felt *we* taxpayers deserved better for our money. Is that going to be a repeating theme!

In and out of holding I went. This line, then that line, and then the first line again. The first line at Jasco was manned by a gruff, fifty-something guard who screamed at me, "What affiliations?"

"Huh?"

"What affiliations do you have? Can't you hear, step up here and answer me when I talk to you!"

I responded, "American College of . . ."

"No, you idiot!" He screamed. "Gang affiliations."

"Oh." I shrank into my shoes, "Uh, none."

After filling out every possible form and talking to half the COs (Correctional Officers) in the state, I fell back into the holding cell, only to find another sack lunch. Finally, around 8 p.m., I was escorted to my new cell by a disinterested CO, juggling my plastic bag of possessions and the "new" blanket and sheet they'd thrown to me, only to encounter my first "cellie."

He must have anticipated my arrival, because he was talking loudly to anyone who would listen—except there wasn't anyone in the cell, or anywhere near it. He was deeply engrossed in a discussion with someone "up there"—someone he alone saw.

Sleep deprivation must explain this, I thought. During the thirty-six hours since my last slumber, I'd traveled but a few miles, but eons in distance through the penal system. Surely that must be why my head was spinning—sleep deprivation, not the apparently psychotic gentleman into whose space I had intruded.

Just let me sleep . . . please!

In spite of the constant babble from my cohabitant, I did manage to sleep that first night—in fits and spurts—always guarding against the possibility of his rants and rages turning their attentions to me. This vigilance was not easy in a six-by-eight-foot concrete cell, adorned with only a stainless steel sink and toilet. Still, even fitful sleep was much needed. "To die, to sleep no more . . ." I whispered to no one in particular as I drifted off.

When I awoke, stationed where I had left him, my cellie was pacing back and forth within our small enclosure, continuing his in-depth discussions with someone "up there," punctuated with bursts of laughter directed in no particular direction. I sat up and hung my legs over the side just in time to see the heavy metal door automatically release and open slightly. My companion bolted to the door, opening it further. He picked up one of the two plastic trays resting on the lowest shelf of a rolling cart just outside our door, next to a huge hulk of a guard.

"*You! On the bunk,*" the hulk shouted. "*Do you want chow or not? Get off your ass and take a tray!*"

I hurried to my feet and grabbed the second tray. As quickly as I did, the door automatically closed just as it had opened and I was left in the quiet of our cell . . . except for the constant conversation. I decided to enter the confabulation, "When do we get to shower?"

My query was met with another burst of laughter. His chatter continued as if I wasn't there. I wished I wasn't. Every so often, he would quiet down and just take a pause, but I don't think he ever stopped. He quickly resumed with an explosion of laughter or cursing, or what seemed like quite serious dialogue. This went on for the better part of three days, day and night, at any and every hour. During that time, the only break he took was to go to the bathroom. Whew! He was human. Or at least he had human bodily functions. Hygiene, though, wasn't high on his list of priorities, as he never once brushed his teeth or hair and was not given the opportunity to shower—something I desperately wanted not only for him, but for myself.

Finally, at three-thirty in the morning of the third day, as I peered from under my one thin blanket, the door automatically opened and my cellie departed into the unknown. I couldn't help but relax as I fell back asleep. Where he went and why, I had no clue, but he never returned.

The next six days I was completely alone. I learned to establish contact with those in the next cell over by talking through the return vent in the wall. These unknown prisoners told me about how to "bird bath." You sit on your toilet and using your plastic meal cup, pour water over your head and elsewhere, with or without soap, depending on whether you had it or not—I didn't.

The water came from the small sink next to the toilet. It would not be such a bad bath—if the water were hot, or at least warm—at least you could knock off the top layer of grime. But I'd arrived in the cold of January and, lucky for me, the hot water had been broken since October. So much for "not a bad bath." Even though water was cold and went everywhere, it wasn't an entirely bad system.

I scrubbed determinately hard, trying to scrub off my situation. On the ninth day, the day "the kid" joined me, a porter came to my door and asked me if I wanted to shave. Did I! I was accustomed to daily hygiene—not just for work, and I enjoyed taking a long, hot shower. My introduction to the porters was a Godsend. I found out they were inmates, but inmates with "experience"—no first- termers. Acts of kindness go a long way.

In the state of Jefferson, there are two such "Reception Center" prisons for men—Jasco and Jaleno. Everyone entering the JDCR—that's Jefferson Department of Corrections and Rehabilitation—begins their journey into hell at one of the two reception centers. I had been deposited in Jasco, not by my choice, but by the state's. They owned me and everyone else in the system.

When I say "own," I mean own. Lock, stock and barrel, morning, noon and night and everything in between. They tell you when to eat, what to eat, how long to eat and when you're done. They tell you when to be on your bunk, when not to be, and when you *can't* be. They tell you what you can have in your locker, what you can't, and whether you can even *have* a locker. They determine what's legal to possess and what's contraband. They tell you what to wear, and when and where to wear it. They tell you where to go, when to go there and what to do when you get there. That is, if and only if, they decide they want you to do something. Or maybe not. Some are just told to *stand there*. They tell you what jobs are available and what jobs aren't, and whether you can have a job at all. They don't seem to care if you're qualified for something, or even if you have a professional license on the outside.

So who's "they," by the way?

About thirty minutes later, the porter reappeared, the door opened and I saw the first semi-friendly face in nine days. The porter, my new best friend, handed me a cheap, double-bladed plastic razor and told me I had fifteen minutes to shave before he picked up the razor. Next, we would be allowed fifteen minutes in the shower. "We" were all the cells on our upper tier. After shaving, I damn-near needed a transfusion from the cheap-razor cuts and nicks. The door popped open again and I fell in behind a line of inmates heading to what I hoped was the shower. I was right, except as I started to get in, a large Black guy screamed at me to get the hell out and down to the "woods" shower.

That was not my first introduction to the concept of race in prison, but it was my first application of its use as it pertained to hygiene. Apparently, there was another shower for me and "my kind." I quickly spied "my people" clustered around three showerheads on the lower level and I scurried down to the safety of the "woodpile."

"Wood." I subsequently learned, is the term used to describe a White man in prison and derives from the pejorative "peckerwood." How and why, you say? Well, according to a *National Geographic* article from the late 1950s or '60s, a "peckerwood" was an affectionate appellation used to describe a sawmill worker in Arkansas. Since most of the inmates in Arkansas at the time were White, poor, and possibly all related, others began calling them by the name.

According to the most credible reference, *Wikipedia*, the term "wood" found its way into California prisons in the 1940s, initially meaning an Okie from the San Joaquin Valley in California. Being from Oklahoma, this didn't sit too well with me. So, I researched further only to find the term was used by White supremacy groups, such as skinheads and others. Tattoos of woodpeckers frequently adorn their members. The so-called "peckerwood gangs" are well known in California and deal in drugs, primarily methamphetamines.

As it eventually found its way into other states and their prisons, like some sort of infection, the term was shortened to "wood" or "woods," if there was a gathering—or is it a gaggle or flock—of "woods." The dictionary says it's a derogatory term for poorly educated, rural White southerners. After gathering my evidence, I judged it to be a moniker more likely of derision than affection.

Peckerwood has found its way into the movies and television. It's been heard in skits on *Saturday Night Live*, on the cable TV show *Sons of Anarchy*, and in movies such as *The Right Stuff* and *Back to the Future*. All in all, I quickly got the sense it was not necessarily a good thing to be a *wood*.

However, I didn't care about politics right then. Sorting out the niceties of racial politics could wait. All I wanted was water—warm, wet water. My time in this prison pond and under the "waterfall" was brief, but heaven sent. Soap of the darn-cheap variety was also provided. I lathered up and enjoyed this short reprieve from hell. Refreshed, I headed back to my cell with a new-found appreciation for yet another taken-for-granted luxury—showering.

The kid—my new cellie—having arrived earlier that day, shot out of the cell before me and arrived back ahead as well. The lucky boy got a shower on his first day. Looking at me, he asked, "Don't you have a curtain?"

"Huh?"

"A curtain. To screen off the toilet. You know, so I don't have to watch you use it."

"Uh . . . no, I guess not." I was clueless.

The kid didn't wait for an answer. He was on his knees, tearing up his sheet, making a curtain. Somewhere he found a paperclip to secure the sheet to the vent at the top of the wall above our sink and toilet.

"There," he stood back. "That oughta do it," and with that, sat down to test-drive the facilities. There was a loud, gaseous rectal eruption within seconds and I ducked under the sheets, without even a feeble attempt at putting on clothes—what was the point?

"You been to medical yet?" the kid queried to the tune of more restroom relief.

"Medical?"

"Yeah, where they ask you a bunch of questions, then draw blood and take x-rays," the kid replied. "You've been here ten days and no medical. Man, these fuckers are backed up," releasing his final fusillade. No sooner had he finished than the door opened and a porter stepped inside and handed us several small pieces of printed-paper. Since the kid was still seated, the porter passed them in his general direction, frowning and muttering, "*Agua*, man. *Agua*," as he left.

"*Agua?*" I inquired.

"Yeah," laughing. "When it stinks, that what guys say to ya. I ignore the fucks."

Useful information, I concluded. *So when our six-by-eight-foot space becomes fragrance-challenged, all I have to do is say, yell, 'agua,' huh?* Very useful.

"These are for you," the kid said, tossing the papers at me. "One of them is for medical in the morning. Now you'll see what I mean. These fuckers. You just wait."

Those were the last words I heard from my companion—last words, but not sound. Soon the small cell was awash with snoring. The kid was asleep—meaning I might never be again, based on the rumbling thunder. I drifted off sometime later.

After another fabulous morning meal of mush-oatmeal several days later, a CO summoned me for escort to medical. I shuffled through the just-opened door. What I quickly discovered is that in a Level Four prison all prisoners are escorted everywhere they go, or perhaps I should say, *taken*. Reception-prisons were considered Level Four—the highest level of security—because they house the most serious felons among the least.

"Walk in front," the correctional officer ordered. "And put your hands behind you and keep 'em together." With that, he directed me down a long, outside walkway to the medical facility. On arrival there, he passed me off to several other COs and they seated me in a hard wooden chair. The door opened and a pleasant-looking woman waved me in. From her ID badge I noted she was a psychologist. She asked me about four questions, filled out a long form and shuffled me back to the chair. This process happened about three more times, but with different paper-shufflers asking me three or four questions each on various topics, none of which seemed related or appeared to be remotely connected to medicine.

After about an hour, a door opened and a stethoscope-around-the-neck guy in a white lab coat beckoned me into his office. *Finally a doctor*, I thought. *Wrong!* The nurse practitioner asked me the same standard three or four questions and told me to stand up. As I stood, he listened to my heart for about ten seconds, put his hands on each side of my groin, and asked me to cough.

"What are you doing?"

"Checking for hernias," he answered, almost indignantly. "You got a problem with it?"

"That's not how you check, you . . ." I stopped mid-sentence. "Nothing," as he continued his "exam."

"You're good," the nurse practitioner snarled. "Take this slip and go to the next room. They're gonna draw your blood."

"When do I get the results?"

"We'll get back to you," hurrying me out and closing the door.

Bloods drawn, chest x-ray taken, TB skin test applied, and three hours wasted. Not that I had anything better to do with my day. I was returned—*escorted*—to my cell.

There are different levels of prisons—a classification of sorts. That is the primary purpose of the reception center—to classify you—medically, criminally, psychologically, educationally, religiously, gastronomically, culturally, and several other -*ly*s, no doubt. I soon learned there are four levels of prisons—a mark of one's criminality, I suppose. Level One is the least "criminal," Level Four the most.

I soon learned the true nature of your crime had little to do with the level where you were placed—unless you were an ax-murderer. Let's be realistic, there are ax-murderers and the like. And there are plenty of other folks who need to be in prison, too. But there aren't many ax-murderers in here or on the streets, for that matter. So, as part of that classifying, "they" put everyone together in a reception prison, until "they've" had a chance to sort everything and everybody out. That meant I might have occasion to mingle and philosophize with ax-murderers and other serious offenders during my time in Reception.

I never met an actual ax-murderer, but I did meet several plain-old, normal murderers during my reception time. They weren't nearly as worried about me being around them as I was.

What did worry me was politics—not the "who's president" kind—but the type that almost got me killed or maimed. My youthful cellie introduced me to a twenty-something-year-old gang-banger from Fresno who made it crystal clear (as in methamphetamine, for which offense he was in our company) he was in charge. There is a hierarchy in each of the cell blocks and yards, divided by races, but the same in many ways. This junior whipper-snapper "elected" himself the White leader for the nine of us on our upper tier and cell block. As required by prison "etiquette," I was to take orders from him. To say that we had different interests and thoughts about that is an understatement. I thought I was nice about it, but I attempted to make it just as crystal clear that I was not interested in the politics or hierarchy.

Big mistake.

In prison, you get poked and prodded, not just medically, but psychologically, your level of education determined, whether you need a special diet or have religious needs, and lots of other testing. I guess I didn't qualify for any of that—other than medical—because I seemed to pass all the others with flying colors. Next thing you know, in a relatively short two months I was finally seen by an actual doctor of the M.D. variety. At least the certificate on the wall said so, even though you couldn't prove it by his demeanor or technique—he was not of the variety I was familiar with. Turns out, he didn't like the medications I was taking for high blood pressure even though I'd been well-controlled for quite some time, and he decided to make some changes.

Little did I know, but the reason for that was none of the medications I took were listed in the prison's "formulary." We're not talking fancy, expensive medications—no, my meds were garden variety, generic, older medications—but medications not available in the prison system. It seems the prison formulary was limited to about one hundred medications. After a week on my new meds, my blood pressure was really messed up. That wouldn't get straightened out for about six months.

I thought that was the worst of my problems. Not so, according to my new prison physician, who shall remain nameless. It appeared that I required a colonoscopy before I could be fully medically classified. Let me say, you haven't lived until you undergo a prison-issued colonoscopy.

For the uninitiated, a colonoscopy is a procedure to detect colon cancer, inflammation, or other maladies lurking inside one's poop shoot—basically, it is designed to intimidate and embarrass you on a good day. They (a rather different set of "theys") shove a flexible scope up your rectum for about eight feet, suctioning, biopsying, and generally snooping around for about twenty minutes, or until they get bored. At that point, they slowly take it out, I'm not sure whether that's for pleasure or malice, as they take one last look at your colon before waking you up. Oh, you are asleep for most of it, thank goodness. This procedure doesn't happen until you complete the really bad part, the preparation for it—cleaning out your colon. The prep flushes out everything—and I do mean everything—by way of a few pills and a bottle of 7UP® that really is magnesium citrate, along with about four gallons of water. About twenty minutes later, you start to run as fast as you can to the closest toilet and evacuate your colon, intestines, pancreas, liver, spleen—you name it, it comes out until you are "clean." Then you do it all again.

About eight weeks after my arrival, my descent into colonoscopy hell began, beginning with the prep. After taking the initial prep in medical—observed to ensure I actually took it—I was escorted back to my cell block to find all my possessions (not much) thrown into a plastic bag and located just outside of my cell. Just prior to leaving for medical, my cellie and I had discussed my lack of enthusiasm for our "leader." I guess he told this "fearless leader," who decided I couldn't stay in "his" area. In my absence, they simply decided to roll up my stuff, informed the area CO that they would beat me up if I wasn't moved, and deposited my belongings outside the cell. On my arrival, I was commanded by the CO to sit at a table until I could be moved. The alternative, I later discovered, was they planned to assault me on the yard for the offense.

They may have handled their problem with me, but a new one was rapidly swelling to the front—the colonoscopy prep given to me about twenty minutes earlier. I begged the guard to put me somewhere before I created a real scene by ruining not only his day, but also his common area. Fortunately, he found an empty cell in another area and I moved in—immediately affixing myself to the toilet.

There's a unique aspect to prison toilets. They can be set to flush only a limited number of times per hour and set to pause for a specified period after you flush. The intent there is to give "them" an opportunity to retrieve anything an inmate might have discarded into the toilet—like drugs, drug paraphernalia or other contraband, or one's cellie—before it all goes to the sewer. Sounds like a good idea . . . unless you are on the throne in preparation for colonoscopy. It that situation, you'd really want the damn toilet to flush a lot . . . and often. Luckily, the CO assigned to my preparation area had recently undergone the procedure and was sympathetic—a rare occasion in prison. After setting my toilet to maximum flushes and with no delays, I was allowed to turn my bowels inside out to my heart's content—I think I purged my heart, too!

At three-thirty the next morning, I was awakened and—after being strip-searched, dressed in a paper gown, bound and shackled at the legs and waist, and my arms handcuffed to the metallic waist band—taken to a private hospital in a nearly town to undergo my colonoscopy. Once inside the procedure room, I was placed on all sorts of monitors, an I.V. line started, and the joy-juice anesthesia medications begun. All of this, while remaining shackled—that's leg shackles, arms chained at the waist, even after the I.V. was established in one of my arms. As I said, you haven't lived until you undergo a prison colonoscopy. God forbid I should escape while under anesthesia. I thought I had died earlier. This really closed the coffin.

As fate would have it, my colon and all my organ-partners were normal, and I was returned to my new cell in one piece—one frayed and tattered piece.

"Hey, they just called you to go to medical," the guard greeted me.

"You have got to be kidding," I responded as I collapsed on the lower bunk.

The door opened and the CO beckoned me out to return to medical, same drill and routine—escorted the entire way. As I trudged through the door, the doctor greeted me with a short critique about my blood pressure and needing to change my meds around—again—not one word about my just-completed colonic inspection. I nodded in agreement without listening or caring. *High thee to a nunnery and get thee hence* was all I could think. All I wanted was to get to bed and recuperate from the trauma.

On return, someone informed me "yard" was in a few minutes . . . and it was mandatory. I didn't care. I insisted I was too sick to go and, luckily, they relented—this time. As I hobbled to my bunk, sleep was my only concern.

"Yard" is when inmates are allowed to spend one hour together in an exercise area—the *Yard*. Your housing area is referred to as "A" yard or "B" yard, and so on. I was initially housed in "D" yard, in D3 before my transfer to D4 following the colonoscopy prep incident. Going to yard is about the only time everyone incarcerated on one yard is allowed to be together—and for good reason. In my time at Jasco, there were seven opportunities to go to yard and five of those times resulted in "yard down" situations.

"Yard down" is when a fight or other disturbance breaks out, signaling to the correctional officers a need to respond. That response is *en masse*, with weapons, chemicals, and my personal favorite—O.C. pepper spray. *O.C.* is the abbreviation for *Oleoresin Capsicum*, a hotter-than-hell pepper, its heat measured at about 2,000,000 Scoville units (by comparison, a habanero pepper is rated at about 350,000 units).

It's called "yard down" because everyone of the inmate species is expected to prone out on their bellies—on the ground. Those who don't are considered the combatants—and most often are. Normally, I would be thrilled to get outside, and bask in the bright sunlight and fresh air . . . a chance to activate my vitamin D. However, my enthusiasm was tempered by the lingering fog of tear gas, mace, and pepper spray. Also, the pugilism was not to my pacifist way of thinking. I soon learned it was the dispute resolution technique of choice in prison. New and old scores were settled, drug debts repaid and, frequently, the mutual assailants just wanted to beat the crap out of something or *someone*. I understood the frustration and emotion, but not the chosen method of release.

What I came to cherish in Reception was the time of day mail was delivered. Reception centers allow no telephone calls and no visits initially. Your only means of contact with the outside world, also known as your family and friends, is via the U. S. Postal Service. Although much maligned, the postal boys became my lifeline—they kept me from going "postal." Getting mail in wasn't a problem, and I lived for mail delivery; however, writing and posting letters out was. Reception inmates had no paper or writing implements—until they went to canteen. The system didn't allow you to go to canteen for the first few months, and sometimes not at all. You scrounged—for paper and pencils—anything that made a mark and anything to make that mark on. I even had my wife mail in paper. Because Jasco Reception was run as a Level Four facility, inmates weren't allowed pens—they might be used as a weapon. Who was it that said, "the pen is mightier than the sword?"

The four different levels of prisons also affect your life significantly. The ax-murderers and others residing in Level Four facilities don't get many privileges, live in cells that are locked down frequently, and are escorted everywhere. Inmate-manufactured weapons are a serious problem. Yard is infrequent and each one is isolated from the others. Dayroom privileges rotate between the inmates, so there are limited numbers present at any one time. Showers are limited to once every three days—even less frequently during lock downs. COs can only search an inmate's cell once a month, but it is a more thorough search. Politics rule in Level Fours and Threes—

dayroom, telephones—you'd better know the rules. There's no significant difference between a Level Four and a Level Three facility other than who's incarcerated and for what offense(s). Sentences there are long and security is maximum and lethal, with electrified fences and COs armed to the teeth with automatic weapons in the towers. Violence begets violence.

Level One and Level Two inmates have jobs, usually live in dorms, have many more privileges, like access to the canteen, the yard, and the ability to receive packages from the outside, and are generally less violent, resulting in fewer lock downs. Everyone—inmates and staff—is going home, it's just a matter of when. Inmate movement in these facilities is also much more relaxed and less scrutinized—but scrutinized nevertheless. All said, it's no "country club" as the media sometimes lead the public to believe.

Once inside the canteen, legal writing pads and the inside of a pen—the flimsy plastic ink-filled part, but not the hard plastic surrounding body that could be weaponized— were available. In the beginning, I begged and borrowed pencil stubs, in order to write long, impassioned letters on scraps of paper to my wife, family, and anyone else I could think of and whose address I recalled. I am truly blessed with wonderful family and friends, most of whom wrote back. It's funny how people think *their* daily routines are boring—and they probably are when they're living it. For me, the monotony became my salvation. Gradually, I came to realize I wasn't dead.

Actually, after these few months inside prison, I was still dead, but maybe, just maybe I could be revived. What I now realized was that I had a goal: to survive. Goals are things worth attempting; their attainment, fulfilling.

Survival is a primitive instinct. Our species, like all others, depends on it. It is as old as life itself. Survival is primitive, unrefined, and crude, as well as rudimentary, unsophisticated, and simple. It is ingrained in us, but the desire for it can be lost. God knows, this place was all that. Survival is not comfortable or easy, but it is a livable condition. Survival is to persist, to resist and to conquer. To attain survival is to outlast, outlive, and outsmart. That eventually became my mission—to overcome my circumstances, no matter what challenges or setbacks "they" threw at me.

Almost immediately upon sentencing, I had become so depressed, as the old proverb says, I couldn't see the forest for the trees. More pragmatically, I couldn't see the end—the end of my time in here, or if there ever would be an end. The day I died,

I did so because I couldn't see a future . . . my future or any other kind.

My world had imploded into a black hole of depression, understandably perhaps, but a paralyzing, dark pit of misery, hopelessness, and despair just the same. From the depths of my hole in a lonely cell at Jasco Reception Center, State of Jefferson, on planet Earth, my death sprouted a nascent seedling of life, a glimmer of light shining through the blackness I felt. My wife, watered by my family, nurtured by my friends, and fertilized by my stubbornness, planted that seedling of hope. Slowly it dawned on me that these bastards were not going to defeat me. My life would not be defined by the headline: **Criminal**.

Ultimately, I came to the realization that this was merely a pause in my life. Punctuation—a comma, a semicolon, even a dash, a hyphen, or an ampersand—anything but a period. *I was alive and I was determined to survive!* That primal instinct had been kick-started.

"Hey, O.G.," the kid intruded into my ruminations. Several weeks had passed since the germination of revelation. "Can I have some of that tape?"

Suddenly I understood why he wanted the tape. The kid had been writing someone, with a dictionary in hand. He labored for several hours to complete a short letter, like virtually every other inmate. What he didn't strain to complete was a detailed drawing of a woman he gently taped to the back of the correspondence. The kid wasn't all hard edges, all the time. He had family, friends, or someone. That humanized him—as it did me. He had someone to live for—as did I. Some of the best art and artists I've encountered were in prison. Unfortunately, the talent is often squandered on tattoos, but it is still incredible art just the same.

Humanity lives, even in prison. Its only route of expression seemed remote—via the mail. Live, in person contact was what I craved . . . to be able to touch someone—my wife, a friend, anyone. Three months after arriving at Jasco, and a few minutes short of total insanity, I was allowed my first visit—a thirty-minute, through-the-glass event. The sensuality of touching someone's hand through thick glass I'd seen in movies and always found "mushy" was now, in that place, anything but. Our hands lingered over each other's at the beginning and at the end of our visit. This was the only occasion that time raced while I was in Jasco. Thirty minutes passed in an instant. She lit up like sunshine and I'm sure I did as well. This was who and what I had to live for. *Revive me, defibrillate me, do something, because I'm coming back!*

With each passing day, I found a new sparkle in the sun, in people, even in the COs. The depression gave way to a tentative positivism that longed to break through. For the first time in nearly a year, I was alive and felt like I could survive. My immediate goal was to transform "could" into "would." I knew there would still be days of darkness. But now I was inspired by the possibilities, by the challenges of survival and the payoff of my release.

"There's a fine line between the darkness and the dawn," songwriter Jimmy Webb penned. I was determined to step across the line from the darkness into the light.

The kid left me in the third month. Apparently, he'd been in prison before, what a surprise. Since the system did keep track of previous "residents," he left before me. He never learned where Iraq was and I still had to spell half the words in his letters for him. I laughed as I recalled the other nickname he had given me—"*Spell Check*." At all hours of the day or night, inmates would shout from their cells, "Hey, *Spell Check*? How do you spell blah, blah, blah." "*Spell check*, can you blah, blah, blah."

He still believed he would get that G.E.D., in spite of the odds against it. I still hoped he would, but I was dragged back to reality by his departure. It accompanied me being moved out of my cellblock to another. Only then did I find out that I had entered the "system" in a lockdown building—*D yard*. Little did I know that, the first thirty-seven days I was incarcerated I hadn't been out of the cell except for very brief circumstances because of gang violence. No wonder the yard went down on the few occasions we were let out.

Even though the days barely crept by, I had been in Jasco for three months, colonoscopy completed, my other testing completed, my meds were completely screwed up, and I was still not getting canteen or visits. Then, in rapid succession, I had a visit, received canteen privileges and purchased a few items—mostly hygiene stuff. It's amazing how a few creature comforts will improve your outlook on life.

One day in April, I found out I was being sent from D yard to A yard, with a short stop along the way in B yard. Of course, I went to the store about ten seconds before the move, just so I could lug my acquisitions about a half mile to my new "home"—A yard. There I was assigned to a cell, and found an older guy who was clearly befuddled, looking around the cell as I dropped my stuff.

Determined not to call him "O. G.," I introduced myself to "Tom." He was at least ten years older than me—proving that age is no deterrent to imprisonment. He was even older than that in neurological age. When I asked him if he'd been to medical, he assured me he had—even holding out his hand, full of pills to prove it. One was a seizure med I recognized, along with the standard cholesterol and blood pressure meds. When the formulary only has a few medications, it's easy to spot the ones you know. More disturbing was his assignment to the upper bunk and I to the lower. *Upper bunk—with seizures?* I couldn't catch a break. I insisted he sleep on the lower bunk. I could envision him having a seizure, rolling off the top bunk, splitting his head open and me being accused of assault or worse. Call me paranoid about the penal system, but my limited experience with it had already educated me. No, I'd once again lose my lower bunk, this time for a righteous reason.

Over the next four or five weeks, Tom and I were moved to six different cells—a total of six but actually moved many more times as we were moved into the same cells more than once, each time for a day or two at most. Packing light was the rule at Reception, so it really wasn't a problem, as each move was inside the same A yard complex.

I learned Tom had been a stock trader and both he and his wife had been convicted of some heinous white-collar crime related to stocks. Not Bernie Madoff bad, but bad enough that the State of Jefferson felt locking up a seventy-plus-year-old (and his wife as well) for ten years was justified. Based on his thoughts and stream of consciousness, I was sure he was suffering from early Alzheimer's disease. Thank goodness, he's off the streets and not wreaking havoc on the good citizens of the state.

Throughout our many moves, we were generally allowed one hour of dayroom. During those prized hours, the inmates housed in my tier of cells were allowed to mingle and play games. I renewed my chess skills, being pounded into oblivion by all-comers. It's fascinating. All these inmates who can't spell, can't add or subtract, and can't find Iraq or any other country, including America, on a map can play chess, pinochle, and damn-near any other game you can think of like grandmasters. I'm told you can measure how long someone's been incarcerated by how skillful their chess game is. This time also afforded me the opportunity to get my hair cut for the first time in three months. Inmate barber's skills left much to be desired—unless you wanted a buzz cut. Still, I was most grateful and less shaggy.

The worst part of my time in Reception was the not knowing. What was happening—in the world, to my family and friends, and to me? After all the sorting out is completed, you just sit, not knowing, waiting. You don't even know what you're waiting for. When you don't know, time stands still. I discovered what everyone was really waiting for was to leave Reception. That depended on a "counselor" advising you—yeah right, *advising*—OK, telling you when and where you were going. Every day, the inmate rumor mill spread the question, "Have you heard anything?" Each day the response was long, involved and rambling, ultimately distilled down to "No."

After 118 days, 14 hours, I was summoned with ten minutes' notice to see a "counselor" who it turns out was a counselor's *assistant*, meaning I'd waited 118 days and 14 hours to see not the top dog, but the top dog's lap dog. My counseling session lasted less than five minutes. It turns out the top dog I hadn't seen was more like a dachshund in the penal system dog world—a "CC-1" I later learned, which stood for *Correctional Counselor-Level One*. If I could have touched him, I would have hugged my CC-1 assistant Chihuahua, because I was leaving in the morning for someplace called JRC—Jefferson Rehabilitation Center—a Level 2 facility, in the southern part of the state, in a city less than forty-five minute drive from where my wife lived.

Next morning, at the regulation time of 3:30 a.m., I was rousted by what inmates call the "Goon Squad." Placed in the standard-issue holding cell for about four hours, I was strip-searched, shackled, but *not* stranded for long, when I met the black-shirted officers of the transport division (these guys were a different rock band altogether). There were no smiles—they were all business. We were quickly loaded onto a rickety-old bus with blacked-out windows for transport to our new venue. There were about ten of us, guarded by a driver and three others.

The bus had a metal screen in the front to prohibit us from approaching the driver or guards—like that was even a remote possibility while shackled at the ankles, waist, and wrists. Just behind the last row of seats was another metal cage where one of the three guard positioned himself, along with an arsenal of weapons. My personal favorite was the loaded shotgun lying on a small shelf aimed towards the front, separated from my head by a thin piece of sheet metal. Yeah, as we started up and the bumps increased from the lousy bus suspension, I sure was glad that shotgun was pointed right at my head. I sure felt safe.

The trip south took four hours. About half way, we stopped at a fast food joint so the guards could eat—in front of us, of course—while we were given the standard-issue brown bag. Tough to eat in shackles and waist cuffs. I passed. What I really wanted was to get off the damn bus and away the hell from that damned shotgun!

We made it uneventfully to Jasco Rehabilitation Center, a.k.a. JRC. It was about four in the afternoon and I figured I'd be wherever I was being placed soon.

Wrong!

Five hours later, after shuffling through the standard five lines and four or five questions in each, we were each given one set of new clothes—"blues"—a blanket, a sheet, and our possessions in a plastic bag. I was handed over to a JRC correctional officer for the short escort to my new dorm.

I'd finally arrived in real prison.

Chapter 4: And In the Fourth Month, He Arose from the Dead...

He restoreth my soul: he leadeth me in the paths of righteousness for his name's sake. ... I will fear no evil: for thou art with me

"Show me your paperwork," insisted a grizzled man, looking years older than his age.

"Let me put my stuff down." I was exhausted, sleep-deprived, and just plain sick of it all. "Which is my bunk?" fully expecting the upper, given my history with prison accommodations.

"You're the lower—sixteen low. You can unpack later. I need to see your paperwork."

"What paperwork?" I'm sure my muffled sigh failed to conceal my exasperation.

"A 128-G, or sentencing sheet," the unshaven, balding man of the moment replied. "O.G. You been down before?"

"Down?"

"In prison. This has to be your first term," titling his head.

"Yes," I loosened up a little, does that make a difference?"

"Yeah. It means you don't know shit. I'm the White *MAC* rep for this dorm. Actually, the White dorm rep. Did you learn anything about the rules in Reception? Races and stuff like that. Where are you coming from?"

"Jasco. Can you not call me *O.G.?* Yeah, I learned a bit about races there." *Did I ever*. "MAC rep?" Little did I know, at Jasco I had only completed elementary school—perhaps only kindergarten. This was an institution of higher learning.

"We'll see about that," sighing. "You're an O.G., so get used to it. Everybody'll call you that. *MAC* is Men's Advisory Council, but I'm not that. I'm the White dorm rep. Got it?"

Not really, but I pretended. I thoroughly hated the term O.G. I gotta find a way out of that. "I've been up all night and I just want to sleep. Uh, what's your name?"

"I'm Doper," the inquisitor sighed again. "You'll sleep later. Right now, I need your paperwork and the CO wants to see you after that."

"Listen, Doper. I have no clue what papers you want but you can have anything I have," handing him all the official documents I had in my possession. Funny how as you traverse the system you accumulate a sheaf of various official-sounding documents, with bureaucratic-sounding titles like *128-G* and *812* and . . . those are the only ones I can think of right now, because I'm tired. Come to think of it, that's one step higher than dead, so I'm making progress.

"Go see the CO," my exasperated leader commanded, and waved toward the other end of the dorm while gathering the pile of jumbled papers. "I'll see if I can find something in here. Are you a pervert?"

"Huh?"

"Never mind. Go. *Go!* And take your ID."

The CO was sitting behind a desk in the small office at the front of the dorm. I walked in and started to introduce myself when he barked, "*Knock before you come into my office! You're an inmate, nothing else,*" and returned to reading his magazine.

I stepped back, now standing outside the open doorway, and knocked. "You called for me?"

"Yeah. I haven't read your file yet, so just tell me," looking up. "You got any issues? You know, drugs, enemies, debts? Are you a pervert or sexual deviant?"

That's the second time I've been asked the question—the answer must be important in here, I concluded. "No," I was thinking. "I'm not a pervert. I don't use drugs and . . . what else?"

"I'm pretty easy to get along with," Correctional Officer M. Punkin, or so said the name embroidered on his green jumpsuit uniform, "Not many rules."

All the COs wore these olive drab jumpsuits, adorned with a heavy leather "Sam Browne" belt toting a retractable baton, a canister of O.C. pepper spray tethered from the belt to their leg, at least one pair of handcuffs, and an assortment of personal items. Embroidered above the pocket on the right chest was their first initial and last name. No one used first names for security reasons—we couldn't know our COs' first names because we might ask a friend or relative to find them for nefarious purposes—like I have nothing better to do than hassle some CO who has my fate in his hands or his family.

A slightly pudgy man in his mid-forties, Punkin had a seemingly tough exterior which, I suspected, was probably a lot more bark than bite. "Talk to your dorm rep about my rules. Out of bounds is my pet-peeve. You go out of bounds, I'll march you up and down the dorm butt-naked.

"I hate noise, too. No loud music. And smoke in the bathroom," he resumed reading his magazine.

"I don't smoke, and I'm . . ."

"Yeah, that's what you all say," and without so much as looking up in my direction, Punkin gestured towards the door. "Talk to your rep. Lemme see your ID?"

"Yeah," handing it to him.

"You have to have an assignment card," he said as he handled the card.

"What's that?"

"Every inmate is assigned a job. So you have to have an assignment card on the back of your ID," as he taped a piece of yellow paper to the back of my ID.

"But I don't have a job yet, do I?"

"Of course not. You'll get one when you go to committee," slightly perturbed. "That's why I'm putting you down as *Unassigned*."

"Unassigned? If I don't have a job, why do I need an assignment card?"

"Because *Unassigned* is your job assignment, at least for the time being," Punkin let out his breath. "And because I said you needed it," tossing the card back in my general direction. "Now get it of here!"

As I turned to leave, I noticed Doper had quietly sneaked up behind me, and stood just outside the office door. When I stepped through the portal, he put his arm around me, and asked, "You wouldn't have a shot of coffee for me?"

"I don't drink coffee. You were outside the office . . ."

"Yeah, your shadow. Damn, I could sure use some coffee. How 'bout a candy bar? Look, you don't want to go around the COs without a shadow—someone to make sure you're not telling them the wrong shit, got it?"

"Got it. But what's a shadow? Sorry, I don't have a candy bar, either. I haven't been to the store . . ."

"Shadow, you know, don't go around COs without a shadow—someone to make sure you're not snitching. Oh, yeah, the candy bar. That figures, coming out of Jasco. I found your paper. You're good. Lemme see your ID."

"Now what?'"

"Nothing. I just want to see your pretty face," chuckling a bit. "Damn, that's a rough one, isn't it?"

"Yeah. Why won't they let you smile?"

Have you ever wondered why the pictures of inmates look so mean and menacing? Well, they take a new picture of you everywhere you go. Of course, they don't take you for a photo until you've been up all night and half the next day. You're unshaved and not recently washed. On top of that, if you even try to smile, they tell you not to. So almost every ID picture is that of a greasy, unshaven, harsh-looking criminal staring into the camera, frowning and tired. No wonder the public is scared.

"I dunno. Go get some sleep."

Finally, I could lay my head down. I threw my one sheet over the supposed mattress and within a few minutes was fast asleep. About an hour later, I was aroused from a deep sleep by a noise less than three feet from my head. I opened one eye and shut it again almost as quickly. What awakened me was someone kneeling down next to me, in the alley between my bunk and the one next to it, shooting intravenous heroin.

The inmate looked up, "Hey," he whispered, and immediately went back to his task of finding a vein.

"Uh . . ."

"Sorry to wake you up, man. I'm 'Tiny.' I won't be long . . ." his speech slurring as he entered nirvana, and fell back against the wall. This inmate was no ordinary man. A White guy in his mid-thirties, Tiny had extremely fair skin, except for the ruddy cheeks that looked like someone was constantly slapping his face, and he weighed at least four hundred pounds. When he slumped to the ground, the room shook. I dropped my head back in exasperation. Is there no peace?

The eighty-eight man dorm was outfitted with forty-four double bunks, each with about a three-foot alley between two bunks, sometimes a little more, sometimes a little less. Talk about living on top of each other. The metal support bars of the bunks usually had cloth bags lashed in various fashions on the inside of the front and back. You stuff your belongings into the bags—along with other things as well, I soon learned, some legal, some rather dubious.

JRC is an old, rundown wreck-of-a-facility, which was actually built in the late- 1920s as a hotel, complete with an adjacent lake. With the coming of the Great Depression in 1929, the luxury hotel business became an unneeded extravagance. The place was abandoned and fell into disrepair until the U.S. Navy took over the facility in 1940 or so, converting it into a hospital during World War II.

The Navy made its wartime renovations, used and abused it, and subsequently abandoned it in 1959. It sat fallow until the state bought it, or condemned it, or somehow came to possess it in 1962, and converted it into the low-level prison facility that it continues as today. Initially intended for drug rehabilitation, the place gradually deteriorated (as did its clientele as well) and, in the process, the population became more criminal than addicted. Today, it consists of four different inmate Yards, A, B, C, and D. Yards A, B, and C are regular housing for regular inmates. The D yard houses "SNY" inmates—the acronym for "special needs yard."

As I later discovered, it turns out that the majority, perhaps as much as sixty percent, of inmates in this great state "go SNY"—they ask the state for protection. Protection from other inmates, themselves, and who knows who or what else? It seems a bit redundant to me that more than half the prison population are in protective custody, kept away from the minority who aren't, but what do I know. At JRC, the SNYs are housed in another building up on the hill. Everything there is separate—canteen, visiting, committee, COs—you name it. "GP"(General Population) inmates can't go anywhere near an "SNY" without an escort and without being placed in handcuffs. Except that you can on occasion.

Each Yard was comprised of "temporary" buildings, wooden single-story units built on foundation slabs, except for Yard A. Facility A, a.k.a. "The Hotel," was *not* actually the former hotel, but another building that sits behind it and was some kind of support building for the original hotel, which now serves as the prison administration building.

All the structures at JRC are in various stages of disrepair, "The Hotel" has been condemned by OSHA for over twenty-five years. Not a day goes by when the plumbing or electrical or something breaks. Ah, "The Hotel"—my new home.

"*Jew* go *comida?*"

I cracked open an eye, noticing a pimply-faced countenance staring down at me about three feet away. "What time is it?"

"*Jew* get up," he smiled and turned to leave. "*Yo soy tú* bunkie. *Mi nombre es* Face."

"English, do you speak English? I don't speak much Spanish." And I don't much care for Spanglish, either.

"*Si*, of course. My namb es Face. I be jour bunkie. *Rapidemente*," Face said, walking away. I sat up, realizing now it was the next morning. Although the sun was barely peeking through the heavy-metal screened window, it was definitely daylight. Focusing, I found a clock on the wall that read 5:43. Based on the light situation, I assumed that was a.m. I fell into my blues as Doper found me.

"You met Face? All that damn Paisa does is play his damn guitar," Doper complained.

"He has a guitar'?"

"Hell, yes. Can't play worth a shit, but he tries. Don't tell me you play?"

"I'm a keyboard player, but I know a bit about the guitar." I was being modest. I'd played in bands since my teens and watched enough guitarists to pick up a lot more than "a bit." I also taught music theory and harmony—it is a passion.

"Well, we have a ten-to-ten, so don't violate it," Doper counseled.

"What's a ten-to-ten?"

"From ten at night until ten in the morning we try and keep the noise down."

"Huh, good idea. I'll bet . . ."

"Nobody pays much attention to it but us *woods*, so you pay attention to it," Doper was staring at me as we walked up one flight of stairs to the chow hall. "I hate that damned guitar."

We were funneled into a line and approved for entry by a CO—approved to get a tray from a small window. The CO wanted to see your assignment card to get in and checked to make sure no one was taking out contraband. They also ordered inmates to tuck in their shirts, checked to see if we were wearing socks, if we had any visible signs of injury, and generally hassled each of us as we went through the line, under the threat of getting a *115*.

After getting our trays, we were directed to a large hall filled with four-seater metal tables. I quickly learned you fill every seat in order, regardless of race, creed, or color—under threat of a *115* again. You have a limited time to eat and that concept is reinforced by circulating COs constantly prompting you to hurry. For those not so inclined to eat fast, there are "slow tables" where inmates are shuffled to and isolated—another form of embarrassment and humiliation, if you let it get to you.

A *115* is a disciplinary write-up. It's another form—actually a JDCR 115 "Rules Violation Report" (RVR) form. I would later become all too familiar with this form in my soon-to-be-assigned job. If you get a *115*, the state in its infinite wisdom conducts a hearing before a "Senior Hearing Officer" (a.k.a., a CO ranked Lieutenant or higher), who determines whether or not to add time to your sentence. They can't actually "add" time, but since everyone comes into the system from the beginning with a time-off credit of between fifteen and fifty percent of your sentence, they have the ability to rescind what the court gave you.

How much of a reduction of your original sentence depends on what type of crime you're sentenced for and how the judge felt that particular day. Don't scratch your head too long, it gets worse. If you're a druggie and were sent to prison as part of a "civil commitment", whatever that is, you don't even have a sentence, so they can't take part of it back. Our drug-addicted brethren can get away with petty offenses and misdemeanors without the risk of lengthening their stay.

Usually at a *115* hearing, they throw in "Suspension of Privileges" as an added penalty, too—meaning no canteen, packages, yard, telephone use—that kind of thing, and frequently include a dose of "Extra Duty," meaning you get to work for some CO for around forty additional hours over the next month. You may be assessed up to forty hours, but in reality you actually only work maybe ten hours or so and the CO credits you for the whole amount. It all sounds rather confusing, but before long I would know more about the process than I ever cared to know.

Let's see, what's the motivation for all this discipline? It gets the inmates stirred up and unhappy, increasing their stress, which typically leads to violence as the consequential release. The COs crack down on that, guaranteeing their job security and demonstrating that inmates are animals who must be treated as such. It's a nicely orchestrated but vicious circle.

It's also another lesson about incentives. The justice and prison systems—are they the same or different systems?—are full of misaligned incentives and ambivalences.

That isn't new or news.

Since time immemorial, humankind has struggled with its ambivalence over dealing with society's outliers. This societal "disconnect" with the judicial system is what I'll call the "Throw Away Effect," where society wants to segregate its criminals and forget about them. Previously, more "primitive" societies segregated prisoners not only physically, but also demonstratively (or, as a "deterrent"), by executing them in a public and gruesome manner, mentally segregated them further—"that isn't me."

I submit that there is no real deterrent effect. There wasn't then, and there isn't now. I submit that precisely the opposite is the resulting effect. By publicizing crimes, criminals, and their demise, we frequently encourage "copycats," encourage deviant behavior (the sexual pervert being aroused by the execution), and accomplish the reverse of what was intended. And, despite the obvious fallacy, we continue to do so. If painful, horrendous executions prevented similar crimes, why do they still occur?

"Hey, are you gonna eat that?" I was yanked back to reality from my mental musings.

Looking up, I noted Doper looking at my tray, coveting what I hadn't yet eaten—which was most of the substances deposited on the tray. Maybe it was just me, but since my arrival at Jasco, I had dramatically cut back on eating. The food wasn't what I was used to, wanted, or could tolerate. It wasn't anything snobbish—I just couldn't stop thinking about what it was I was being given to eat and where it came from.

"Go ahead," I motioned to Doper. Before I'd even finished speaking the last syllable, my tray was scraped clean onto his.

"Anybody else want some of this?" Dopers offer was declined—a privilege of rank, I surmised.

Yeah, since my arrival at the Los Diablos jail until now, I'd lost around thirty pounds. It was unnecessary weight I needed to lose—just not lose it this way. My stomach had shrunk and even when I wanted to eat more, I couldn't. The only time I would "pork out" was during my every-two-week visits—and I didn't even know about those yet!

"Hey, Doper, how do I get visits here?"

"Gotta be approved."

"The visit or the visitors?"

"I dunno. Nobody ever visits me," Doper replied matter-of-factly. "Ask the counselor."

"Huh?"

"You're gonna see our counselor sometime in the next week or so, unless he's on vacation again. The bastard's never here."

"Jes, *pero* when he ees, he be *no bueno*," Face jumped in.

"No shit," Doper echoed. "He's supposed to be on our side—yeah, right. He don't do shit, but he's all we got. Unless you *602* it."

"What exactly is a *602?*" I'd heard the term since Reception.

"You don't know about a *602?*" Doper looked at me. Then he and Face were laughing at me.

"Hey!" he shouted to the next few tables. "The newbie here don't know about *602s*." Turning back to me, "I'll introduce you to Leonard. He's the *602* King."

"Hi, I'm Leonard. I've probably written more *602s* than anybody you'll ever meet."

I hadn't noticed him standing behind me as we got up to exit the chow hall. A thin-as-a-rail man in his mid-forties, long black hair beginning to gray, with a ponytail hanging down to his lumbar area, Leonard continued, "Let me know when you're ready to write someone up. I hate the bastards," his eyes starting glisten.

"Sure. But, what is it?"

"A *602?*" Leonard broke into a wide grin. "My masterpieces," walking next to me as we re-entered the dorm. "I gotta go to work. We'll talk tonight when I get back. Start thinking about who you're mad at and what you want to say."

"But is that the only purpose, to let someone know you're mad at them? Who's 'them' anyway?"

Laughing, Leonard gathered his lunch and headed out of the dorm to work. "Rookies. You gotta love'em." I was left with more questions than answers—again.

"*16 LOW!!*" The CO bellowed as I flopped onto my bunk. What's he screaming about now, I shuddered, then I closed my eyes. I was still tired from yesterday's long day.

Not for long.

"HEY!" the guy in the bunk next to me yelled. "Can't you hear him calling you? You gotta go see the CO when he calls."

Now it dawned on me. The CO was calling *me,* as I scrambled to my feet.

"Take a shadow," advised a tall, Black man in the bunk next to me, 15L. "Be careful with this CO. He's a mean sum bitch."

Most in the dorm had left for work—most—but not my leader. "I think I need a shadow, Doper." He casually got out of bed and followed me to the CO's office.

"Yes, sir," I opened the door.

"Knock first, when you come in my office," the CO screamed.

I retreated and reentered, this time knocking as I noticed Doper chuckling under his droopy moustache, all the while staring at the CO.

"Sorry, sir. You called?" You'd think I'd learned that lesson.

"Counselor wants to see you. Right now. Here's a pass. Go!" with that, he resumed looking down at his computer monitor.

"Excuse me, but where do I go?"

"Herring, get this moron to the counselor's office," CO Pike glared at Doper.

"Herring?"

"Yeah, that's my last name. Jeff Herring. Now you know why I like Doper."

No, I didn't.

After leaving the office, Doper told me to put on my blues, take the pass, and go two flights up, one flight past the chow floor. I was supposed to knock on the door marked "Talch."

I wandered through the stairwell up two levels as directed. The stairwell is one scary place. I didn't know yet why it was, but it already gave me the creeps. Imagine a three-foot wide 1920s hallway used by the service staff of a hotel. Dank, dirty, dark, and claustrophobic; I was soon informed it also was where inmates beat up other inmates since it was . . . confining, shall we say?

The counselor waved me into his office, air conditioner blasting on full. Even though it was only late May, it felt good. "You're going to committee next Tuesday. Probably take five minutes at most since you're new and your file's pretty clean. Any questions?"

Uh, yes. This was all Greek to me. "What's 'committee?' What happens there? Do I need to do anything to get ready for it'?"

My CC-I leaned back in his chair, put his hands behind his head, and frowned. "You don't know shit do you?" Without waiting for an answer, CC-I Talch began his lecture on "Committee 101."

"Every inmate goes to classification, that's UCC not ICC, on arrival and again annually."

"UCC?"

"UCC stands for Unit Classification Committee. That's where you're going. ICC stands for Institutional Classification Committee. You're not going there."

"But . . ."

"Don't ask."

The purpose of the Unit Classification Committee, I learned, is to assess where you are in the penal process and determine if any changes in your program need to be made.

"At your initial committee, you'll be put in a job, told what your privileges are, and whether or not you're P-coded," pausing to let that sink in. "The Facility Captain runs the show. As your CC-I, I'll be there, as will a CC-II, along with who knows who else if they come from Education."

My mind was swirling with questions, and confused by he jargon. "*P-coded?*"

"Just means your points can't go above eighteen and you can't go to a Level One."

"Points?"

"Yeah. You didn't know you have six points? Normally, you'd be sent to a Level One with under eighteen points, but P-coded means you're permanently stuck at nineteen. It's a way we keep you in a Level Two. Each year, if you're good, your points drop by six. So you can go to a lower level."

"But not me?"

"Not you, right. You're P-coded."

"What are the criteria for getting P-coded?"

"Technical stuff. You wouldn't understand."

"*Why am I P-coded? Try me,*" I challenged.

"Any other questions?" Mr. Talch had moved on.

"Do I get any requests about jobs or about my privileges? What privileges are we talking about?"

"You'll get put on a job list. If you have requests, you may get it, or not. Everyone usually starts out in the kitchen or as a dorm porter. Looking at your T.A.B.E. score, you'll be perfect for the clerks list. Privileges, man. Canteen, packages. That kind of stuff."

"T.A.B.E. score?"

"Remember that three-hour written test you took in Reception? That's a T.A.B.E. test. It stands for Testing of Adult Basic Education."

Oh, yeah, that "three-hour test" which took me forty-five minutes to finish, I reflected. "What about visits?"

"Family or regular," Mr. Talch wrinkled his brow.

"What's the difference?"

"Man, if you don't know . . ." his voice trailing off as he remembered I was a newbie. At least he was patient. "If you got visitors at Jasco, they had to complete a visiting form. It's still good here and at any other state prison. I noticed in your C-file that you're married. If it's true, then you can get family visits."

"Is that what I think it is?"

"And just what do you think it is?" He was playing with me, or so it seemed.

"Conjugal visits. With my wife," I answered confidently.

"Conjugal, oooh, a big word. Yeah, that's what it means, although you can have others besides your wife, like kids or parents, as long as they're relatives and approved."

"I'll stick with my wife for now," the first thing that caused me to smile even remotely. "Yeah, big word. I know a few more, too."

"I'll bet," Talch smiled. "Well, you're in luck," throwing me a four page packet of papers to fill out. "Bring these back to me and if you're approved, you can have a couple of days away from all this—every three or four months."

"That sounds like heaven."

"Not exactly, but it's the best I can do," Talch stretched his arms over his head. "I know your story. I even saw you on the news. You got screwed but it is what it is."

"No kidding," trying not to be too sarcastic. "Don't believe everything you read . . ."

"In the papers," Talch interjected, "or in your file?"

"I just want to get by without any hassles and go home someday."

"Someday? Aw, four or five years isn't so long."

"It is when you're over sixty." Just thinking about that long a time wiped the smile off. "Tell that to my wife."

"I get it. Just stay out of trouble and the time will pass quickly. Find something to do. You'll get a job—not the one you want, you'll get that eventually—but find something to keep your mind in the game."

That was the best advice I'd heard since entering the "system." "When's this committee?"

"Next Tuesday. You'll get a ducat."

"Ducat? I know what a ducat is and I can't believe you have them in here."

"It's a pass to move around the institution," Talch smiled. "It'll come the night before. At least it should. You never can tell."

"But a ducat is . . . never mind," I stood to leave. "Thank you. This has been informative."

"Huh?" Pausing without looking up. "It's my job."

As I left, all I could think about was the term—*ducat*. Why was a pass called a *ducat*? I would learn soon enough in three days, when I was handed my ducat on the Monday night before committee. I received a three-by-five inch gold-colored piece of paper—a ducat—for committee in the morning.

You see, a ducat was a gold coin used in medieval Europe. Gold coin, gold-colored paper—why not? I soon learned that prison also had blue ducats, red ducats, and white ducats, each with different meanings. Oh, by the way, the gold ducats were phased out in my third year and replaced with the red ones. So now, there's no actual association with gold or coin in prison ducats. Go figure.

The next morning, I sat waiting for two hours before being called into committee. When you don't know squat, it's all pretty intimidating. I entered a small office presided over by a Correctional Officer of the Captain variety. Mr. Talch was there at the head of the table and did most of the talking. Also there was a third person, I discovered later, who was the facility CC-II.

There are five CC-Is in Facility A, supervised by one CC-l1. Each of the three "watches" had multiple COs, one Sergeant, and one Lieutenant, and overseeing them all was the facility Captain, who actually presided over two facilities. First Watch is from ten at night until six in the morning. Second Watch is from six in the morning until two in the afternoon and Third Watch is from two in the afternoon until ten at night. And I thought a watch was worn on the wrist. Very confusing at first. Then again, everything was confusing to this newbie.

In committee, I was told I was *P-coded*—I still didn't really understand what it meant or why—and that I was in privilege group *A1A*, whatever that was, and that they would get back to me about my job assignment. About a week later, they got back to me. I got another ducat—a white one—telling me I was assigned as a porter. Oh joy! What did that mean?

Dorm porters are responsible for keeping the dorm and bathroom clean, and I use that term loosely. How clean depends on how angry the particular porter in question feels that day, or any other excuse to interfere with his motivation. I learned just how filthy we humans can be and just how little it bothers some people.

I kept missing Leonard. I really wanted to find out what these *602s* were that I'd been hearing about since Jasco. Finally, about the same time I went to committee, he sat down with me one night after chow.

"Leonard," I initiated my query. "What can you tell me about these *602s*?"

Leonard was sitting on his bunk, making alterations and sewing on a pair of state-issue pants. He looked up and cocked his head sternly. "Do you believe?"

"Do I believe what?"

"Are you a man of God?"

"I think so," hesitating. I'd been reading in my CR Bible each night and struggling to more clearly define what I believed and what I didn't. Reconciling religion and science was my current dilemma. "Why?"

"I found the Lord about five years into my term," his sternness evaporating. He seemed pensive for a few quiet seconds. "I've been going to a nightly men's Bible study group. That's why you've had trouble finding me. Think you might be interested?"

"Religion is a personal thing to me," replying calmly. "I'm sorting through a lot of my feelings. Maybe down the road. I'm trying to re-discover God again."

"Reborn?"

"Not exactly. This whole prison thing. It's a wake-up call from God, I think," I continued. "I was raised as a Presbyterian, but haven't been into it much until . . ."

"All of this? Yeah," Leonard added. "Crisis brings God into focus for a lot of people in prison, including me. I've been down sixteen years now."

"Wow," I couldn't help being impressed. I'd learned that it's not kosher to ask someone why they're in prison, or what their crime was, so I didn't. "You're pretty young. I'm guessing . . ."

"Forty-three," Leonard interjected. "I was one bad-ass dude and one bitter son-of-a-bitch for the first five years or so. Then I met a couple of LWOPs and they led me to the light."

"LWOPs?"

"Life-Without-Parole guys. Lifers. LWOPs. Man, you got a lot to learn," Leonard smiled for the first time tonight. "Sometime we should talk about God. But for now let's stick to *602s*. So who you wanna write up?"

"Nobody really. I just don't understand . . ."

"Look, it's us versus them. They try to get out of giving us what we deserve and try to get out of doing anything. The bastards," Leonard was getting wound up. "If you don't get a package, or if you don't get the job you want, or if you don't . . . if you don't . . . Well, you get it. We can't let these bastards take advantage of us."

"Is that really the Christian thing to do?"

"Yeah, well, I slip a little every now and then," Leonard smirked.

"But what are you really trying to accomplish?"

"Huh?"

"It seems to me you're angry at the system and trying to give 'it' grief. All that does is piss 'em off, right?" My reasoning was coming in spurts. "Except it doesn't get you anything but trouble from them. Who is 'them' anyway?"

"*Them?* All the bastards."

"All what *bastards?* Who are you . . . *we* . . . fighting? And why? All I want is to get out of here as soon as possible and in one piece," I continued. "I'm assuming you do, too?"

"Yeah."

"If you want to get your package, or whatever, writing a complaint isn't going to get it, is it?"

"They have to answer a *602* in fifteen days," Leonard argued. "That's in Title 15. Fifteen days or you can appeal it."

"But you still don't have your package, right?"

"No, you don't."

I stood up, pacing slowly in the narrow alley between Leonard's bunk and the next one. "What's 'Title 15?' Anyway, if you want your package—what's a package?—if you want it, sugar works better than vinegar."

"Title 15 is the Jefferson Code of Regulations for Crime Prevention and Corrections. It's the law in here, for us and the green meanies," Leonard's eyes tracked me as I paced. "Sugar, huh? Just what sugar do I have? They have all the power. We're nothing. They hate us, abuse us, and could care less about us."

I stopped and looked Leonard in the eyes. "That may be true, but they're still human, susceptible to human nature. We have to find what makes them tick, what they're interested in, what motivates them."

"I'm not talking to the cops," Leonard was firm.

"But you do every day," I persisted. "We all do. Yeah, it's business mostly, but it doesn't have to be. Intelligence, that's what we're gathering—Intel."

"What are you talking about?" Leonard appeared confused. "Intel?"

"The left hand doesn't talk to the right. We gather a little information from the left, feed it to the right, and get some more info. Intel, that's what we end up with—information." I counseled. We sat quietly for a minute. "Back to *602s*. When you get it back in the fifteen days you say they have to complete it, what does it say?"

Leonard sighed, "The bastards usually make some lame-ass excuse for why they didn't do what you asked for, or tell you it's the wrong form, or some other bullshit excuse."

"But it is a *602*. That's the right form you said?"

Leonard scowled and said, "Of course it's the right form—except it really isn't. It's called a *602* because that's what it *used* to be."

"What?"

"Yeah, a *602* was a *602* form until about five or ten years ago when they did away with it. It's a *Form 22* now," Leonard explained. "There's still a *602* form, but it's only for appeals. If you ask for a *602*, you really want a *Form 22*. If you get an actual *602* and send it through, you'll get it back asking where the *Form 22* is and a nasty comment about not using the right form."

My head was reeling. "Let me see if I understand. If you want to complain about something, you ask for a *602*—it's called a *602*—but it's actually a *Form 22* you want, if you want to get something. So you fill out the *Form 22*, not the *602*, even though it's called a *602*."

"Right."

I was reminded of the Abbott and Costello *Who's on First* burlesque routine.

"If you do fill out a *602*, it's only for appeals. So how do you know when to appeal? When you get the *602*—the *Form 22*—back, saying you're rejected and that pisses you off and you want to appeal it." I took a deep breath, and continued, "Where does the real *602* appeal form go? Who gets it?"

"Whoever originally rejected your *602* which is really a *Form 22*."

"The same person?"

Who gets the check? I don't know. Third Base!

Leonard nodded his head. "Yep. There's actually an appeals section on the *Form 22* you fill out after the first rejection. It's only after the *Form 22* comes back rejected that you fill out the *602*."

"*The real 602?*"

"Yeah."

"Does anybody ever get an answer?"

"To what?"

"A real *602*, I mean a *Form 22*, or, well, both?"

"Not if you *602* them."

"Then why *602* anybody for anything?"

"'Cuz Title 15 says that's what you gotta do if you wanna complain about something." Leonard was beaming now. "I'm the best at filling them out. I hate those bastards."

"So you never get your package?"

"Not usually." Against my better instincts, I decided to ask more. "What is a package? Everyone keeps throwing that term around."

"Each quarter, an inmate can have his family or whoever order him a *package*. It's outside food, hygiene things, electronics, that kind of stuff," Leonard advised. "You can only order thirty pounds, but it's a Godsend. When they don't get it to you or they lose it, you write a *602*."

"You fill out a *602*—or a *Form 22*—or a whatever, because that's what Title 15 says to do?"

"Right."

"There has to be a better way," I mumbled. "You want to get your package, knowing someone seems better than filling out endless forms."

"Yeah, but I won't talk to the bastards."

"But that's why you never get your package."

"No," Leonard countered. "I don't get my package because the bastards never respond to my *602s*."

"I thought you said you were the *King of 602s*."

"I am. But that doesn't mean they answer many of them."

"I thought you said they have to answer them—in fifteen days?"

"I did, but they don't."

"I gotta think about this," I shook my head. I really just wanted to get away from the discussion. If there were even an ounce of truth to what Leonard had said, this was truly insane.

As I wandered towards my bunk, I came upon Face, Tiny, and Doper in deep conversation with another inmate. As I walked by, one of them motioned me into their conversation.

"Settle something for us," Tiny stared at me. "Doper says you know a lot about the real world. Well, Face and Pitr are . . ."

"Excuse me," I interrupted, "who's Pitr? Do you mean Peter?"

"Me," the third inmate in the discussion chimed in. "It's Pitr, not Peter. A long 'I', not an 'E'."

"*E-i-e-i-o*," I muttered under my breath. "Well, Pitr, uh, nice to meet you. What's the question?"

"OK. Here's the deal," Pitr began. "Tiny overheard a new guy talking to another guy about his genitals—the new guy said he was a nurse or something and . . ."

"No, a tech, an x-ray tech," Tiny chimed in.

"OK, a lab tech," Pitr continued. "Anyway, here's the question. The guy was asking the new guy if he would look at his penis, being in the medical field and all. The new guy must've said yes, because they took off for the jack-shack."

"The what?" I frowned.

"The jack-shack, you know, the mop closet."

No, I didn't know. Was he ever going to get to the question? As the story droned on, I started drifting off. I had questions, too, and no answers. Is punishment meant as a deterrent or not? Is incarceration for punishment or rehabilitation? Who and what determines what is or is not a crime? Should causation be a factor in whether or not an act is a crime and should it mitigate punishment? I've only scratched the surface in a few areas of my ambivalence. I had so many questions my head hurt. Did I have any say in answering them? I remembered my main objective was to survive.

"So, what do you think?"

"Huh?" I was drawn back to the present, a discussion with Face, Tiny, Doper, and Pitr.

"Does that make him gay?"

"Uh . . ." I hadn't listened to the last part and I was regretting it. "Run the last, just the last, part by me again."

"So the new guy—the lab tech or whatever, who said he was in medicine—if he checks out the other guy's private parts—his unit—does that make him gay?"

"You are kidding, right?"

They weren't. All four were staring at me, waiting for my response.

"First of all, the new guy's a doctor, not a nurse or a lab tech or an x-ray tech. A doctor with over thirty years of experience,"

I took a deep breath, and continued, "I know him pretty well. No, he isn't gay, and examining someone doesn't make you gay even if you aren't in the medical field."

"Are you sure?" Doper spoke for the group.

"I'm sure. Tiny, did you see who was talking to the new guy?"

"Not exactly."

I quickly came to appreciate just how "not exactly" most second-hand accounts like this actually were, and how frequently they would be the case.

"Interesting," I addressed the group. "So you don't really know who the new guy is—the one doing the examining?"

Four heads shook left-right in unison. This was my introduction to the inmate rumor mill.

Every organization has its own rumor mill . . . hospitals, manufacturing plants, offices, government bureaucracies . . . all of them. The inmate variety is a particularly virulent strain, since it is often propagated by misinformation to begin with, by poorly educated inmates with poor communication skills in the first place. One inmate *thinks* he heard something—but of course can't remember it correctly—then, adding his own take, tells another, who does more of the same when he passes it on, and soon enough you have, well, what had unfolded right in front of me now. Little did they know, but I had also observed the same incident.

"Are you talking about the new guy asking or the new guy telling?" Pitr asked.

"Either one," I replied, "because it makes no difference. Let me help you out. I'm the one who was giving the advice to an inmate who asked me if he had cancer."

"You?"

"*Jew?*"

"Yeah, of course, *him*," Doper silenced the others. "Who are you?"

"I'm . . . do you want my real name or what everyone calls me?"

"What's your handle?"

"*Doc.*"

"Doc?"

"Yeah. My name is . . ."

"You're really a doctor?" Pitr raised his eyebrows.

"*¿El médico?*" Face echoed.

"What the hell are *you* doing here?" Tiny's eyes lit up.

"Yes, I'm really a doctor, and it's a long story. But that's why I'm called *Doc.*"

"Doc. Well, I'll be," Doper murmured.

Pitr whistled and Face whispered, "*El médico.*"

This conversation, however, was not entirely benign; as I was slowly adjusting to my new surroundings, something else was occurring within me. Although I hadn't realized it at the moment, four months into my sentence, I was returning from the dead.

Chapter 5: Drugs, Sex, and Rock 'n' Roll

Yesterday . . . all my troubles seemed so far away.
Now it looks as though they're here to stay.
Oh, I believe in yesterday.
Suddenly . . . I'm not half the man I used to be.
There's a shadow hanging over me.
Oh, I believe in yesterday.

—Yesterday
Paul McCartney, The Beatles

There were boom-boxes to the left of me, boom-boxes to the right, and here I am, stuck in the middle of them all. Sounds a lot like a song from the '70s, but it was the truth. To walk down the center aisle of my—or any—dorm was to enter a cacophony of noise . . . a.k.a. "music" . . . but mostly noise. When I get out of here, I made a mental note to myself, *the thing I want most is . . . quiet!* As I walked past a bunk, there might be classic rock, rap, hip-hop, juju, you name it . . . it was all noise.

But blend them all together simultaneously and you have prison.

Prisons certainly aren't monasteries. As a child of the '60s, I consider myself damn-near enlightened, certainly on the good side of the Bell curve. And as a child of the '60s, I'm also one helluva judge of good music, a bit of a trivia buff, and a student of the culture. Why not? I lived it, like so many other *Boomers*. That also means a certain familiarity with the cultural hallmarks of drugs, sex, and rock 'n roll. My familiarity wasn't as important as that of my fellow travelers through the penal universe. Their familiarity with the finer points of this trio of distinguishing cultural features would come to impact virtually every aspect of my remaining time, every single day, from daily dorm life, to work, and nearly every moment in between.

Purple Haze was in my brain,
lately things don't seem the same,
acting funny, but I don't know why,
excuse me while I kiss the sky.

Purple Haze was in my eyes,
don't know if it's day or night,
you've got me blowing, blowing my mind,
is it tomorrow, or just the end of time?

— Purple Haze
Jimi Hendrix

"Doc! *DOC!!*"

I could hear the shout from half-way down the dorm hail. *What now?*

"Doc!"

This time called by another voice from the same general direction.

Two distress calls—this was probably an emergency. I took these as my cue to respond, sliding off my bunk and walked toward the inmate bathroom area. As I approached, three inmates of the *woods* species bolted out the entrance.

"Doc! It's Tiny!" one screamed. "*Come here—quick!*" Based on my short dealings with Tiny, a.k.a., Rick Dantropoulos, I had a pretty good guess at why I was being called. The three escorted me into the shower area where I found the showers pouring over a hulk of a man slumped against the back wall, water running everywhere—on him, the walls and the two other inmates hovering over him.

"Let me guess," coming closer to the mass of flesh on the floor. "He slipped in the shower?"

"Doc, you gotta help him," one of the shower companions spoke while slapping him hard. "He puked and then fell out."

People are strange when you're a stranger,
faces look ugly, when you're alone...
When you're strange, no one remembers your name.
When you're strange...

— People are Strange
Jim Morrison, The Doors

I moved alongside my new patient. He was slumped over with his head resting on his chest—his very large head. He was not his normal white with ruddy complexion, but a dusky, blue from head to toe. Having seen this too many times to count in the ER, I grasped both sides of his mandible at the angle in front of his ears and gently lifted his head, extending his neck while thrusting his jaw forward, while not so gently easing him to the shower floor.

Executing this maneuver, my rotund mortal soul took a gasping breath, drooled down his face, and lightly thrashed about. His color dramatically improved in seconds as I motioned the others to step back.

"Give him some space. What you have to worry about is an airway problem. With his head slumped down on his chest, he can't breathe. No breathing and soon you're dead," pinching his chest to create a painful stimulus. That will help him wake up.

"Whoa, dude. The colors. What happened?"

"You're asking me?" I couldn't help shaking my head. Turning to the assembled gathering, "Who was with him?" No one answered. "C'mon guys, you and I both know what this is. How long ago did he use?"

"Well . . ."

"Anybody else? If he OD'd, then it must be good stuff, so others may OD as well." Good stuff. Did I just say *good stuff*? Heroin? "Get some cold water, not this hot shower water. Throw it on his face. I'm guessing we don't call the medical people, right?"

"Hell, no," someone offered. "They'll roll him up. C'mon, Doc. It's Tiny."

About this time, Tiny opened his eyes and smiled. "Whoa, dog. That was some light show," vomiting all over himself, and smiling the entire time.

"Tiny," I threw more cold water on him, to shock him medically and to express my frustration personally. "You OD'd. You gotta be more careful. Do you know any old heroin addicts?"

"Huh?"

"Do you know any old heroin addicts?" I rendered his response. "No, you don't. They're all dead. You will be, too, if you aren't more careful." I was sick of seeing young people in the prime of life ruined by a veritable cornucopia of substances—some old and traditional, many newer and more lethal.

I was a mixture of anger, sadness, and frustration—all related to this incident and others. Slowly, Tiny's level of consciousness improved, and within a few minutes he was standing as if nothing had happened. This wouldn't be the last time I encountered one of my compatriots in the throes of substance abuse. It was the *du jour* issue of each and every day. He stumbled back to his bunk. I pleaded with the others to watch him and not let him sleep for at least an hour.

Tiny was a good fellow of Greek extraction and the facility supply clerk. Other than a "little" heroin habit, he was quite helpful to me over the first few months. The facility supply clerk distributes office-type items such as pens, paper clips, Post-it® Notes, and the like—all useful, I came to understand, in the material-poor environment of an old prison. Much of it contraband for inmates to possess.

God bless the boys that make the noise on Sixteenth Avenue.
—Sixteenth Avenue
Lacey J. Dalton

I love music, all types of music—rock 'n roll, country, blues, rhythm and blues, jazz, even classical . . . especially classical. As a kid, I took classical piano lessons until eighth grade when I mustered the courage to quit—what thirteen or fourteen year older wants to practice piano when there are bikes to ride, baseball to play, and footballs to toss. That keyboard abdication lasted about six months—until *The Beatles* hit America.

In the ninth grade, I started my first band and rapidly moved up the band ranks. By tenth grade, my high school band of five guys was experiencing major success. By my junior year, we toured in a three-state area and frequently opened for big-time acts.

We were damn good; I was hooked. Rock 'n roll attracted me in the beginning because I was blown away by the harmonies *The Beatles* used. There were others, but I was definitely a "Fab Four" fan. Several of my bandmates went on to professional music careers, with one actually winning several GRAMMYS. McCartney's lead vocals—the nuances and subtleties—were my template. By college, I was writing and recording while still playing in bands—now my fraternity house band. That led to writing, directing, and producing USO tour shows during the Vietnam War years. There's not a military base in the southwest I haven't played.

There were some nice fringe benefits, too. Music gave me a way out of the house in high school, financial independence—we made a lot of money in those days—AND the bonus of attracting girls in droves. I can remember singing, *"I Saw Her Standing There"* and having girls scream at me. Man, *was I hooked!*

> *I was feelin', so bad. I asked my family doctor just what I had.*
> *I said, "Doctor—Mister M.D.—can you tell me, what's ailin' me?"*
> *. . . All I really need . . . is good lovin'.*
>
> —Good Lovin'
> The Young Rascals

At some point, however, I decided I had a one-in-a-million chance of really making it big in music. Based on those odds, I chose to pursue other interests; that meant my other passion . . . science. Next thing you know, I was in pre-med. That also wasn't bad for finding women—no longer girls, I'd grown up.

I continued playing, but more time was spent getting into medical school, which happened in 1970 after three years of college. I got in a year early, still playing music, but now seriously hunkered down to study. At the end of medical school, and during my surgical residency, I wrote a Broadway-style musical with my writing partner that ended up off-Broadway—waaaay off, in fact.

Nevertheless, I can safely say that music profoundly shaped my life, and it continues to do so to this day.

> *One is the loneliest number that you'll ever know.*
> *Two can be as bad as one,*
> *it's the loneliest number*
> *since the number one.*
>
> —One
> Three Dog Night

I find music very personal. When I listen to music, I can't do anything else. I concentrate on it, study it, and I can't listen with distractions.

In prison, the purpose of music is distraction. Most inmates have a radio, CD player, or a combination of the two, and many listen to their music with headphones. Guys walk around or lie on their bunk with ear buds and a radio, completely in a zone. Similarly, you can order a personal thirteen-inch TV—flat-screen to boot—to watch with your personal headphones. Unfortunately, too many of the inconsiderate persuasion choose not to use their headphones. This allows/forces the entire dorm to participate in their listening experience.

> *After midnight, we gonna let it all hang out.*
> *We gonna have some talk and suspicion,*
> *we gonna put on an exhibition,*
> *we gonna find out what it's all about.*
>
> —After Midnight
> J. J. Cale and Eric Clapton

But . . . and a very big but . . . all things have their time and place. Two a.m. is not the right time, and this sure as hell wasn't the right place. Music blasting on boom-boxes at all hours of the night and day is not my favorite time. Of course, it does fit with the drug profiles of the players. So much for the ten-to-ten rule. Doper was right when he said no one paid attention to it. It was *supposed to be* a quiet time from ten at night until ten in the morning—for sleep, rest, whatever. I do love music, but I practically hated it by the time I left JRC.

The COs could care less . . . about music, noise, or much of anything . . . especially at night. Oh, the occasional CO would not take kindly to the noise, walking through the dorm and screaming at an inmate or two, then disappearing back into his cocoon of an office. On rare occasions, they actually confiscated a boom-box, TV, or radio. The loss was usually temporarily; it wasn't hard to convince another CO to give it back, perhaps as early as a few hours later that same day.

"Doc," came a timid voice.

"Yes," I looked up to see Stinky, another *wood* from the "woodpile."

"Can you come see Tiny?"

I bolted up from my bunk. "Is he breathing?"

"Oh, yeah," Stinky nodded. "He just wants to give you something." Stinky was a quiet, stay-to-himself kinda guy, a bit older than most others in our dorm.

I wandered over to Tiny's bunk and found him lying on his back. He motioned me closer.

"Doc," Tiny whispered. "Here are some pens," tossing me his precious cargo of writing utensils. "I saw you're about finished with that one in your pocket. Can I have it when it's done?"

"Uh . . . sure," I was confused. "You want a pen with no ink?"

"Yeah," motioning me closer, "One more thing. I want you to have my jack-shack spot tonight."

"Uh,. . . "I paused. "I don't know what to say." I really didn't. But I recognized it for what it was: a thank-you.

The jack-shack, as it is called, is really the mop closet off the inmate bathroom. It has a closeable metal door that usually has a blanket covering the view. Inside is a large sink and basin for mops and several places to hang them next to a large window with the obligatory metal security screens. Mop storage is the shack's designated purpose—more personal things are its primary *raison d' etre*.

> *Baby I'm hot just like an oven, I need some lovin,*
> *And baby, I can't hold it much longer,*
> *It's getting stronger and stronger,*
> *And when I get that feeling,*
> *I want Sexual Healing . . .*
>
> —Sexual Healing
> Marvin Gaye

One of my biggest fears about prison was sex—the uninvited sort. With all the TV shows and myths, who could blame me? Visions of homosexual rape danced along with visions of sugar-plums in my brain. To be sure, it is a reality in higher-level facilities, but not so in my experience in a Level Two. That isn't to say there is no sex.

The SNY facility has *special needs* all right. One of them is to house members of the LGBT community—Lesbians, Gays, Bisexuals, and Transvestites—of all flavors and persuasions. Several COs regaled me with stories about having to work in those dorms at night. They always made sure to jingle their keys when walking through the dorm for count or any other reason. Even the COs didn't care to see what went on when the lights went out.

Getting "up the hill," as Facility D was called, was usually an obvious matter. If you requested protective custody, or the court ordered it, you started off "up the hill." If you began in the General Population and felt threatened, or if you decided you'd had enough of being in a gang, you were sent there as well. Just asking for SNY meant, at the minimum, an interview with custody staff to determine whether you really qualified. Supposedly, once you go there you're expected to not participate in gang activity or other nefarious goings-on. *Yeah, right.* I'm sure it is toned down, but prison is still prison and boys will be boys—unless they're not.

You'd think determining whether someone is a boy or not would be easy. Not so fast. Like everything else in JDCR, there are mixed messages and mixed incentives, where easy things are hard and vice-versa. Toss in institutional and personal indifference, and mistakes become commonplace. On occasion, a new inmate would be deposited in the dorm that, by all measures, is drop-dead gorgeous—pretty hair, make-up, and perfect breasts—the whole package. The whole package, that is, until you look under the hood—like when they go to the shower. Only then do you discover that this beauty has a penis and scrotum.

Turns out there are a fair number of, how can I say this, "conflicted" inmates who have only partially undergone sex-change surgery, and are now taking female hormones and living the role of a female, except for the fact that they come equipped with a few extra parts. As enlightened as I believe I am, it is still a bit more than creepy standing in the shower with a "woman" who has a penis.

JDCR considers you a male if you have a penis. It places these poor, mostly-female-souls-in-almost-every-way in a male prison—one with lots of testosterone. They are usually moved to an SNY facility—after the apparently obligatory stop in a General Population dorm. This accomplishes the requisite embarrassment and humiliation for the inmate/victim and provides a topic of conversation for the rest of the dorm for a few days. These "girls" are lucky if they escape without being assaulted.

Speaking of hormones, there is simply a lot of testosterone in prison inmates *and* correctional officers (including the female-variety)—way too much testosterone. Prison is also a young man's game—hence, one of the results of all this testosterone floating around is a need to release it. That's where the jack-shack comes in handy. It is a palace of relief for those so inclined. I was not.

Any relief is welcome. Some exercised, others ran—both on the yard. Others found a release spiritually, or through reading, and some found release through substance abuse. Competition for time in the jack-shack was fierce. You didn't walk in when the door was closed, and there was an unwritten rule about not talking too much about the place to begin with. It also doubled as a smoke-hole, drug-shooting gallery, interrogation room, and, on rare occasions, as a mop closet.

Combine testosterone with frustration, stir in a little underlying anti-social behavior, add a pinch of gang ethos, and you have the recipe for prison turmoil. Throw in a CO with similar hormonal overabundance to heat the pot and it doesn't take much imagination to figure out why prisons are in a constant state of tension that erupts in violence from time to time. And that doesn't take into account the incentives issue.

"Doc, stay out of the bathroom after count," Doper advised one night.

"Why?"

"You don't need to know. Just a little discipline." I found out when someone got into debt and couldn't pay, they got a free, all-expenses-paid trip to the bathroom where three fellow travelers flailed on him for a set period of time, say thirty seconds. The idea was to inflict the damage in places not obvious to the COs. Sometimes it worked, sometimes it didn't. Why or how someone could get himself in debt in prison, you ask? Drugs. Almost always related to drugs.

> *It is my duty to completely drain you,*
> *travel through a tube and end up in your infection. . .*
> *With eyes so dilated, I've became your pupil,*
> *You've taught me everything without a poison apple*
>
> —DRAIN YOU
> NIRVANA

"Doc!" Someone called in the distant part of the dorm. I was beginning to hate hearing my name—this place was worse than the ER!

I looked up to see who was summoning me and saw no one. Then I heard it again, except this time it wasn't "Doc" I was hearing, it was "Dog."

For the first few months I jumped every time I heard "Dog," thinking it was Doc. "Dog" is simply slang for a person, or in this case, a person of the inmate species—also known as "homey," "dude," "my home-boy," and a few others I won't mention. You hear, "Say, Dog?" and, "Hey, homey?" or, "My home-boy" this or that. I had trouble enough remembering real names and now I had to learn slang ones.

"Doc, you awake?"

This time it was really me who was wanted by Stinky, leaning over to see if I was awake, apparently not noticing my closed eyes. Another prison pet-peeve, "seeing" if I'm awake when clearly I'm not, accomplishing the task of waking me without the appearance of interference.

Frowning as I opened my left eye, squinting into the sunlight, "Yeah, Stinky."

"You got a minute to talk to me?"

"Sure." One thing you get used to in the emergency room is frequent interruptions—of sleep, train of thought, consciousness—I couldn't escape that even in here.

"I'm an ex-junkie. I'm not proud of it, but I did kick it," Stinky nodded his head in satisfaction. "I dropped out of high school and I don't know much from books. I got all my school from the streets. Anyway, I want to get my GED. I was wondering if you could help me. You know, be my tutor."

"I'm flattered," I demurred. "But to what end? Why earn your GED without a plan to do something with it?"

Stinky stared back for a minute then looked me directly in the eyes. "I do have a plan, Doc. Yeah, I was a major league druggie, but I stopped several years ago. My brother-in-law has a job for me in construction when I get out. That or maybe even something from my work in here. I'm a dental technician in the dental lab here. I never was a very good criminal anyway. The only time I broke into houses was when I was high, you know, looking for the money to buy more drugs.

"All that's in the past. It's sad isn't it? Look at Tiny. The big goof is too young to know how he's screwing up his life with the drugs. You know what he told me? He said he came to prison because it's easier to get drugs in here . . . and cheaper, too. He's homeless."

"Was," I countered. "He's here now."

"Yeah, but he's here on purpose."

"How can it be more available in here?"

"Doc, you're a rookie," Stinky laughed. "How do you think it gets in?"

"I never really thought about it."

"Well maybe you should," Stinky continued. "Yeah, Tiny slept on the streets, had a full-time job, and was even making good money. He had a membership at a gym and showered there every morning after working out. Then went off to work. Used all his money for drugs. Said they cost too much, so he committed a robbery to get in here."

"They knew that in court?"

"Knew it? Doc, it happens all the time," my companion carried on. "Judges are part of the problem. They don't solve the drug problem, they just shuffle it off to the prisons. Same thing with crazy people."

"Wow!" he'd given me something to think about. "What are you studying now?"

"English, math, geography. The damn math is kicking my butt."

"I've got a map for geography and I'll brush up on math." I hadn't looked at basic math in at least forty years. "You got a textbook I can take a glance at?"

"Sure," Stinky's eyes twinkled. "I'll bring it home from class tonight. Maybe we can set up a schedule for each night?" Stinky turned to leave and stopped. "Thanks, Doc. I know you'll be a big help."

> *Mirror on the ceiling, pink champagne on ice.*
> *And she said, "We are all just prisoners here, of our own device."*
> *And in the master's chambers, they gathered for the feast.*
> *They stab it with their steely knives, but they just can't kill the beast.*
>
> *Last thing I remember, I was running for the door,*
> *I had to find the passage back to the place I was before.*
> *"Relax," said the night man, "We are programmed to receive.*
> *You can check out any time you like, but you can never leave."*
>
> *Welcome to the Hotel California,*
> *such a lovely place, such a lovely face.*
> *There's plenty of room at the Hotel California.*
> *Any time of year, you can find it here.*
>
> —Hotel California
> Eagles

Before Stinky asked for my tutoring help, I had been thinking or trying to sleep. Now he'd given me something else to ponder. How in the world do all the drugs get in here? Over the next few years I learned a lot about how drugs get into prisons—several more mixed incentives. In lower level facilities, like JRC, believe or not, "associates" will drive by after dark and toss a football out a window—onto some area of the prison. These aren't NFLers and they aren't playing a game, well not exactly a sporting game. Inside the football, someone can pack an incredible amount of illicit substances. Gives new meaning to the term "going deep."

Another way is an outside visitor coming for a nice weekend visit—legal and above-board—until they pass banned stuff to an inmate. The inmate gets it back to the dorm by rectal packing—placing the wrapped package up their poop shoot, or swallowing it and waiting for it to pass. It is a game of sorts, since inmates are strip searched before leaving the visiting area for just this reason. In my legitimate visits, I witnessed several incidents that bothered the hell out of me.

Several stand out in my mind. A mother brought her newborn one-month old along for the visit. Inside the infant's diaper, a "special delivery bundle"—and not the baby—drugs. Give me a break! The tragedy is that there are no winners—other than the JDCR.

The inmate gets busted while in prison, something the system frowns on in a major way—a big write up, thrown in the hole, more time added to the sentence. His significant other, the mother of the child—maybe his, maybe not—is arrested on the spot, and she, too, likely ends up in prison. Neither gets help dealing with their addiction other than from JDCR, which translates into not much, if that much. The poor child loses both parents, and in the absence of another family member becomes a ward of the state—transferred into a different governmental bureaucracy, and probably being primed to follow in the footsteps of one parent or the other.

One of the coveted jobs in JRC was being assigned as a warehouse worker. Even a prison needs supplies and everything passes through the warehouse. That includes food, office supplies, and inmate packages—all beginning their journey into the system by being logged and inventoried into the JRC computer system. Inmates were not allowed access to the Internet or to sensitive computers, but inmates were responsible for moving this entire inventory around, storing it, and logging it. "Free staff"—civilians who work for the JRC and have various levels of expertise in the assorted places they work, supervise the warehouse. I say "work," but it's the inmates who do all the work and the "free staff" simply sit around collecting their state-issued paychecks.

There are numerous "opportunities" for an inmate to intercept items mailed to the warehouse and handle those packages personally. One fellow I came to know worked there until he "lost" a rather substantial shipment of "personal property" of the contraband class, which led to an untimely assault by several disgruntled inmates. It also resulted in his termination from the warehouse—not an uncommon occurrence. There are COs in the warehouse, but mostly they are there to check inmates in and out—conduct strip searches and the like, looking for contraband.

The Supreme Court ruled on the legality of strip-searches in the early 2010s and one of the reasons given for approving its use was for protection of the officer—yeah, right. Even the officers I asked laughed at that.

The method of entry for drugs I found most astounding, or perhaps not when you take the time to think about it, is by Correctional Officer. I guess all humans are subject to the frailties of humankind, including those sworn to uphold the law. Maybe that's another reason I've become more than a bit jaded by this whole "justice system" idea. During my time at JRC, I observed two separate arrests of officers on scene. Not only drugs, but other illegal contraband, such as cell phones and tobacco were being smuggled in. Until I came here, I was unaware that prison guards are not allowed to bring anything to work and are subject to random searches and seizures. Of course, the inspections were infrequent and most officers did bring in a few items. One of my favorite COs had his Bible confiscated at the gate as "contraband." I wonder what Jesus thinks of that?

> *Trying to keep my head up living do or die,*
> *My momma says she fed up and late at nite she cries,*
> *I got all the odds against me somebody tell me why*
> *sitting in the penitentiary trying to survive.*
>
> —INCARCERATED
> X-RAIDED

The Black man living on bunk 15L leaned forward and whispered. "You be careful of that White boy," he cautioned, motioning towards Tiny.

Over my first few months, I came to value Sigmund Tree's counsel. Tall, lean and about sixty, he was one loud son-of-a-gun, and a sports nut. You could hear his booming voice anywhere in the dorm, and its volume remained the same most of the time, whether he was talking to you from two or twenty feet away. When he got quiet, I really paid attention.

We made friendly wagers on games and he gave me his unique insight—a Black man to a White guy. He'd been "down" about six months longer than me, on this term. Sigmund helped me understand as best I could the psychology of the dorm and its inhabitants. A barber by trade, he fancied himself quite the ladies' man.

"He's a HAIR-ON addict, I tell ya. You be careful with them HAIR-ON boys. They'll steal you blind."

"HAIR-ON? You mean heroin?"

Yeah, HAIR-ON, what I said," Sigmund countered. "Hell, them bastards'll get you hooked. Doc, don't you listen to him."

I knew not to argue with Sigmund lest he'd get louder. Sigmund's advice on "HAIR-ON" and its believers, however, was right on the mark. During my time, I developed a healthy skepticism for much of what the users had to say. Sad, but true; they would give you things when they weren't using, and lie to or steal from you when they were. Sigmund leaned back to watch basketball—I was never a big b-ball fan—and was soon snoring.

He challenged me to start thinking about drugs and race. Blacks primarily used tobacco and marijuana—tobacco is illegal in prison, so it's the same as a drug here. The *woods* were the main tobacconists, along with being purveyors of methamphetamines, the poor man's cocaine—and trafficked a sprinkle of heroin on the side. Mexicans of the South-Sider persuasion were heavy into heroin, but only occasionally meth and tobacco; American Indians, heroin and meth. The Paisas—Mexicans who really *are* Mexicans—don't use much of anything. That's because *they sell it* to everyone else.

What we have here is a smorgasbord of substances to abuse and a telltale way of telling who's using: *Who's up at 4 a.m.?* The ones who wake me up! Since tobacco is not allowed, there are no cigarettes. The tobacco is of the god-awful variety, brought into the prison in bindles—glorified wads of the leaf wrapped in cellophane. Next, this was rolled into a smoke using toilet paper as a substitute for cigarette rolling paper and lit by creating a "lighter."

The lighter is two raw wires someone inserts into a wall socket, creating a spark that ignites wadded up toilet paper. Or trips the circuit breaker, plunging the dorm into darkness. The TP slowly burns and provides lights for several inmates. This also generates a fair amount of smoke and the occasionally flame—I guess the COs didn't care, because I never saw them look specifically for a lighter. They found them, of course, but more often by accident. If as much creativity were channeled into legitimate endeavors, a Nobel Prize could come from JDCR (or just about any other prison) someday.

I always wondered where the drugs, including tobacco, were hidden once they made it into the dorm. The use of the human anatomy came into play frequently—the rectal cavity being the most common. Sometimes they'd swallow it for transport, necessitating a delay until it passed through their GI tract. Other times the rectum was used for straight storage. Medically speaking, the rectum can hold a large amount—stool, drugs, whatever. Even weapons have been stored there, too.

I've developed a much better appreciation for the unclothed body search and its purpose.

> *The best things in life are free.*
> *But you can keep 'em for the birds and bees.*
> *Now give me money . . .*
> *Money don't get everything, it's true.*
> *What it don't get, I can't use,*
> *now give me money . . .*
>
> —Money (That's What I Want)
> Berry Gordy and Janie Branford

"*¿Medico?*"

I cracked my eyes to see Face, staring over me. "It's Doc, Face."

"*Sí, medico.*"

I did a partial sit-up, leaning on my elbows, "What's up, Face?"

"Dis *es mi amigo*, my friend. He has *el guitaro.*" Standing next to Face was another Paisa.

"A guitar? You want me to play it?"

"No," Face continued. "*Jew demonstra* him?"

"Huh? I don't know," I hesitated "You mean teach him? What's your real name—*¿como se llama?*"

"*Mi nombre es Martin, pero . . .*"

"English," I stopped him. "My Spanish isn't good enough to understand you yet."

"*Jew* play guitar? Doper, he say *jew* play guitar. *¿Es verdad?*"

"I really play piano—keyboards, but I know guitar."

A big smile crossed his face. "*Jew* teach me?"

"Sure," I relented. "You teach me Spanish and I'll teach you guitar—music theory and harmony, not so much how to play a guitar, more what to play. OK?"

"*Perfecto. Jew es el mejor*—da best."

Over the next couple of years, Martin and I became good buddies. I think I taught him more guitar than he taught me Spanish, but what the heck. By the time he left two years down the road, he knew his way around a guitar, could rattle off the circle of fifths and tell you the "one" or the "five" chord in any key. Even after he left, he wrote me from Mexico City to tell me about teaching guitar to his nephew. We stayed in touch for several years.

> *Glowing and burning, blinded by thirst,*
> *They didn't see the stop sign, took a turn for the worst.*
> *. . . He said, "Call the doctor, I think I'm gonna crash" . . .*
> *Life in the fast lane.*
> *Surely make you lose your mind.*
> *Life in the fast lane.*
>
> —Life in the Fast Lane
> Eagles

A few weeks later, I was lying on my bunk reading when I heard the running coming towards me.

"Doc, DOC!" Stinky screamed. "It's Tiny. He's . . ."

I knew instinctively what it was, as I slipped into my shoes and following the herd back to Tiny. He was prostrate on the floor, sprawled between two bunks, cyanotic and, this time, pulseless. There would be no thank you pens today. "Call the CO," I barked. "Tell him it's a medical emergency."

"We can't call him . . ."

"Get the damn CO," I shouted. "This guy's dying. Got it?"

I lifted his jaw to create an airway as before and grabbed two hands from a bystander and clasped them to the side of Tiny's large head.

"Hold his head like this and don't move."

I hovered over his chest and began compressions. "Come on, Tiny. Not like this," I muttered.

Then I noticed my used pen lying next to him, modified into a syringe—that's why he wanted it. Sharing needles and syringes was as common as dirt in here. No one seemed to care about infection.

At least a minute transpired until CO Pike sauntered over, looking down at me straddling the massive hulk.

"Shit!" he was now fiddling with the alarm on his belt while reaching for his radio. "Medical Code One in 104. Man down," Turning to me. "Do you know what you're doing?"

"Hell, yes!" Stinky answered. "He's a damn doctor."

At least two or three more minutes passed before a medical team arrived. I tried to tell them what happened, but was cut off. The Sergeant accompanying them screamed at me, "On your bunk. *All of you—on your bunks!*"

As I left, I couldn't help saying to the medical staff, "Give him some Narcan." One looked up at me like I was from Mars and looked back at his co-worker. I headed for my bunk. After about fifteen minutes, an ambulance crew arrived and Tiny was placed on a gurney and taken away—no small task getting this hulk onto the gurney and down the flight of stairs. Several days later, I heard Tiny had survived, but was still in the hospital. Maybe he'd learned his lesson—doubtful. Remember, there are no old heroin addicts.

> *Tell him to wait right here for me,*
> *or, I'm gonna kick tomorrow*
> *... I'm gonna kick tomorrow ...*
>
> —Jane Says
> Jane's Addiction

I spent most of my free time writing letters and lying on my bunk listening to music. My first package included a CD player and several CDs. You're allowed ten CDs maximum, so there's quite a bit of bartering and trading in CDs throughout the facility. Few were interested in mine—several classical compilations—Beethoven and Bach, and good-old rock 'n roll of the classic variety—so my collection remained intact.

Not so, my CD player. Sigmund warned me about those "HAIR-ON" boys. Unfortunately, I had to learn the lesson for myself. Not only are they known for thievery, but spending all their resources on drugs meant they had little in the way of possessions—like CD players. So they begged, borrowed—and stole. My stuff usually came back . . . usually, but not always. My Christian rule is charity towards all until you take advantage of me. After that, no more loans of equipment. My poor CD player made it the entire four years. Its power source did not. Power sources are good for lots of illegal activities. The last two years I had to listen to my CDs using rechargeable batteries. A CD consumed the batteries in about an hour. The radio portion lasted much longer. I learned to listen to more radio.

> *You can't always get what you want . . .*
> —You Can't Always Get What You Want
> The Rolling Stones

Martin was not the only prisoner interested in music and the guitar. One year a famous professional musician came to visit around Christmas and brought with him a donation—fifty Fender acoustic guitars. These were worth around two hundred dollars each. The gift was intended for those interested inmates in the SAP program—the Substance Abuse Program. Our rock star benefactor had known the demons himself and wanted to contribute to those who had committed to trying to get better. The day he donated the guitars was the last day anyone saw them.

The warden had them confiscated "to check for contraband." They never made it to my SAP friends. Yeah, that was great for morale at Christmas.

> *If you want to hang out, you've got to take her out*
> *. . . Cocaine.*
> *If you want to get down, down on the ground*
> *. . . Cocaine.*
> *She don't lie, she don't lie, she don't lie*
> *. . . Cocaine.*
>
> —Cocaine
> J. J. Cale and Eric Clapton

About six months later, someone got a call from Tiny. He had been released and was living in a drug rehabilitation halfway house and, apparently, doing well. I pray he remains that way.

Lying on my bunk now, Tiny wasn't my concern. I needed a haircut in the worst way. Not seeing or knowing where to turn, I approached Doper and asked him.

"I'll cut your hair," Doper offered. "Tomorrow morning in the game room."

"What time?"

"Doesn't matter. Just find me."

The next morning at ten, I located Doper running around the dorm and managed to get him to pay attention for a moment—lately his attention span was extremely short. In a few minutes, he returned to the game room with clippers and a large comb.

"How do you want it?"

"I want to keep it close to how I wear it on the outside," I requested. I tried to be my "normal" self. "So just touching my ears—kinda long for in here."

"No problem," Doper was already combing through my hair. It was long since it had been at least two months since my last cut. Over the next full hour, I watched with increasing anxiety as he buzzed, combed and buzzed off more. "Just trying to even it up," was a frequent response. Finally, he held up a mirror for my inspection. "It's perfect," Doper trumpeted.

I gulped as I looked. "A little short," I choked. "Uh . . . thanks." What I saw was as short a buzz-cut as possible. Doper's attempt to even it up was successful—it was evenly non-existent. It took three full months to grow it long enough for even a trim.

When I walked back to my bunk, I passed Stinky who whistled and shook his head. "Ooooh, nice haircut. Who'd you piss off?"

"Well, I needed it cut. Doper volunteered."

"Today? Are you nuts? Don't you know he's tweakin'?"

"Tweaking?"

"Yeah, he's been up for three days tweakin'—meth. He's whacked out on crystal."

"Crystal methamphetamine? Oh, geez," me, an ER doc and I didn't recognize it. No wonder his attention span sucks. Another drug lesson learned. No haircuts by meth-heads. Check.

The pounding headache from the smoke and noise was a daily ritual. Even though many smoked in the bathroom considerately, others puffed at their bunks. Occasionally wouldn't be so bad. But one of the real medical tragedies is the number of smokers in prison—in my dorm, nearly everyone smoked, regardless of race. I'll bet 60 or more out of 88 smoked. I initially tried to tell people about it, but to no avail. Combined with the cacophony of various musical styles, also known as noise, made for one helluva headache. Is there no relief?

"Doc," Leonard walked over to me one evening. "I have a surprise for you."

"Great," I was cynical.

Leonard threw a wad of plastic at me and then a cloth item. "I thought you'd like these earplugs, and I made my Christian brother an eye blinder."

I jumped up and hugged him. It was great, not cynical great, *really great!* Surviving my death just got a little easier. May God bless Leonard.

> Well my mind is goin' through them changes,
> I feel just like committin' a crime,
> Every time you see me goin' somewhere,
> I know I'm goin' outta my mind,
> Well my mind is goin' through them changes . . .
>
> — THEM CHANGES
> BUDDY MILES

Chapter 6: R. E. S. P. E. C. T. — Find Out What It Means to Me

This concept of surviving weighed heavily on me, especially in the first few months. What was I surviving? I didn't know squat about this place, this system or any person in it. I felt like I had a pretty good handle on why I wanted to survive, just not how. My first few weeks and months were dedicated to the basics—food, water, shelter—that was Jasco. Finally, at JRC, I was beginning to emerge from my death to realize I was alive and ready to rejoin the human race—to survive. I first experienced "respect," or more accurately, "disrespect" at Jasco. Now at JRC, the true "strain on the brain" began.

The dictionary defines respect as: "1. To feel or show deferential regard for; 2. To avoid violation of or interference with; 3. To relate or refer to; 4. Polite expressions of consideration or deference. Synonyms include esteem, regard, appreciation, affection, deference, veneration, praise, admiration, approval and others". Where do I begin?

"Aw, shit," Sigmund scowled, making eye contact with me. "You watch out for that boy," gesturing with his head to the bunk on his other side. "That Rico is a bad-ass sum-bitch."

I whispered, "Who's Rico?"

"That crazy Samoan sitting over there drinking. He's got the pruno out. He's bad enough sober. You mix in that pruno and he's trouble, I tell ya. Big trouble."

"Samoan? Pruno? Give it up, Sigmund. More information."

He leaned in closer and whispered as best he could, being a loud-mouth. "That crazy Samoan is the head Mexican. Not the Paisas, but the South-Siders. He's got a screw loose or something."

"Wait a minute. He's Samoan, but runs the South-Siders? How can that be?"

"'Cuz he's one mean sum-bitch," Sigmund snarled. "Don't know nothing 'bout why them crazy Mexicans picked him, but they did. Give him pruno and he's an even meaner sum-bitch."

"Pruno?" I was curious, but I didn't want to try it. Based on my experiences already, anything inmate-manufactured meant bad.

"All that fruit we get at chow in the morning," Sigmund instructed. "They collect it and mash it up—homemade moonshine. That's why them COs check for it in the morning—don't let you take it out. It gets out anyway, 'cuz they don't be checkin' too hard. Don't you be getting into that shit, Doc. You wanna get CO Punkin pissed off, let him catch you with pruno. He'll tear the dorm up, throw the pruno all over the floor and make somebody clean it up on their hands and knees. No sir, don't get messed up with that shit."

"No, no. Not me. I'm just curious . . ."

There was a loud scream, not what you normally hear because noise attracts attention—abnormal noise does, not the usual all-the-time noise. This was more like an old Western Indian war hoop type scream.

"Oh, shit," Sigmund shook his head, jumping to his feet. "We best get outta here."

I followed him as he left the bunk area. I wasn't quick enough. Rico fixed his gaze on me, raised his head and bellowed. "Who the hell are you?"

"I'm . . ."

"Don't you have any respect? Do you know what I'm talking about?"

Just then, Doper rescued me, sliding alongside me. "Rico," stepping between the two of us. "Leave Doc alone. He's a *wood*. He's my problem."

"You be damn-sure you keep him on a leash, away from me," pointing at me as we left. "No respect, I tell ya. He has no respect."

We entered the game room—Doper and I, not Sigmund, since he couldn't come in the Whites' and Hispanics' game room—and Doper motioned me to a table. "What'd ya do to piss him off?" Doper was mildly perturbed.

"Nothing. Sigmund and I were talking and he was telling me to stay away from this guy, Rico, especially when he's drinking. I guess he made some pruno or something. "

"Stay clear of Rico," Doper advised. He was straight today—no substance use. "He's a piece of work. Spent way too much time on a Level Four yard. Don't know what the hell he's doing here, but he is. So give him a lot of space." Doper got up and left me with my thoughts.

Survive? With this maniac around? Survival just got a lot tougher. That's when I looked up the definition of respect. Was I missing something?

Later that night I was lying on my bunk reading when Rico stumbled over, still quite inebriated. "Lemme borrow your light," he slurred.

"I'm reading. Maybe later," I replied.

"I don't give a shit! Lemme have the light," Rico demanded, nearly falling as he spoke. "You have no respect. None, you piece of shit." By this time, several other South-Siders had come over and were trying to lead Rico back to his bunk. He broke free and stepped back towards me. "I want the light," pointing at me. "Now."

I didn't see any way out of it without a major escalation. "Here," handing him the portable reading light. "Can I have it back when . . ."

Too late. Rico had staggered back to his bunk. Within fifteen minutes, he had passed out. The entire dorm breathed a sigh of relief. Of course, no CO noticed anything. So what's up with this respect issue? I'd tried to avoid interfering with Rico and I damn-sure was polite. I figured I must be missing a definition. It turns out the definition of respect is in the eye of the beholder. What I discovered is that the synonym for respect in prison is "what I want," or "my way or the highway." Oh, and might may not make right, but it sure does rule in here.

The next morning Doper was waiting for me to wake up when I opened my eyes. "Did Rico take the light last night?"

Rubbing my eyes, "Yeah, how did you know?"

"In this place, I know everything," Doper growled. He can't disrespect another race like that," standing up as he spoke.

"Wait a minute. I've got enough trouble with him already. I don't . . ."

"It's out of your hands. It's a racial thing now," Doper advised.

"Should I write a *602* or. . . "

"You dumb-fuck," Doper glared back at me. "You *602* the COs and staff, not another inmate," turning away.

"But I thought. . . "

"Well quit thinking. And don't loan your shit out unless I say it's OK. Got it?" Doper was gone before I could let out my whimpering, "Yes."

That night a very sober Rico came over to my bunk, along with Doper and several others. "I, uh . . . I wanted to apologize, you know, say I'm sorry for taking your light." Rico handed it back to me and added, "I got a little carried away, I hear. Won't happen again." He looked at Doper who subtly nodded his head. Rico was gone as fast as he had appeared.

I tried to turn on the light but it wouldn't come on. I opened the back and noticed the two rechargeable batteries were missing. Great. They're precious as gold and expensive, too.

"What now?" Doper watched me fumbling with the back cover.

"The batteries are missing."

"That son-of-a-bitchin' Samoan," stomping off in Rico's direction.

I decided the better part of valor—not to mention the better part of my health—was to not follow. When I woke up the next morning, the two batteries were sitting on my bunk. Doper later re-emphasized his "no loaning stuff out" policy, at least to Rico. It wouldn't be my last encounter.

At breakfast that morning, Doper sat with me. "When we get back to the dorm, you and me need to have a talk about the rules in the dorm." Stinky trailed along with me. Doper turned to him, "Come help me explain the facts of life to Doc, especially about Rico." Looking at me, "Rules, Doc. We have a few things to discuss."

"OK," I wasn't so sure it was.

Stinky sat down on my bunk to my left and Doper to my right. "First of all, you didn't do anything wrong with Rico," Doper began. "But everyone's gonna think you did because it's Rico—too bad, but that's your tough shit. Suck it up, he's an asshole. Each race kinda sets its own rules but a lot of 'em are the same. The *woodpile* likes to all go to chow together because there are fewer of us. That way if a fight breaks out, we're all together. "

"You won't be much help in a fight," Stinky interjected. "Too old."

"It's also against my . . ."

"Cut the crap," Doper cut in. "If I tell you to fight, you fight, got it? Anyway, be careful dealing with other races. I don't even play games with other races—it just sets up too many problems. Like, what if they're cheating? How ya gonna say that without starting a fight?"

"Playing cards—I sometimes do with a few Paisas, but even them, you gotta be careful," Stinky added. "No sharing food with Blacks, but it's OK with Mexicans, although I get nervous about doing that with 'em, too. You're just better off . . . safer . . .

sticking with other *woods*. You know we have a game room for Whites, Mexicans and Paisas only, right?"

"Yeah," I allowed. *Did I ever*. It's kind of a refuge. "But . . ."

"And don't let Blacks sit on your bunk," Doper decreed. "Or others either. They're basically Blacks."

"Or smoke with them," Stinky instructed.

"I don't smoke," I was relieved. "I've seen different races sharing the same needle to shoot drugs. That's OK, but sitting on a bunk isn't?"

"Yep. Drugs are different," Doper continued. "I'm not opposed to smoking with 'em if they got the tobacco, but you're really not supposed to."

"So doing drugs and smoking—things that are bad for you and can kill you—are OK to share, but not things that don't hurt you—like sitting on a bunk, or eating something—that's forbidden?" I was beginning to show my skepticism of these rules. "That doesn't make sense."

"Yeah, it does," Doper lowered his voice spoke deliberately and slowly, "because . . I . . said . . it . . does. Understand?"

"When you're on the yard, hang with people you know, Whites, maybe a few Mexicans, but keep your eyes open," Stinky warned. "If this were a Level Three or Four, you couldn't go anywhere without someone else. You go to take a piss on the yard and you better be with someone. Even taking a drink from the water fountain—you take someone. Otherwise, you get the shit beat out of you. It's not so strict here at a Level Two, but it's still better if you take someone with you in case a fight starts. Have you seen a fight yet?"

"Well, at Jasco there were a few skirmishes, but nothing really serious," I responded. "At least it . . ."

"Ever seen someone stabbed, Doc?"

Now I was a little miffed. "Guys, I worked full-time in a busy ER for over thirty years. I'll bet I've seen more stabbings and shootings than either of you two."

"Don't be too sure, Doc," Stinky speculated. "I'll bet you haven't seen anyone shot with a block gun, huh Doper? You even know what that is?"

Doper was smirking as Stinky asked his questions. "Big-ass shotgun that shoots a piece of two by four at you. Hurts like hell and breaks bones." Doper moved closer. "You've seen it all in a hospital, but not in a prison, Doc. Big difference. They don't come running to save you here. They come if they get around to it. I'm guessing you think the guards are here to protect you, don't you? Let me tell you, they start a lot of the shit and sure as hell don't stop it until they're good and ready to."

"They'll talk to you nice one minute, but'll turn on you the next," Stinky counseled. "There's a green line between us and them. Don't cross it."

"What do I do if something happens?"

"Follow what everybody else is doing," Doper directed me. "When something happens on the yard, the cops'll call 'yard down'. That means everyone gets down on the ground. Anyone who doesn't is fair game and believe me, these bastards enjoy taking out their frustrations on you."

"Anybody left up is fair game," Stinky added. "You'll know what's going on by how many are left standing. It's about discipline. There's a code. If you screw up, first it gets handled in the dorm—usually burpies or some kind of exercise. It goes up from there. The other night, remember when you were told to stay out of the bathroom after count? That's because the South-Siders were disciplining someone. The bathroom is to settle individual issues—two who want to fight it out—or to discipline someone. But always the same race. It's usually for a set length of time, like twenty-three seconds of three-on-one. If it's more serious, someone will get beat up in the stairwell. That's to take them out."

"Always within your race," Doper emphasized.

"Yeah," Stinky continued. "If you see two different races going at it, that's bad. All other guys in each race are supposed to join in—it's a free-for-all riot. Great fun. Doesn't happen very often."

I hoped it would never happen. "What do I do? I won't fight."

"You'll do what I say. You fight," Doper again commanded. "Aw, maybe not. I forget you're an O.G. Just stay on your bunk, but try to find some other White guys to protect you."

"On the yard, if a fight starts—usually happens just before yard's over—that may be an intervention to remove someone."

"Huh?"

"It's usually three-on-one," Stinky went on. Three guys, sometimes more, gang up on one guy to get him removed from the yard—really from the prison. They all go to a SHU. I know, you don't know what a SHU is. It stands for Segregated

Housing Unit. It's the 'hole'."

"They cuff 'em all up and take 'em to the Program Office, interview 'em and roll 'em up. Some Lieutenant or Sergeant will question them. Most keep quiet—not all," Doper droned on. "A roll up is when the cops do a *114* on you and transfer you out of here."

"What's a . . ."

"A *114* is the form that gets you transferred," Stinky picked up on my education. "Man, you don't know anything. It's OK, Doc. I didn't either. Before they transfer you, the cops shake you down for information. Grill you good. You get locked in a cage for a few hours, butt-naked . . ."

"Don't bullshit, Stinky," Doper stopped him momentarily. "I got locked in the cage for over twenty-four hours last term."

"Twenty-four hours? Huh. You beat my record," Stinky laughed. "Anyway, the cage is a metal box about two feet by two feet—damn claustrophobic—where they keep you until they haul you out of here for a SHU term. You might stay in the SHU for ten days, maybe six months, or even a year, depending on what you did."

"He ain't goin' to no SHU," Doper grinned sarcastically. "That's for us. If the yard goes down, Doc, you go down. And don't wear headphones or earbuds on the yard—you can't hear anything with them on. The cops'll take them and bust you. Keep your eyes open, too. Pay attention to who's in front of you and who's behind you. There's lions and antelopes in the jungle, and you ain't no lion, Doc."

I agreed. I'm no lion. I was much less enthusiastic about going to the yard at all. "So what do you have to do to get disciplined?"

Both of them laughed. Stinky looked at Doper, "Debt mostly. That and disrespecting someone gets you in the most trouble."

"About this issue of disrespect . . ."

"Sometimes you don't even know you're doing it," Doper cut in. "Everybody does it, but guys like you in particular. Because you got all that schooling, you got this superiority about you. It's gonna get you in trouble. That's probably why Rico doesn't like you."

"But I haven't said two words to Rico."

"Maybe that's the problem, you haven't talked to him," Stinky insinuated.

"No," Doper waived him off. "It's better if he stays completely out of Rico's way."

"About this discipline," I tried to draw them back to my concerns. "You said debt and disrespect. This disrespect seems to be not giving somebody what they want. And debt—I assume you mean drugs?"

"Drugs and other things, like tobacco, canteen, or packages can get you into debt," Stinky thought a second. "But mostly drugs."

"You ain't gonna have a debt problem, Doc," Doper hinted, "You're a rich doctor. Your problem . . ."

"Whoa," I stopped him. "I used to have some money, but the lawyers took almost everything I had. What was left, the banks took. My house was foreclosed, and my wife had to sell most of our personal stuff just to eat. So don't get any ideas about that rich B.S."

"Ooooh, I touched a nerve, huh," Doper gave me faux sympathy. "Even if what you say is true, nobody's gonna believe you. We all think you're rich, so you'll get hit up for lots of stuff."

"You said, 'we', don't you mean 'they'? You think I'm rich, don't you?" Now he was outed, too.

"What of it?" Doper got testy.

"Let me tell you again—I'm not rich. I lost everything." True, I'd lost most of my material possessions, but I'd found that I still had what's really important—family and friends. I closed my eyes and reflected on that until interrupted.

"Look," Stinky continued. "All Doper is saying is to be careful. We have a 'no debt' policy in this dorm. That means . . ."

"It means no debt, and I mean it. Not for anything to anybody," Doper was adamant. "You may not have money, but you're a smart guy. I'm not worried about you getting into debt, I'm more worried about you loaning shit out and getting scammed. If you have any doubts, come to me or Stinky. As to discipline, you're an O.G., so I'll cut you a break—yeah, yeah, you don't like being called O.G., I know—this time you should be glad. Like I said, I'll cut you a break because you're old—and because you're a first-termer and supposed to be smart. Try not to say anything without thinking." Doper stood up, indicating he was done with our little talk.

"Just ask me about stuff," Stinky stood up, too. He patted me on the shoulder and gave a wink.

They both left me alone with my thoughts. I got the business about debt concerns, I really did, but this respect—disrespect—thing, and all the discipline rules . . . most still didn't make sense to me at all. I kept coming back to the why—why is violence the dispute resolution mechanism for everything in here? On that, I would need to reflect.

The key to surviving seems to be adapting to your circumstances. Physically, that means food, water, and shelter. Mentally, is going to be my challenge. I've always been one who has to understand the root cause of things in order to embrace them. My entire life is being turned upside down—what I believed and what I didn't. Understanding the causes, the reasons, that was going to be my key to survival. I don't have to agree with them, just understand and accept them for now.

How I reacted and changed would determine whether I survived. I was determined to make it for the same reasons I found to be important—family and friends.

I didn't have long to wait. Rico stumbled over a few nights later and demanded my light again.

"Rico, I've been told not to loan out anything, sorry," I feigned disappointment.

"What? Says who?"

"I've been told to . . ."

About that time my head jerked to the right and my glasses flew about ten feet as Rico slapped me—open handed, but hard—and I was immediately quiet. Rico stood there for a few seconds and then turned to walk away. He knew he'd turned a corner in more than just a physical way. I sat there hoping no one had seen, but several had.

Sigmund was shaking his head and leaned in to me. "I told you that Rico was trouble. Now the shit hits the fan."

"Isn't there anything I can do to stop this nonsense, Sigmund?"

"Ain't nonsense, Doc," he raised his voice, insuring others would hear, "it's out of your hands."

Later that night, Doper, Stinky and several other *woods* presented themselves to inspect me and to take my emotional temperature. Satisfied that I was not hurt in a major way, I was told in no uncertain terms to stay on my bunk and be quiet. There would be no apologies this time. After count when the lights were turned out, I heard a commotion in the bathroom. Sigmund whispered that the South-Siders were disciplining Rico. They do it to avoid an all-out fight between all the *woods* and South-Siders—part of the rules.

Who decides when he gets the discipline, since he's the leader?

The next morning, Rico didn't go to chow, staying in bed. I saw him in the bathroom and observed why—two black eyes and several small lacerations around the lips. If he goes to chow, the COs will see him and tear up the dorm looking for perpetrators. They'd strip everyone down to boxers and inspect each person, looking for bruises or swollen hands—telltale signs you were in an altercation. To avoid that, Rico just stayed in the dorm and mostly on his rack.

A few days later, four COs entered the dorm quickly and headed straight to Rico's bunk, rousting him out of bed, standing him up, handcuffing him and escorting him out. About thirty minutes later, CO Punkin unlocked Rico's locker and emptied its contents into a large plastic bag, taped it closed and dragged it to the office. All very neat and surgical—well, almost. Several *woods* told me what it all meant, and then Sigmund translated what they meant.

Rico had been "validated," meaning he met several criteria confirming his gang status. Once an inmate is validated as a gang member, they're sent to a SHU and eventually on to a higher level facility. I was told a confidential informant is usually involved. I can't say I was unhappy to see Rico leave. I'm guessing there were any number of informants ready and willing to "help" the process along.

One night, Sigmund sat on his bunk after lights out, rolling a cigarette. "Doc, I gotta smoke and the bathroom's busy, so you gonna have to put up with it."

"Please, Sigmund can't you wait a minute?"

"Aw, hell," Sigmund grunted. "Damn doctors," tucking his contraband behind his ear. "You lucky I'm a respectful bastard."

Yes I am. Sigmund was one of the few who was considerate and respected the rules—and my health—by not smoking at the bunk. Too many others didn't. I found myself leaving my own bunk to avoid the smoke on a 24/7 basis. I was learning that consideration is different than respect. Consideration is a human concept, respect is a prison concept. Consideration, or thoughtfulness and mindfulness of the needs or feelings of others, is compassionate. Respect—as practiced in prison—is hollow.

Artificially dividing human endeavors because of race, or ethnicity was declared unconstitutional and illegal in the 1950s. Prisons and prisoners apparently didn't get the message. Not only did they not evolve out of that archaic humiliation, it is actually worse now than it was in the 1950s.

Drugs, gangs and debt have always been a part of prisons, but not to the extent they are now. They are a primary reason for the exacerbation of racial tension. Violence is as common as water. Race is used now as an excuse as much as a reason.

"It's a Black day!"

"No, it's Whites!"

The screams grew louder as the TV room debating club met at its usual morning time. In order to maintain racial and ethnic harmony in the TV schedule, each race gets to determine what channel is viewed on their designated day, the schedule derived from a rotating calendar. The harmony is frequently punctuated by staccato bursts of fortissimo shrieks each morning, "Black," "White," "Mexican," as each of the designated races vies for position—the "Paisas" and "Others" losing out since they are absorbed into the "bigger" races.

I am so past the division of humanity into races, since genetics proves it to be artificial. One would think a written schedule would solve the argument—not so, as the discussion only changes from what race day is it, to what numerical day of the week it is. Inmates rarely know what day it is—since for many their routines are the same day in and day out. Only the few with watches or who live for a weekend visit arbitrate the disagreement. What a perfect example of racial and ethnic harmony, just as our country's founders intended.

"Sergeant IN THE HOUSE!" someone yelled as I was reading on my bunk.

Sigmund leaned over to me, "That's one crazy bitch."

"Who?"

"That Sergeant," Sigmund replied. "Sergeant Whining is her name—I. Whining. You wait and see. She's nuts."

"Sit up, all of you," Sgt. Whining screamed. I found out for myself what Sigmund was talking about. "You yahoos think you can pull the wool over my eyes. Well, not this time. "

"What's she talking about, Sigmund?"

"Who knows?"

"Six feet, that's all you got. If it doesn't fit in six feet, I take it. Any less and . . . I'll think of something," as she walked slowly through the dorm, pulling a wooden box behind her.

"Oh, shit," Sigmund's favorite expression seemed appropriate. "If all your stuff don't fit into the box she's draggin' around with her, then she's gonna take it."

Sgt. Whining was eyeing inmates and their bunk areas as she walked, stopping every now and then. "You!" she pointed at an unfortunate inmate. "Into the box." We felt like sheep waiting for the slaughter. She strutted like a Nazi officer picking out souls for the gas chamber. 43L began pulling out possessions and stuffing them into the small box she towed. As the boxed filled, the inmate squashed the contents down, desperate to keep his few belongings.

Six cubic feet is a *very small* space. When contents neared the top, the Sergeant, smiling not-so-benignly, tapped the wooden side. "Stop!" She thrust a retractable baton into the chest of the designated victim. "The rest, in here," pointing to a large rolling bin the dorm CO was pushing behind her. Into the bin went the remaining possessions. The rest of the dorm hunkered down trying to avoid eye contact or whatever they could divine as her method for choosing—including me.

"Oh, one more thing," pausing a few bunks away. "There's a big food sale coming next month. It's for the warden's favorite charity. Lots of food and sodas. Buy up, boys, it's for a good cause. The more you buy, the happier I get." After a few more bunks, she grew bored or something and left as quickly as she came.

"Bitch," Sigmund exclaimed, loud enough for several to hear, including CO Punkin.

Punkin chuckled under his breath, shaking his head. "I'll get the stuff back."

"What's with this food sale, Sigmund?"

"They do it every six months or so," Pitr interjected. "The food beats the hell out of what they serve here."

I scratched my head, "Yeah, but if they just confiscated a lot of stuff because it takes up too much room, where does all this new stuff fit?"

"First it fits in my stomach," Sigmund laughed. "Them soda pops, they do take up some space."

"Funny how they don't care about taking up space when it's for their food sale," Pitr added.

I was suspicious, "Is it really for the warden's charity?"

"Who knows?"

"Who cares? Beats the food here," Sigmund agreed.

I was puzzled. "One of the items in the package catalog is a storage bin for under your bed."

"Yeah, so what?"

"It's approved—all the stuff is approved in packages—right?"

"Yeah. "

"So if it's approved for us to have," I reasoned, "that means we're approved for more than six feet—the stuff under the bed alone is more than that."

"So?"

"If it's approved, how can they take it?"

"'Cuz she's the damn Sergeant," Sigmund sniffed. "She can do anything she wants. They all can." Pitr nodded his head in agreement.

"Why don't we *602* it?" Leonard would be proud.

"Good luck," Pitr mocked me.

"You just tryin' to attract attention, Doc?" Sigmund frowned. "Them bastards make the rules, break the rules, and then tell you it's your fault. The rules are there to outline how they're gonna get you . . ."

"It's an advanced warning," Pitr added, "of what they're gonna do to you. Here are the rules and there's no way you can abide by them. You go and write 'em up on a *602* and it's like you're giving them permission to mess with you."

"I thought that's how we complained about things?"

"It is," Sigmund continued. "But it isn't. You can write 'em up, but if you do, they won't answer it. You write 'em up and you just told them you're a troublemaker. Don't make waves, Doc." The same advice I'd given Leonard.

"Sigmund's right. Don't make trouble," Pitr counseled. "Don't let them know you even exist."

"How do we get anything changed?"

"We don't. Sure as hell not by writin' a damn *602*," Sigmund lobbed a ball of spit into the trash.

"But . . ."

"YARD!" CO Punkin screamed.

The dorm nearly completely emptied in about fifteen seconds, inmates racing to get out of the dorm. I was caught off guard, not ready, but quickly caught up with my dorm-mates. Yard was at once good and bad. Good for exercise, activating one's vitamin

D in the sun and, for me, a chance to be alone as I ran and walked on the track.

I spent much of my day and especially my yard time searching for "me" time and space. Bad because I was frequently interrupted on the track, especially once I got my future job. And especially because of the disciplinary issues that occurred on the yard. Since incidents usually happened near the end, I looked forward to the start of yard and not so much the end. I always breathed a sigh of relief when nothing happened and I made it safely back into the dorm—only to encounter the reasons I left in the first place.

I developed a routine on the yard. When I first arrived at JRC, I could go whenever they called it—two hours on our day, at least two out of three days—one of the perks of being "unassigned." Once I received my job, that opportunity diminished. I savored my alone time on the yard, having been reduced to just once or twice a week after I was assigned.

The yard has a quarter-mile track—typical of JRC, it's ten yards longer than an actually quarter-mile. The track surrounds two softball fields and a central soccer field. Around the outside of the track are various exercise bars and metal tables. The yard is supervised by two COs, and many more available as back-up with a call by radio during an incident. When running smoothly, I was able to run smoothly. Being an older model human, my knees appreciated me running in quarter- or half-mile bursts rather than all at once. So, I would run a lap or two, and then walk one. There is also a small stadium adjoining one of the softball fields with stairs for running wind sprints up and down. My yard time was devoted to fantasizing about life on the outside and, eventually, to plan my future.

"YARD DOWN!!" screamed a CO into a bullhorn. With that, most on the yard sat immediately wherever they were—all but four stationed at the far end of the track, three pummeling one. This was my first "yard down" and I was glad it was a good one hundred yards away. A long distance for viewing, but I quickly learned pepper spray wafts across that distance rather easily—not much, but just enough to taste it.

I didn't notice, but Stinky was sitting about five feet from me. "Good boy, Doc. Stay close to me. This should be over in a few minutes."

"What's up?"

"This is a removal," Stinky advised. "See the one guy the three are thumping on? He owes about $250 for heroin."

"South-Sider?"

"Yep. Tough to go through withdrawal in the hole."

"Don't they get medical help?"

Laughing at me, "Help? Are you kidding? You're lucky to get chow. I remember back in 1998, thinking I was gonna die. Crapped all over myself, freezing, then burning up. Went on for the better part of a week."

"Geez."

"He'll be fine," Stinky lectured. "They'll probably keep him there a month or so and then ship him to a Level Three. Have you met Jaime?"

"No. Who's Jaime?"

"One of the Paisas in the dorm. Just thought you might have heard his story. No big deal."

I sensed there was more to this Jaime than Stinky was letting on. With the yard "down," however, it was the wrong time to pursue it.

I simply hate violence. That sentiment would harden throughout my time incarcerated. As the yard was released, I trailed the others heading back to my dorm. How was I going to confront the violence? How was I going to deal with it? I flopped down on my bunk and randomly opened the Bible to a verse:

> *Rescue me, O LORD, from evil men.*
> *Protect me from men of violence*
> *who devise evil schemes in their hearts*
> *and stir up war every day*[1]

---

1 Psalm 140:1-7, *The Holy Bible,* New International Version.

Chapter 7: *Medical Misadventures, Dental Decay*

*Surely goodness and mercy shall follow me
all the days of my life*

As a board-certified emergency physician, I'm used to being in control—not just of the emergency department, but of life itself, and *my life* in particular. Loss of control is damned hard for any doctor to accept, and I'm no exception. Prison means the utter loss of control, of my personal surroundings, friends, and family. Particularly problematic was loss of control over my health—it nearly drove me crazy—which was not a far drive.

I'd heard disaster stories about the medical care in the JDCR prison system. I'd vaguely heard about lawsuits as well, but I had no personal experience by which to judge. That changed the minute I landed at Jasco. My confidence in their stewardship of my health dropped precipitously . . . and immediately. It fell even further upon my arrival at JRC.

If I was going to survive upwards of five years here, I had to survive the medical and dental care. Since I'd decided to survive, I was able to look forward to life after JRC—unless they killed me first—that is, inflict a medical misadventure. Realizing that, I became determined to take back as much control of my health care as possible—not an easy task by any means in a state bureaucracy that didn't care about me (or anyone else). Control. It's all about control.

Remember the fiasco with my blood pressure? I certainly do. Well, I decided taking control of that was my first priority. Soon after arrival at JRC, I had my chance when I was called for my first visit to the medical facility. After the obligatory two-hour wait, I was ushered into a small examining room where I encountered a forty-something year-old Vietnamese-American, Dr. Duong, sitting at the small, cluttered desk with an ancient computer adorning one side. I decided not to lead with my secret profession to see if he would discover it in the record, and to see how he reacted to inmates. I was pleasantly surprised by his demeanor and even a slight smile. His medical knowledge seemed adequate, even concerning blood pressure management. Then we got down to medications—medications *he* wanted to adjust.

"I'd like to change your blood pressure medications." Dr. Duong suggested. "You're on a beta-blocker and something else—I can't read it. I'd like to . . ."

"Doctor, I'm a doctor," I interrupted. So much for staying stealthy. If he couldn't read what medications I was taking I sure as hell wasn't going to let him guess. "I appreciate the fact that you're in charge of me while I'm in JRC. However, I intend to leave here at some point and have a vested interest in my health. If I may see your formulary book, I will make my own recommendations."

"You can't see the formulary," he replied tactfully.

"Why not?" I couldn't help myself—this was my health, after all.

"Inmates can't see our formulary."

"So it's OK for you to prescribe medications to inmates, but they can't know what they are, or if there are alternatives?"

"Oh, no, I mean yes. We tell you what they are . . ."

"But not the alternatives?"

"Correct," Dr. Duong was shifting in his chair.

"Then I'd like you to tell me all your available ACE inhibitors, Calcium Channel Blockers and Angiotensin Receptor Blockers, please."

Dr. Duong hesitated and leaned back in his chair, thinking. After a short period, he picked up the formulary book and handed it to me. "Take a look at these."

Mission accomplished.

Some are willing to bend the rules—lesson learned and filed away for later use. Together we agreed on a regimen of an ACE inhibitor and a Calcium Channel Blocker, both at low doses. Subsequently, Dr. Duong remained flustered each time I saw him. I still hadn't had a physician, including Dr. Duong, truly lay hands on in a real physical examination. I'm not sure to this day if they would find anything if they did.

I know my body well enough to take care of it. In four years plus, they never found a walnut-sized, benign tumor I discovered when I got to Jasco. God forbid I wasn't in medical control—like most other inmates. I knew it was benign, but they didn't know about it at all.

Over those first few months, I came to respect, and even admire, Dr. Duong. Unfortunately, after those first few months, they transferred him elsewhere, and a Dr. Mee replaced him, followed the next year by a Dr. Ram. Respect and admire them, I did not.

Sitting on his bunk next to mine, Sigmund was waiting for me to return from medical. "Them bastards'll screw you up. Be careful of them bastards."

"Sigmund, you're suspicious of everybody." I shared his suspicions, but I wanted to hear his reasoning.

"I'm not lettin' those bastards touch me again, no sir, not again."

"Again? What happened?"

"I took off my shirt and all he could do was look at my chest scar," Sigmund growled. "Didn't pay any attention to my hernia."

"Chest scar? Did you have heart surgery?"

"Hell, no," Sigmund laughed. "I was drinkin' with some buddies one night and I just passed out. Woke up in some damn hospital with about a hundred people hoverin' over me. One said I had a 'urism' or something. Cut me open from top to bottom."

"Let me see your scar." Sure enough, they had cut him from top to bottom—from the sternal notch of the chest to below his xiphoid process—surgery known as a thoracotomy. "Sigmund, if it wasn't heart surgery, was that 'urism' a thoracic aneurysm?"

"Yeah, a 'urism'. They kept tellin' me I couldn't smoke, but I fooled 'em. Hell, I was smokin' the next day."

"Great. The next day after aneurysm surgery. Great." As I looked closer, I noticed his abdomen. All he cared about was a small umbilical hernia. What I cared about was the pulsatile, rhythmical heave-ho in his lower abdomen. "Sigmund, have you ever noticed how your belly bounces?"

"Yeah. I dance to the beat," laughing and wheezing.

"Well, if you want to keep on dancing, you better show that drummer to the medical folks upstairs." I watched it for a short while—bump, bump, bump, bump—very rhythmical at 80 beats per minute or so. "Sigmund, can I examine your abdomen?"

"Sure. You're a damn doctor. Why not? Gotta be better than those bastards upstairs." He stretched his six-foot-five-inch frame on his bunk.

"You must've been around fifty when you had the thoracic aneurysm, right?" I began gently probing his abdomen with both hands, putting him at ease before really checking it. You don't want to palpate an aneurysm too much.

"Yeah, forty-nine."

"Anyone ever ask you about a disease called Marfan's?" I was scrutinizing his upper abdomen first before moving down—normal liver and spleen, no upper pulsations or tenderness. Sigmund had long, gaunt extremities, especially his fingers. He resembled Abraham Lincoln with hollowed cheeks and wrinkled skin, gangly and thin except he was Black—a Black Abraham Lincoln.

"Hell, I don't know. You're the doctor. It sort of sounds familiar. Why?"

"Forty-nine's pretty young to have an aneurysm in the chest. Marfan's is a genetically acquired disease and it causes aneurysms. Lincoln probably had one in the head. "

"I'll be damned. You doctors are full of sh . . ."

"Sigmund," I stopped him. Palpating lower, he had a definite right-of-the-midline lower abdominal pulsatile mass consistent with an abdominal aneurysm. I'd felt enough. You have to go to medical as soon as possible. Tell them you need an abdominal ultrasound looking for an aneurysm."

"Write it down, man. I can't remember that kind a stuff."

"It's important, Sigmund. It's life-threatening," scribbling down my diagnosis on a scrap of paper. Was it ever. If an abdominal aneurysm is greater than five centimeters, it has a high likelihood of rupturing within a year—curtains time. This one felt at least five centimeters. Coupled with his history of a thoracic aneurysm, I was extremely nervous. Given the JDCR's general lack of medical concern—or is that lack of concern in general?—I could envision it rupturing some night and me being accused of causing it somehow. Sigmund wasn't worried nearly as much.

"Let me think on it. I gotta smoke." With that, Sigmund wandered off to the bathroom—considerate at least. Turning as he rounded my bunk, "Oh, you got a ducat, Doc. You got a new job. You gonna be a clerk." He wheezed as he laughed.

I looked on my bunk where Sigmund had pointed and sure enough, there was a white ducat. "Reception Clerk" was printed on the front. *What the hell is that?*

The next morning at seven a.m., right after chow, I hurried excitedly to the Facility A Program Office and presented myself for duty—that's the A Yard office. Turns out each facility has an inmate office—the Program Office—where inmate-clerks create and type disciplinary reports and generate the volumes of paperwork that every bureaucracy must produce in order to be a bureaucracy.

JDCR is no different, although having worked in a medical bureaucracy for a long time, the JDCR documents are uniquely tedious. Since each facility has a Captain overseeing the entire facility, as well as a Lieutenant and a Sergeant for each of the three shifts who are in charge of the day-to-day operations, there are a fair number of people generating mountains of monotonous, droningly dull forms, rules, and regulations. Into this world, I was now assigned.

The inmate-clerks are divided roughly along the same lines as the custody staff—except when they aren't. There's a Captain's clerk, and two or three Lieutenant's clerks per shift. No one is assigned to First Watch—they wake up a Second or Third Watch clerk if they need something. There are also two reception clerks, of which I was now the newest, whose job description continues to escape me to this day.

Like many of the clerk jobs, their primary purpose appears to be to dig a hole and fill it with someone else's dirt, much like the scene in "Cool Hand Luke" . . . or, more accurately, someone else's paperwork. The problem with being a reception clerk was that no one could tell me what or where *my* dirt was or in what hole to put it. In short, *there are no reception clerk duties.* Neither the Captain's clerk nor the Lieutenant's clerks could tell me what to do, or none *would* tell me.

As it turned out, the reception clerks are supposed to help the counselors—the CCIs—with anything they need . . . except they don't want any help because they don't trust the clerks, especially newly assigned ones, and don't have anything even for a trusted one. So, for the first few weeks, I went to work in the morning, stared at the walls and the one Lieutenant's clerk who was there every day, until I couldn't take it anymore and I'd leave. After those first few weeks, I began bringing reading material, but even that gets old after a few hours.

The more I familiarized myself with the Program Office, the more I noticed the only one doing anything—or for that matter the only one there most times—was the one Lieutenant's clerk, Lee, a pompous, arrogant, know-it-all Black gentleman in his late thirties. He would glare over his glasses at the least attempt at conversation or question about whether he needed any help. That got old fast. Lee and I—and everyone else he encountered—would soon have major-league issues. Aside from his personal superiority, he intentionally made things so unpleasant that anybody who wandered into the office, calculated or not, would suffer the slings and arrows of his outrageous fortune. After observing him for a few weeks, it became obvious he was doing it on purpose to make sure everyone left him alone—conversationally and physically. By doing all the work, he thought he made himself indispensable. I soon discovered he was also running several scams—selling office supplies and "chronos" to inmates.

Chronos are multiple-part forms we clerks generate for various reasons, such as permission to go to visiting wearing normal shoes rather than state-issued ones. The most coveted chronos were those that authorized possession of a previously confiscated TV or radio, ordered an inmate a double mattress, or requisitioned a lower bunk. Like most flim-flam artists, Lee—and others before and after him—profited from the fraud with or without realizing many of the documents they sold were invalid or obviously fake. Since shoe chronos and mattress chronos, even lower bunk chronos come from medical, a program clerk would need to fix it up to look like the real thing.

That required something in short supply at JRC—*smarts*. Lee had more than most, so his scams worked for the most part. I spent my first months observing, and learning from his bad examples. After about two months, I was promoted to Captain's clerk, the position in which I remained for the remainder of my time at JRC.

As fate would have it, becoming the Captain's clerk was one of my salvations. Lee paroled out of JRC—not for long, but that's another story—and suddenly I was the most experienced Second Watch clerk. Rapidly, I not only became the most experienced clerk, I was also the only clerk. I've always done well when thrown into the fire and this was a major conflagration.

Clerking is *not* neurosurgery. I've done that, and believe me, JRC clerking isn't even in the same universe.

But I digress. The former clerk, Lee, paroled alright. His freedom lasted all of eight days before he was picked up for being near a school. It seems Lee was required to wear an ankle bracelet as a condition of parole and, in spite of that, he wandered too close to a bunch of third graders. Apparently, he was a child molester—the kind that's supposed to go to the SNY yard—but JDCR managed not to put him there. Another rule broken.

As I rapidly fell into a routine, I was able to figure out another of Lee's reasons for running everyone else away. By having all the COs, Sergeants, and Lieutenants reliant on you to do their paperwork, they mostly leave you alone. They say familiarity breeds contempt—in here familiarity breeds survival.

"Doc," Stinky met me at the door coming back from work. "We're gonna need to put off tutoring tonight. I gotta work late in dental."

"No problem, Stinky. Hey, how do you get an appointment in dental? I'd like to have my teeth cleaned."

"Appointment?" Stinky stared at me in a way I was beginning to recognize . . . it meant I'd asked another dumb question. "You just fill out a medical 602. They'll send you a ducat in a few weeks."

"*Medical 602?* There's a difference between that and a regular *602?* Is a Medical 602 really a 602 or something else?"

"Yeah, it's a *Medical Form 22*, not a *602*."

"You gotta be kidding me? Another kind of *602* that isn't?"

"Well, it's actually a Form—what's the number?—*7362* . . . it's just called a *602.*"

"I know," sighing. "Because that's what it *used to be* years ago and now it's not."

"Something like that," Stinky smiled.

"It takes two weeks?"

"Or more. Get one from the CO. Just ask for . . ."

"I know. A *602*."

"No, man," Stinky smiled more broadly, "a <u>Medical</u> *602.*"

I fell back onto my bunk. I had the same headache starting again. Later that night, I negotiated my way with the CO to the correct form, filled it out, and planned on waiting two weeks.

Six weeks later, I got my dental ducat. Oh, and I didn't have a shadow when I got the form—I rarely did, nor did anyone else.

When my dental day arrived I meandered down to "the lowers"—that's the B and C Yards, where the main medical and dental facility is located—and entered a queue of about a hundred inmates waiting to be seen. Several hours later, I was placed in a real dental chair. Thirty minutes later a real dentist—at least that's what the wall certificate said—passed through long enough for a cursory examination and advised the dental assistant that my teeth were acceptable for cleaning. Apparently, one's teeth must be approved for cleaning and only if they pass muster—people with bad teeth that really need dental care aren't "eligible" to be cleaned.

I guess I'm fortunate? I've got yellowed, crooked teeth, and probably should've had braces when I was a kid—but I don't have one cavity. I brush and floss them. In the JRC dental points system, I made the grade—but not so fast.

I was scheduled for the cleaning three months into the future. After going through the same waiting routine three months later, I was given an adequate cleaning by the head dentist, who recognized me from TV, prompting another discussion of my case with a stranger. Each year I went through the same rigmarole to get my teeth cleaned.

Oh, that these were my last experiences with dental. However, about a year away from release, at one of my many clearance exams for cleaning, the dentist—a different one each time—told me I had a small cavity. Low and behold, they filled it right then and there. All's well that ends well.

I wished.

During my second year one early evening about thirty minutes after dinner, while lying on my bunk reading, I had a sharp, right-sided pain, not bad at first, but worsening to severe over ten minutes or so as I kept shifting on the bunk trying to find a comfortable position without success. I couldn't stay still.

My biggest fear was having a serious medical problem while under the jurisdiction of the JDCR. I could control the day-to-day stuff, but something serious—like this—I wasn't too confident. For that reason, denial was a major emotion. After several hours of pain, I launched myself towards the bathroom to make a deposit—of the vomiting type; dry heaving after completely expelling the contents of my stomach, I knew I was reaching the limit of denial.

Since onset, the pain was now more sharp, hurting when I took a breath and more in the front of my right upper abdomen. I'd seen this enough in the ER to know the differential diagnosis—gallbladder versus kidney stone. Since it seemed more anterior rather than posterior, and since its onset was thirty minutes after dinner, I was leaning towards a gallbladder attack—acute biliary colic with or without a gallstone.

Damn. That meant transport to outside medical, I feared. By now, it was around nine at night. I struggled to convince the CO I needed to go immediately to "urgent care" in the lowers. That meant more paperwork for him, thus, his reluctance. God forbid it was something serious which would mean even more paperwork!

I was given a pass to walk the mile to "urgent care" where an angry nurse met me at the door of the one small room. Apparently, she was angry because I caused her to have to do something for which she was actually being paid to do. She took my blood pressure and announced loudly that it was elevated, then asked whether I took BP meds.

"Yes," I answered, but then I informed her I had also vomited the medications during my stint in the bathroom.

In response, she sneered and commented that if I'd take my meds as directed my blood pressure wouldn't be elevated and didn't I know better. I guess she skipped the lecture in nursing school about how pain was a significant cause of increased blood pressure—not to mention skipping the day they lectured on compassion.

No physician exam or evaluation by a physician was made, but an apparent phone call to one was. I remained seated on a bench, waiting to be stripped and searched, after which I would be wrapped in a paper gown for transport to the local county hospital. Yeah, I was a real threat to society at that point—writhing in pain on a bench.

After squirming around for another hour, I survived the twenty minute ride to the never-to-be-named hospital. One thing about being a prisoner, you do get whisked into the ER without delay—once you get there. After the obligatory vital signs by a nurse, a typically harried ER physician evaluated me very briefly. I was well-known for being fast in my ER career, but this guy flew in and out quicker than crap moves through a goose.

I tried to cut through the small talk—there was none actually—letting him know I was an ER doc and thought it was my gallbladder, or possibly a kidney stone, and that I needed an ultrasound. Dressed in a paper gown and shackled to the gurney, I sensed he didn't consider me credible, that and the smirk on his face. Throughout the nearly twelve hours I spent in this facility of healing, it turned out to be the only opportunity I had to share anything with my "attending physician."

At least he ordered the ultrasound. The ultrasound tech scanned and smutched greasy jelly repeatedly to make contact with the probe—all normal ultrasound tech stuff. I asked him what he thought, only to be rebuffed with the standard, "the doctor will tell you, I'm just a tech" routine. Blessedly, on return to the ER from ultrasound, the pain resolved just as suddenly as it had started.

About four hours later, another nurse came in and started an IV in my right arm—my legs were still shackled and my left arm handcuffed to the gurney—and she informed me they were giving me a liter of intravenous fluids. She also placed a "duck" on the rail, that's one of those plastic urine containers the healthcare workers give you when they want you to pee. Now that was an interesting experience, trying to pee in a duck, shackled, with one arm handcuffed and the other attached to an IV. Sure enough, about an hour after the infusion was completed, I had to pee like a racehorse.

Accompanying the intravenous infusion was the return of the pain, less than before but definitely the same pain. There was no one to notify since I never saw anyone—healthcare worker or other—until a nurse came in to have me sign my discharge papers. By then the pain had come and gone several times. Throughout my twelve hours in the ER, I wasn't given any pain medications or anything other than the IV. When I asked the discharge nurse what the ultrasound revealed and asked what my diagnosis was, she looked at me, frowning and said, "All your tests are normal. It's all here on the chart." When I asked for a copy I was told the CO would give it to me on return to JRC.

On return to JRC, my vital signs were faithfully taken again. I was informed my BP was normal and sent on my way—walking back to my dorm and without a copy of my chart. The pain mildly recurred several times over the next two days. I managed to beg a few ibuprofen tablets in the dorm—they give those to inmates when they pull a tooth—and eventually the pain completed subsided. Three days later, I was summoned back to Facility A medical where Dr. Mee asked me how I felt, told me to take my blood pressure meds properly, and that I would be ducated in two weeks to provide another urine sample. When he started to send me away, I intervened and asked him just what my diagnosis was, since all my tests were normal.

"Normal?" He exclaimed. "No, no. You had a kidney stone. It says so right here."

"But I wasn't given a copy of that, and the nurse said all the tests were normal."

"No, you were given a copy," showing me a scribbled signature acknowledging receipt of a copy—not my signature—and pointing to the chart indicating blood on urinalysis and a written diagnosis of "acute ureteral calculus."

"Really?" Now I was really peeing blood. Of course, none of this was told to me here or there.

"Well, it's all written down," Dr. Mee retorted, ushering me out.

"Told ya not to trust them bastards," Sigmund counseled me on return to the dorm. "What a bunch of idiots."

I was beginning to agree with Sigmund.

Remember my colonoscopy during reception at Jasco? Over the next four years I was assaulted repeatedly with ducats ordering stool guaiac testing—that's where *I* put stool on a cardboard card and *they* add a reagent that makes it turn blue in the presence of blood. It's done as an early detection screening test for colon cancer. If it is positive, colonoscopy is ordered. Since I'd already had the definitive test—*colonoscopy*—I couldn't figure out why they kept ordering the preliminary test—the stool guaiac.

Aside from the fact that getting your own fecal matter onto a paper card is not only embarrassing, but also damn-near impossible without inmates thinking you're gay, then you're supposed to take it to the lab—a nice one-mile hike—where it sits for several days. That delay can mean it is inaccurate at the least and a false-negative in the worst case. All of this is unnecessary of course, if you've had the definitive test—*colonoscopy*—which I had, except they had no record of it. It was lost. Gee, what a first in JDCR.

Leonard came by my bunk after work one night. I could see he was agitated and mumbling something about writing another *602*.

"OK, Leonard. What's up? Why all the frustration?"

"They won't fix my hernia," he sighed.

"You have a hernia?"

"I think I do," Leonard responded. "I have this lump and it hurts when I lift stuff. I do a lot of lifting at work. Plumbing is squatting all day and heaving pipe."

"Has medical seen it?"

"Yeah, about a year ago. I keep putting in medical *602s* hoping to get it fixed. I'm gonna have to put in an appeal, I guess."

"Let me have a shot at it. Do you want me to check it out?"

Leonard grabbed my shoulder. "Maybe later. Doc, don't get me transferred."

"How could I get you transferred?"

"If you go to outside medical too many times, they transfer you."

"What? That doesn't make sense?"

"What does?" With that, Leonard walked to the bathroom.

I decided to check into his hernia next time I saw one of my medical acquaintances. Turns out, they did know about his hernia. I was told they were waiting for approval to go to the next step. When I asked what that next step was, they couldn't tell me, or when it might be. Leonard was pleased just the same.

As to this transfer problem Leonard worried about, it turns out that if you go to an outside medical facility twice or more in a year, they label you as having a chronic medical problem and transfer you to a medical prison facility. That's what Leonard was scared of. Except it didn't make sense—what does? If your problem is fixable, like with a minor procedure, why would they transfer you? Especially if your two outside visits were because they are so inefficient that they can't handle the paperwork in one visit.

There are exceptions, like Sigmund, who had multiple outside visits to evaluate and allow them to scratch their heads about what to do with his aneurysm. If anyone should've been transferred for medical reasons, it's Sigmund. But he wasn't. Leonard was.

One night while returning from chow, I noticed an agitated inmate, pounding his head against the bulletin board. When I asked what was going on he started screaming and pounding his header even harder.

"C'mon, man. Why are you so upset?" I worried about the bulletin board as well as his head.

He stopped pounding and turned to look at me, narrowed his eyes as if I were his prey and shouted, "They won't give me a ducat!"

"OK," I stepped back. Lots of crazies in here. "We can figure this out. What's the ducat for?"

He inched closer and yelled, "It's for anger management! They won't give me a ducat for anger management," spewing saliva and resuming his pounding on the wall.

My first brush with mental illness in the penal system had been my first cellmate at Jasco. I never really knew what happened to him. This was my first JRC experience . . . but it would not be my last. "J-cats," "psychos," and an assortment of other names of derision soon entered my vocabulary, though I tried not to use them.

All were designations for inmates classified as CCCMS by the JDCR as part of the MHSDS. When a bureaucracy wants to baffle the uninitiated, it creates an inordinate number of acronyms and slang, no doubt useful to the initiated, but terribly confusing to those I'll label as "normal," whoever that is. MHSDS is Mental Health Services Delivery System, a fancy tag for the social and psychological folks supposedly delivering mental health care. CCCMS stands for Correctional Clinical Case Management System—how in the world does one understand that to be a psychiatric patient designation? It was also known as a "triple-C."

If you have an inmate in the JDCR who attempts suicide and is MHSDS at the CCCMS level of care, a designated, licensed MD (a psychiatrist type of MD, not a GP type of MD), or a PhD psychologist can order placement on suicide watch in a GACH, CTC, SNF, OHU or other appropriate facility. An RN, LVN or CNA can't do that. Got it? Like I said, it's designed to confuse.

"Are you in an Anger Management class already?"

"I dunno, " continuing to pound.

"Well," I probed, "are you triple C?"

"Yeah."

Bingo. "Did you ask to be in the class?"

"Not really. But I want to go."

"And you should, I mean you can," I hastily corrected myself. "Did you ask to be put on the list?"

"Yeah," my associate grimaced. "The CO said I wasn't on the list. When I asked to be put on the list, he said I had to ask them to put me on."

"But how can you ask them without going there?"

"I dunno. The CO laughed at me," my new friend was nearly crying. "I just want to stop being so angry at everything."

"Let me see if I can get you on the list."

My companion stopped pounding his head and smiled weakly, "Thanks, Doc. You're the first person who's listened to me."

That was my all-too-frequent experience with the delivery of mental health in JDCR—*no one listens*. To be fair, it's a problem in the "real world" as well. Our "real world" mental health system isn't really a *system*, and what little resemblance to a system there is, is broken. Practitioners start out well-meaning, until they become corrupted by lack of resources and give up. Add a mental health bureaucracy and payment system with too few beds and too few staff and you have everything necessary to cause paralysis and failure. *And that's the good news on the outside.* Within the confines of a penal system, there is even less motivation and overwhelming numbers to contend with . . . or ignore. The latter is easier to accomplish.

No, I've never been a fan of the mental health system in my years in the ER, and my disdain worsened in here. It is a system well versed in shuffling people and paper around without accomplishing the goal. Many times, it can't even identify what the goal is. The CO laughing at my companion wasn't even in the system, so his disinterest was more blatant. Next day at work, I asked around in medical—my new colleagues there were growing more helpful each visit and I found out how to get someone on the Anger Management class list. In the process, I met one of the psychologists sitting alone with his thoughts in his office—a long line of inmates waiting to see him. I guess he'd seen me or somehow knew who I was, because he beckoned me into his office.

"Am I interrupting?"

"No, not at all. I'm not busy right now," the psychologist beamed. "I hear you want to be in our Anger Management class. It would be great having a professional like you help in the class."

"No, not me," I protested. "It's a guy in my dorm who's been trying to get on the list." I could see the disappointment in the psychologist's face.

"Oh," he looked down. "I'd hoped to elevate the conversation a bit. Are you sure you're not angry about something?"

"Well, I'm sure I am. Aren't we all?"

"That's the kind of thinking I like. We need more of it in the class," becoming more animated. "I'll put you on the list."

"What about the guy in my dorm? Can you put him on, too?"

"Who?"

"The guy I was telling you about."

"What guy?"

"*This guy,*" writing his bunk number on a scrap of paper.

"Oh, I can't put him in the class without a name. Besides, how do you know he wants to come to Anger Management?"

"He's aching to get in. His head hurts to attend, believe me."

Chapter 8: *Bondage and Discipline*

As I finally settled into a personal routine, I turned my attention and survival instincts to understanding the officers in this prison "army"—the COs. Understanding their mentality, structure, and what makes them tick was my objective. The old adage, "those who have the gold make the rules" was rather adaptable to prison. They clearly had the "gold," in this case, keys, and were agents of the state, and the state made the rules, big-time. Ah, but rules are made, at a minimum, to be bent, if not outright broken. The important thing to figure out was who is malleable and just how far the system could be bent without either disrupting or breaking it.

"Doc," the Lieutenant swiveled in his chair to face me, "you're going to be my right-hand man. I gotta trust you, so don't screw it up." Lieutenant Croquet—pronounced not like the French/English ball-and-mallet lawn game, but like the name of the early-American, coonskin cap-wearing frontiersman—was a scruffy old hand within JDCR, having been "in the system" for 29 years; just one year from retirement, all he wanted was peace on his watch—no drama. An unlikely scenario.

"I'll do my best, sir."

Since I was the only clerk now, he didn't have much of choice. As I later found out, the inmate assignment office simply filled slots; they didn't care whether an inmate wanted the job or was qualified for it—only that he was on the list for it, in this case, the clerk's list. That meant there were a fair number of inmates assigned as clerks who had neither the requisite skills nor interest. Combine that with those who wanted to be in the program office for the express purpose of furthering their criminal careers and you have the perfect setup for failure.

When the correctional staff found someone with any particular skill set, they latched onto that inmate in the hopes they had found a life raft of sorts, only to be disappointed . . . frequently. I also discovered that those with significant computer skills—which I have—are a rarity among the correctional staff. The reality was that more inmates than staff had computer skills.

In time, I realized I had the ability to pick the other clerks, if I could find qualified candidates. I learned I could easily manipulate the assignment office. The combination of qualified and interested inmates, however, was the singular problem I faced. I viewed my little office as a sanctuary, a veritable oasis in the midst of chaos and turmoil, and a refuge from the insanity—in more ways than one—of prison. Finding others who had a similar view was my task, but one I was in no hurry to complete. Old Lee wasn't wrong after all. There is a good reason to be the one and only program office clerk.

Over my time in the office, Lt. Croquet was the first, and last, of four Lieutenants for whom I worked. The "ELL TEEs" were rotated at least once a year . . . sometimes even more frequently than that. Those of us on Second Watch tended to do more actual work than the Third Watch clerks, primarily because it was daytime and all the pooh-bahs and οἱ πολλοί ("hoi polloi", literally, "the many") were around—the Warden, Assistant Wardens, and Associate Wardens, even the higher-up Headquarters-types from the state capital on occasion. As each passed through "my office," I quickly figured out that doing stuff for them allowed me to be viewed favorably in return. That can be a real plus in here—inmates refer to it as having a "juice card." I was determined to keep that juice card tucked in my back pocket—not to use it unnecessarily. That would be a waste.

Typical of JRC, when a clerk is assigned, he is thrown into the pool without swimming lessons. You're expected to know all about how to run the facility . . . from the disciplinary reports to the many other daily routines. There are a lot of sharks in the pool. The only things the Lieutenants and Sergeants really care about are their disciplinary hearing reports—the JDCR 115s, 128-As, and 128-Bs typed in proper form and with good grammar. The Sergeants also care about running their particular facility—searches, shake-downs, and overseeing their subordinate COs—lots of paperwork. All the dorm COs seemed to care about is getting their porter schedules, payroll, and various other chores completed, including any copying they may require. They needed the extra time to spend playing games on their computers.

Copying is interesting. The only copier sits in the Lieutenant's office and either a Lieutenant or Sergeant is supposed to authorize *and supervise* making copies. When they aren't around, the dorm CO might unlock the office for copies, depending on who's working. Before too long, all this door knocking and getting permission gets old, so the brass generally prefers to identify who's trustworthy or not. I prided myself on gaining that trust by demonstrating dependability and responsibility. Of course, a lot of inmates wanted things copied, too, and not necessarily the "authorized" variety.

That created a genuine "Dr. Laura" moral dilemma for me: *do I risk getting fired for making an inmate a copy of something that's BS to begin with, or refusing the request and having them pissed off at me?* Once the Lieutenants and Sergeants got to know me, I was able to copy items for inmates occasionally by slipping them in between CO copies. I didn't abuse the privilege like some before, and most likely after, me. Everybody has their priorities—staff and inmates. As Dirty Harry once said, "A man's got to know his limitations."

"You gotta pay attention to the rules, Doc," Sigmund counseled, letting out another of his trademark wheezing laughs. "You can't break 'em 'til ya know what they is."

We were discussing discipline in the facility. Sigmund had become my resident expert. Doper I didn't trust and, increasingly, I rarely found him "untweaked." Stinky and Leonard worked, and Pitr and Face either didn't know or didn't care about discipline—at least not the prison type. The topic of Sigmund's master's seminar today was *Structure and Discipline*.

It was my impression, developed from the first day of incarceration, that the primary deficiency in the lives of the incarcerated is the *lack* of structure and discipline. I'll say one thing for gangs, they provide those two necessary elements of daily life—just not in the manner society approves. Society has its own structure and discipline—in elementary schools, higher education, on the playground, at work, and in virtually all other aspects. Everyone sent to prison is here for a violation of the rules—rules meant to bring order to, or maintain, the structure and discipline of society. Some inmates' violations are more egregious than others, but all are in violation of the larger society's rules.

At least that's the ideal premise. Of course, it assumes those rules have been fairly, equally, and equitably adjudicated—right!?!. Once here, prisoners are subjected to a completely different set of rules, but the structure is delineated with bars, razor wire, electrified fences and gates, and the discipline is meted out by COs. The "rules," although established in black and white, are subject to the individual whims and fancies and interpretations of each CO, Sergeant, Lieutenant, and above—not unlike society, just with different consequences. Break a minor rule, society slaps your hand. Break a minor prison rule—or maybe not even break one at all—and, depending on the CO, one might get a simple verbal warning, a more formal write-up, or suffer a physical assault. On top of this, there are the gang or race rules, with their major infractions such as sitting on the wrong bunk, or sharing personal property, with an entirely different set of penalties.

"You screw up and the cops bust ya," Sigmund opined. "Might tear up your shit or take your TV, but them bastards'll get you. Don't lip off to 'em either. You get caught out of bounds or with contraband and it's a write-up for sure. Don't show up for work or show up late, they might write you up or just yell at you; depends on their mood that day and whether they got any the night before," laughing again until he couldn't breathe.

"Got it. But now that I'm a clerk, I'm starting to see all these write-ups come through for me to type," I was curious. "Some of these COs are frigging illiterate."

"Ill . . . what?"

"They can't write. Do I fix their mistakes?"

"Screw 'em, I say," Sigmund sniffed.

Easy for *him* to say. What I learned was a good clerk had to know when to fix bad use of language, poor grammar, and spelling . . . and when *not* to—or for whom not to. Several of the writers couldn't put two words together, much less a sentence. Then, again, some did put two sentences together . . . or three, four, or more . . . so damn-many run-on sentences; often I could barely discern the beginning or the end, let alone figure out what the intent to communicate was. Some knew it and would ask me to write it from scratch—against the rules, but whaddaya gonna do? Most appreciated my edits, but a few others did their own write-ups and complained if they were altered.

"So, Sigmund," I continued. "Punkin seems like an OK guy. Can I ask him questions?"

"Hell, no! Ask another clerk. Don't ask them bastards nothin'." Everyone in uniform, and select others, were "them bastards" to Sigmund.

"But I'm the only clerk now on Second Watch . . ."

"Ask them Third Watch boys."

"They don't want to have anything to do with me."

"Yeah, them Third Watch clerks are all druggies. You be careful of them boys, Doc. I better not hear 'bout you doin' them drugs."

"Sigmund," staring at him. "Do we have to go over this again?"

"Naw, I guess not, but you be careful. Damn bastards."

The "you be careful" was sage advice. Since there was no one to ask among the inmates, and Sigmund said I shouldn't ask CO Punkin, I decided to figure it out on my own. Out came the Title 15—part of the Jefferson Code of Regulations, or JCR, that supposedly governs the structure and discipline within the state prison system. I spent the next few days reading Title 15 enough to be conversant in the generalities and mustered the courage to ask Lieutenant Croquet about a few specifics.

It turns out there is supposed to be a system of progressive discipline applied to those who violate the rules—beginning with a verbal warning, then a *128* write-up, and finally a *115*. Croquet's advice was to learn the main garden-variety violations, since the majority fall into but a few categories. *128-Bs* are informational only and carry no disciplinary penalties. He also commented that I was the first inmate he knew of who had read any part of Title 15.

I rapidly figured out the *128s* and *115s*. Facility A wrote about fifty *115s* and about twenty-five *128s* a month. Since every *115* results in a disciplinary hearing conducted by a Lieutenant, that means about fifty hearings a month, too. We also did about six to ten *114s* in a month. In the computer I used to type the reports, there were rudimentary templates for each of the 100 or so Rules Violation Reports, or RVRs. I spent the better part of a month modifying those and correcting the inconsistencies and numerous spelling or grammar errors.

Everyone always asked whether my computer had Internet access—no, it did not! Ah, that it did. Even the "help" functions for programs like Excel and Word were disabled on my computer. Inmates are strictly prohibited from accessing the Internet. There's even a *115* for it.

Soon I was ready to tackle the biggies—RVR hearings and *114s*. As it turns out, the *114s*—*lock-up orders*—are easy. When an inmate really screws up or asks for protection, a *114* is created. This document identifies all the many boxes to be checked on way too many forms prior to an inmate being transferred to higher custody. Once this step is initiated for whatever reason, that inmate is stripped down to skivvies and thrown into a cage until he is transferred. That may take more than eight hours—sometimes longer.

No other inmate is allowed in that person's general vicinity and when they are moved, any inmates in the areas they pass through must turn and face the wall.

A *114* usually encompasses several interviews where the staff gathers information—a shakedown cruise. If an inmate is requesting SNY status, before getting it they usually have to give up a fair amount of information—or get thrown back into the general population for "debriefing." If that inmate is making the request because he owes money—a frequent reason given all the drugs—they not only have to give up information, but names as well. If it's a really big case, the ISU, or Investigative Services Unit, personnel get involved. These guys *look* intimidating; they walk around in all black and have a swagger that commands attention. You do not want to have to talk to these guys.

Yeah, *114* "lock-up" paperwork is easy, but not so much for the affected inmate. The main problem with *114s* is that the COs and Lieutenants want them *yesterday* because an inmate is awaiting transfer to higher custody and sitting in a cage. The staff could care less about the inmate in the cage—they just wanted the paperwork done. And it literally is a cage—chain-link fence and all. Feeling sorry for the inmate, I wanted to go as fast as possible so they'd get out of the cage. Little did I know, however, was that most of the time they were being sent to solitary confinement—a slightly bigger cage, but still a cage.

The reason an RVR hearing is so much more difficult is they are long, wordy and document the disciplinary action taken against an inmate, if convicted. It's the reason Lieutenants exist. Without these hearings and the reports, the LTs don't seem to do much of anything else, and that's just the way they like it. I eventually realized that the cushiest job in JDCR is being a Lieutenant. Nobody really knows what they do while they're in their office; they surface occasionally to hold a hearing or go to a meeting.

As best I could tell, the worst part of an LT's job is dealing with the facility Captain. When conducting a disciplinary hearing, aside from the lengthy documentation of the "facts" in a case—facts as told by the Reporting Employee—the hearing concludes with a determination of guilt or not guilty. Most outcomes seem to be pre-determined and the usual result is, not surprisingly, guilty. That means the guilty inmate receives some form of penalties from the LT. The disciplinary sanctions generally fall into three basic categories: forfeiture of credit, loss of privileges, and extra duty. There are other possible penalties for less common offenses, but these three are the ones most frequently assessed in the majority of hearings.

Forfeiture of credit is an interesting concept. Remember, I came to prison with an eighty-five percent sentence—eighty-five percent of five years. Everyone enters with a reduced amount of time to be served—some 85%, others 80% and still others with as little as just 50%—depending on the severity of one's crime(s) and the mood of the sentencing judge on that particular day. So everyone starts out believing their sentence is less than it actually is—another example of placing incentives in the wrong direction—creating a sense of entitlement to your reduction. If an inmate is convicted of a RVR, during the hearing, the SHO (more acronyms!)—that's Senior Hearing Officer—who is a Lieutenant or higher, assesses a forfeiture of credit, usually in increments of thirty days, such as 30, 60 or 90 days. For the most serious offenses, an inmate can be assessed up to 360 days.

Forfeiture is, in reality, an addition of time to what was previously reduced by the court. In other words, the judge credits you with "time off for good behavior" in advance. So you may come in owing the state eighty-five percent of your sentence and, through forfeitures of credit, suddenly find yourself serving more time than when you arrived. Instead of penalizing bad behavior, you would think it might be better to incentivize inmates to be well behaved by crediting them for good behavior *when they do behave well* rather than giving them an "advance" and taking it back if they screw up?

If you thought the courts were the final say when it comes to punishments penal, think again. I learned several years after entering the system. JDCR can actually reduce your percentage on its own from say 85% to 50%. I'm sure there is a manual somewhere with the criteria which spells out how it's determined, but in practice it sure seemed arbitrary to me. Little did I know that it meant I could have had my prison time reduced by JDCR, as happened to several "colleagues" of mine along the way. Ah, the joys of being a "high profile" prisoner.

Of course, having been hit previously with forfeitures of credit, you could be up to one hundred percent. Fortunately, you can't go beyond that (if you could, some prisoners would be serving life sentences for relatively light-duty felonies), at least not without being sent back to court for some new offense. In less serious circumstances, the forfeiture could be restored after a period of remaining disciplinary-free. So what's "less" serious?

After you get an RVR, it's classified by another Lieutenant or higher as "Serious" or "Administrative." If it is a "Serious" RVR, it is classified as an "A" through "F" offense, with the As being most serious. Ds through Fs might have forfeitures restored. But forfeitures for the more serious charges, those in the A through C lists, cannot be restored. That period of remaining discipline-free is problematic for many. The RVRs just pile up. So once you get to one hundred percent, there is exactly no incentive to be on one's best behavior at all; there is no real penalty for behaving otherwise, other than the temporary losses of certain privileges.

Now loss of privileges—like phone, yard, packages and canteen—the good stuff . . . *that* was punishment. The SHO could even assess loss of visiting privileges—to me, that would have been the worst them all. For the duration of the loss, an inmate was prohibited from going to yard, the canteen, or whatever, during the entire time of that period, which was usually assessed in increments of thirty days.

The SHO could also assess "extra duty," meaning the inmate is required to work a certain number of extra hours in his job, or more commonly, performing extra tasks in the dorm such as cleaning the CO office. The extra hours were usually either twenty or forty, and rarely did an inmate actually spend that much extra time working. The supervising CO usually gave an inmate two or three hours' credit for a mere thirty minutes of work. So "extra work" as a punishment was really nothing to be feared.

Does any of this sound like kindergarten?

It was into this world I had descended—or was that ascended?

"Doc!" Lieutenant Croquet bellowed. "I'm doing three hearings this morning. The inmates are on the way, so look out for them and send them into my office when they get here. Sergeant Whiner will be helping with the hearings this morning."

"Yes, sir!" Ever since my first encounter with her during the dorm inspection for six-foot personal property compliance, I shuddered just hearing Sergeant Whiner's name spoken. She did become slightly friendlier once she realized who I was, and I hoped the LT had told her about me. Croquet and I were about the same age—I was a little older, but we both had the same temperament. We hit it off as best an inmate could with a custody staff Lieutenant.

Within a few minutes, the first inmate arrived and I ushered him into the LT's office and closed the door. A thin wall separated my small office without amenities from his larger one with air conditioning and other "luxuries."

As the hearing began, the sounds from the Lieutenant's office were muffled. Soon, the softened noise rose in tenor and tone. A punctuated staccato voice cut through the wall like a skill saw cuts through drywall. I could now hear words and entire sentences.

"Stand up when you talk to the Lieutenant!" I recognized the shrill vocalization of Sergeant Whiner. "And don't say a word."

"But how can I answer without saying a word?" The inmate countered.

"Don't talk back to me!" Whiner screamed. Noticeably absent was the voice of the Senior Hearing Officer—Lieutenant Croquet. As I had come to know him, I could imagine him sitting there with a smirk, taking in the Sergeant's performance.

"It isn't mine."

"Don't you mean 'wasn't' mine? Remember, we confiscated your contraband," Whiner seethed. "We're not in the present tense, 'was' is past tense. You had it in the past, right?"

"No, I mean . . ., no, I do mean no," the poor inmate struggled. "Look, I was at work when the search happened."

"How do you know a search happened? If you were there when it happened how could you have been at work? Are you trying to bullshit me? Do you know who I am? I'll rip you . . ."

"Sergeant," the voice of reason finally came from Lieutenant Croquet. "Let the boy have his say. You were saying, inmate?"

"Sir, I was at work. Everything I know is from the *115* paperwork I was given. Nobody in my dorm even told me about the search or what they found. I . . ."

"Then how do you know there was a search?" Whiner interrupted again. "All you inmates lie like a stained rug under my feet. LT, I can have him taken to the hole . . ."

"Naw," Croquet intervened. "A few hours of extra duty should be enough."

"But sir," the inmate protested. "I'm supposed to go home in a few months . . ."

"Shouldn't've been talking on a damned illegal cell phone then, huh?" Whiner snarled. "You're all alike. Running drugs and calling hookers on your contraband. You make me . . ."

"Sergeant," Croquet barely audible through the wall intoned. "You can file for an emergency restoration of credit," looking at the inmate. "You ever heard of constructive possession, inmate?"

"Huh?"

"Yeah, well I didn't think so," Croquet continued. "That's where something in your area is found—something illegal—and you're guilty of having it even though you didn't really."

"Huh?"

"Huh?" I agreed. I knew a little about the law and immediately began flipping through my Title 15 book for "constructive possession." Title 15 said constructive possession, "exists where a person has knowledge of an object and control of the object or the right to control the object, even if the person has no physical contact with it."

Now I had a few questions of my own, if only I could get into the hearing—which was not at all likely. Questions like, *Did he have knowledge of the cell phone?* If not, *How could it be constructive possession?* Where's the proof he had control, especially if he had no knowledge that it even existed?

"Did you know about that cell phone, inmate?" Croquet asked.

"I know that a lot of guys have 'em," inmate Acevedo replied.

"And did you know where they were kept?"

"Not really, sir. I am . . ."

"Stand up, straight! And address the Lieutenant as 'sir'!" Whiner interjected.

"I did call him sir. I . . ."

"Don't take that tone with me, inmate," Whiner was screaming loud enough I could feel the spit spraying Acevedo's face.

"Sir, I don't know where the cell phone came from. I don't know who it belongs to. I was at work . . ."

"We've been over your defense about being at work," the Lieutenant was clearly becoming bored with the hearing. "I'm finding you guilty on the basis of constructive possession. But I'm only going to give you 30 days suspension of privileges and no extra duty because I believe your story."

"You mean no loss of credit?"

"Oh, no. Forfeiture of credit is mandatory 90 days for a cell phone," Croquet added. "I'm just knocking down the other stuff."

You could hear the dejection through the wall.

"Can I appeal this? Acevedo asked. "Can I file a 602?"

"You can appeal anything. It says so at the bottom of the hearing report."

"But I don't have that."

"You will," the Lieutenant responded. "We have up to 15 days to serve you."

"But I'm supposed to . . ."

"I know. Supposed to go home," Croquet cut him off. "Emergency restoration. Get one from your counselor, your CC-I. Bring it back to me and I'll get it expedited."

"Can I get him out of here now?" the Sergeant growled.

"Yeah," Croquet answered. "And inmate. Get that emergency restoration of credit form. I'll help you with it."

In a few minutes, Acevedo walked slowly out of the office with his head down. Sergeant Whiner continued screaming at him, but it was clear he wasn't listening. I knew all he was thinking of was the 90 days—staying 90 days more in this madhouse. Since I would be typing the report of his hearing, I was curious how this would all look on paper. I doubt the injustice will appear in the dry verbiage. It won't include the intimidation, the lack of due process, the failure to apply the definition of "constructive possession" properly, the monetary incentive the JDCR has for incarcerating inmates for longer periods, or the shear insanity of the process.

What it will include is the pro forma language stating the inmate was afforded his due process rights by being given 24-hour notice as time to prepare his defense, that he was found guilty by the preponderance of evidence presented, even though there was no cross examination of the witnesses and no chance of excluding the evidence, and certainly no proof of the chain of custody of that evidence or its credibility. This was not a court of law, but a kangaroo court.

I lived this life for the next few years. As the senior clerk—when not the only one—I was counted on by Lieutenant Croquet, and the four or five other LTs that passed through the Facility A Program Office. Let's just say that experience did not improve my feelings about the justice system. I didn't think injustice and unfairness could be worse than the court system—not until I encountered the disciplinary system in prison. They truly are the judge, jury, and executioner—with absolutely no real oversight.

"Doc, it's time you relaxed a little," Pitr met me at the bunk one day as I returned from work. "They call you all the time now. You work Second Watch, but they call you on Third Watch. Hell, they even call you for First Watch. You need some time off."

They were certainly "utilizing" my skills and services, if not taking advantage of them. I'll admit it made the time go faster. As I say, the office was my oasis.

"OK, Pitr. Whaddaya got in mind?"

"Play any cards, Doc?"

"I've been known to play some in the past. Why?"

"Well," Pitr began. "Me, Stinky, and Face play Hearts at night. Interested? It'll take your mind off the damned *juras*."

"When do we start?"

"How 'bout now? Be in the dayroom in about five minutes."

Face and Stinky had joined Pitr in the dayroom by the time I walked in. They'd saved a spot for me at the table, There were three tables in the small, cramped room, the other two occupied by a dominoes game and a game of chess. Only the domino players were making any kind of noise—a relief to me. As I sat, I could see the other three sizing me up as a card player. Time to reel 'em in, I thought.

"Tell me about this game—whaddaya call it—Hearts? I think I've played it before with my family. I just can't remember." I leaned into the middle of the table. "Who's gonna deal?"

"Uh, Doc," Pitr took the bait. "I thought you said you could play?"

"It's OK," Stinky chimed in. "We'll teach you as we go along."

"*Jew* knows what *es di* Queen, *jes?*" Face cocked his head.

"Yes, I know what the Queen is." Thirteen points, if I remembered correctly.

"Enough talk," Pitr silenced the room. "Let's cut to see who deals."

"What's that?" I feigned ignorance.

"You don't even know about cutting? High card deals," Stinky shook his head.

I'd set another hook. Face won the cut and dealt the cards. Each player surveyed his hand. I was going to take great delight in messing with them more.

"How do you know who goes first?"

"The two of Clubs," Pitr sputtered, barely able to contain his annoyance, too. "Who's got it?"

"Me!" I threw the two of Clubs on the table, The hand progressed uneventfully with the twenty-six points spread evenly among my three cohorts. They hardly noticed I didn't take a point. I stayed quiet through the next three hands, taking one point in each—one point, enough to prevent anyone from Mooning.

I was analyzing my competition, especially how they passed. I noticed that the player to my left—Face was sloppy in his passing to me. I think he thought he could get away with it because I couldn't play. Time to let him know otherwise. Next time Face passed to me, I was ready to give him an education.

As I inspected my hand after the pass, I knew it was a Moon, even a laydown, but I wanted to draw it out. I had one bad card and it fell on the first trick. Now to get the lead—a lead that would not be relinquished. I intentionally played a trump, knowing they hadn't been broken yet.

"You can't lead trumps, Doc," Stinky scolded. "They haven't been broken."

"Oh, sorry," I smiled. Remain disciplined, I told myself. Picking up the Heart, I played the ten of Spades. Don't give away the strategy yet. "Let's see who has the Queen," I announced. The ten won—not news to me, since I had the Ace, King, Queen, and Jack accompanying that ten. I was actually surprised something other than Spades didn't fall on the trick, but distribution held.

On to the next snare, I played the Ace of Diamonds.

"Damn it, Doc," Pitr cautioned. "A high card like that'll attract heat—you know the Queen or a Heart."

"You're right. I counsel discipline, gentlemen," I picked up the winning trick. All I had left to go with the top four remaining Spades were the top six Hearts. It was a definite lay-down. Still, that was no fun. I played the Jack of Spades. Bingo! I picked up a low Heart.

"Told you," Pitr frowned. "What do you mean by discipline, Doc? Now Hearts are broken. You can play your low one, the nine I think."

"No," I quietly smiled back. "Discipline—stay within yourself. Set goals, that kind of thing," I sighed. "I think I'll lead this back," throwing out the Ace of Hearts, followed dramatically by the King, then the Queen, then the Jack, and finally the Ten and Nine of Hearts. Not waiting for them to play a card, I continued with the Ace of Spades, followed by the King and last, in theatrical fashion, the Queen of Spades. "That, gentlemen, is how you Moon."

"*Jew's* kidding, eh?" Face sprayed saliva as his "J" reached the table.

Pitr just stared at me.

Stinky smiled and shook his head. Finally, he looked up and leaned into me,

"Discipline, huh? You set us up, didn't you, Doc? You knew how to play all along, right?"

"I don't know what you're talking about. But I did have a plan," I smiled back innocently. "Let's just say I'm a fast learner."

Chapter 9: *Infection Detection and Other Farces*

"Calm down, Doc," Pitr hovered over me. I'd come to like Pitr as a person, though not his name. He was a reasonable wind in this storm called JRC. While his allegiance was to the South-Siders—he also wanted to survive—his sympathies weren't entirely aligned with the gang mentality. His semi-literate parents blessed him with this moniker at birth, and, like the rest of us, he didn't have any say in the matter.

Pitr attended high school in the San Fernando Valley area of Los Angeles, California, and actually graduated, a genuine rarity within the Hispanic gang community. Even then, he was only marginally affiliated—again, a simple matter of survival. He was tall, with an early potbelly—a common physical attribute in the Hispanic males I treated in my ER days—mostly from the carbohydrate-loaded foods associated with traditional Mexican meals. Tortillas, beans, rice, and various meats frequently led to what's called "metabolic syndrome"—a combination of hypertension, hypercholesterolemia (high cholesterol), and Type-2 diabetes—and my friend, Pitr was well on the way to this all-too-common Hispanic health curse. Even he participated in the ritual meal eaten by groups of South-Siders—a spread—as soon as we got back from chow. No wonder they develop that telltale protruding gut—eating again after just having eaten.

On this occasion, Pitr was trying to soothe my angst brought about by frustrations concerning the spread of Hepatitis C. Several members of my dorm fraternity came to me individually, as well as in small groups, wanting to know about Hep C. The incidence of this viral infection is reported to be six-in-ten among the incarcerated, no doubt from the high drug use—another serious health crisis largely ignored. Notice how all prison problems are interconnected: drugs, education, health. It's no small coincidence.

"Are you telling me you have Hep C and they aren't offering you treatment?"

Why was I not surprised?

"They talked to me about getting some shots and pills for it. But when they were supposed to start, they all of a sudden said 'no' because they didn't have a doctor or something." Pitr was matter-of-fact in his description.

"So it sounds like they were going to give you interferon and riboflavin," I was asking as much as telling Pitr. "At least that's my guess. They didn't because of not having a doctor? There are several doctors. Are you sure that's what they said?"

"Yeah," Pitr sighed. "They said they didn't feel comfortable giving me the shots without a specialist supervising it."

"Comfortable? You got to be . . ." I stopped myself. "So they're not treating it at all?"

"They said they're gonna watch it," Pitr replied.

"Watch it? Watch it do what?" My blood pressure rising. "Have you had a genotype test or a viral load count?"

"Huh?"

"Never mind," my incredulity was growing exponentially. I did some checking in the medical clinic with a couple of my nurses I had befriended—who told me the physicians didn't feel comfortable giving the Hepatitis C medications without a supervising hepatologist—a specialist in liver diseases. Those guys do genotyping and count viral loads.

Genotyping is a blood test that determines which Hepatitis C sub-type someone has. It's important because certain genotypes are more susceptible to treatment. A viral load is an actual measurement of the number of virus particles observed in the blood. The higher the number, the more damage the virus is doing and vice-versa—lower viral loads are also easier to treat.

The nurses told me they didn't bother telling the inmates what the results were because "they aren't interested." That's probably true, and a self-fulfilling prophecy, unless it is accompanied by a deeper discussion of the disease and its ramifications—something that wasn't going to happen at JRC for sure.

"Do you wanna play cards now, Doc?" Pitr was trying to distract me from the malpractitioners and calm me down.

"Why?"

"Well, you're getting yourself all worked up. Cards might slow you down some."

"Yeah, you're right. This Hep C stuff really pisses me off. Count me in."

I welcomed the distraction; anything to take my mind away from the ridiculous excuses for not properly treating Hepatitis C, especially after 2013, when a cure—not a treatment—was introduced. It's a very expensive cure that all state healthcare bureaucracies are having to deal with. At around $84,000 per patient, this drug alone could bankrupt the states. But not the prison system—because they didn't offer it. Of course, once an inmate was released, the state's other medical bureaucracy—Medicaid—would likely get that privilege.

This disease and its sequelae are a coming epidemic—not just in prisons, but throughout America. It is the prisons, however, that aren't doing anything to mitigate the coming crisis. Not all genotypes were susceptible to treatment until 2013. The ones that are have significant cure rates—good for the patient-inmate and a huge long-term cost savings for the state. Avoiding a liver transplant is in the inmate's and state's best interest.

With the new medications now coming to market, cures for certain genotypes are possible. As expensive as they are, when compared to the cost of a liver transplant, treatment is relatively cheap. Since the state will likely pick up the costs of a liver transplant twenty-five years or so down the road, either through the prison health budget or the Medicaid budget for indigent healthcare, the state would be better off in the long run to treat it now. But that requires long-term thinking—not a bureaucratic strong point.

"So Pitr," I was curious, as we walked to the dayroom for Hearts. "Aren't you guys worried about all the Hep C?"

"I guess. But the state don't seem to be, so why should we?"

There's a lesson in public health administration—stick your head in the sand and the problem goes away. Except that's been tried repeatedly through the centuries with generally poor results. I shook my head.

"But you all know it's bad, right?"

"Sort of. Nobody gets sick from it."

"Yeah, that's because it takes twenty-five years or so to eat up your liver . . ."

"I never liked liver," Pitr commented. "Hey, where's Face and Stinky?"

"Not eating liver, but destroying yours. It can lead to having a liver transplant—if you're lucky enough to get one. Has anyone ever come and talked about prevention?"

"Naw. We just know we got it. I guess we can't play unless we can find Face and Stinky, or somebody else to play."

"You know, it comes from sharing needles, right?" I grabbed his arm, stopping him from looking for the others. Cards weren't important to me right then. "If you didn't share needles, it would prevent the spread."

"Oh, I don't use anymore," Pitr beamed. "I stopped," pulling away from me.

"Yes, but you *used to* and that's probably how you got it in the first place," I gently admonished him. "If others wouldn't share before they got it, then no one would pass it on."

"Doc," Pitr lowered his head and looked at me in a disbelieving manner. "These are junkies. They don't think about twenty-five years from now, they think about their next fix. Most won't be alive in twenty-five years and they know it. Remember what you yelled at Tiny? About why there aren't any old heroin addicts?"

Another public health lesson administered.

"LISTEN UP!" CO Punkin bellowed. "Next Monday after chow will be TB testing. Nobody goes to work, nobody gets out of it."

Since I had been skin tested for TB not to many months ago when I arrived at JRC, I was guessing this wouldn't include me. Wrong.

Monday, after waiting for three hours, I queued up with everyone else in my dorm and trekked to the chow hall. On arrival, I noted several lines, the first appearing to be a prison version of check-in. When my turn came, I told them about my recent testing and was cut off mid-sentence.

"Everyone gets TB testing. It's the law," the free-staff clerk told me, without looking up.

"But I . . ."

"No buts. Everyone. And every year about this same time," she casually answered, handing me a form. "Next."

I traveled on to the next line. One of the nurses I recognized applied a TB skin test, which I knew would be negative. Like the Army, JDCR runs a lot of cattle calls. In my time, I would be a participant in at least twenty or so.

There are other military similarities. The COs are the equivalent of the Army's non-commissioned officer corps, the Sergeants, Lieutenants, and Captains are the officers. The Assistant Wardens and Wardens are the field-grade commanders—

Colonels and Generals. That leaves only the inmates unaccounted for—we are the enlisted men. However, we are not at all a "volunteer" Army. We are more like the Army of my youth—the non-volunteer draftees of the Vietnam era. Like the military, healthcare is shoddy but escapes scrutiny primarily because its subjects are young and healthy. Like the military of the 1960s, drug use and abuse causes more problems than injuries from conflict.

Also like the military, maintaining mental health is a challenge. I hated psych patients in the ER—not the patients themselves, really, but the mental health system . . . or lack of one. A mentally ill patient in an ER was a huge drain on resources, because getting them placed takes an act of Congress. There are only a few psychiatric in-patient beds available, but that doesn't stop psychiatrists from writing "5150" mandatory holds, even though there is no room in the inn. That often meant our psych patients were boarded in my ER for many hours and, sometimes, even days. What I recalled hearing during my time in the ER was that a primary source of psychiatric treatment and housing is the penal system. Now I am seeing it first hand . . . from the inside.

Like my anger management dorm-mate, a significant number of inmates are assigned to mental health services, or "MHSDS." There are intermittent attempts to house the psych patients—I mean, inmates—in the same dorm. They are designated a "hot meds" dorms. In all my time in the ER, I never heard the term, but according to JDCR, certain psychiatric medications require administration in a cooler environment, or so they say. When the temperature climbs to around 100° Fahrenheit, inmates taking medications can't go on the yard and extra cold water is given out—or is supposed to be dispensed.

Placing these inmates in the same housing makes things that much easier—not for the inmates, but for the staff. These inmates still manage to get scattered all around the institution despite the minuscule efforts to keep them together. Just because an inmate is designated as CCCMS doesn't mean he is on any medications. So the CCCMS inmates are also housed in different dorms. Staff knows who the CCCMS inmates are, inmates don't—at least they aren't told, but they know it soon enough by the actions of the CCCMS inmates, hence, the references like "J-cat" and others. As in society-at-large, the mentally ill are ostracized, especially by the custody staff. They steer clear of "J-cats" as much as other inmates do. It's almost like they have an infection.

"Doc," Pitr timidly called. "Can I bother you?"

"Of course you can bother me," I propped myself up on my elbows. "What's up?"

"It's Jaime. You know him, right?"

"Not really."

"Sorry. Stinky said he thought you did," Pitr looked confused.

"He only asked me if I knew him," I replied, another deficiency of the inmate information distribution system. "I've never met him."

"Well, he thinks he has mersa," a confident Pitr declared.

"I'm thinking you mean, M-R-S-A?" I spelled out the letters.

"Yeah, I guess so," Pitr not so confidently answered. "His arm is red. You know."

I did. Another casualty of heroin abuse.

"I guess it's time I met this Jaime, huh?"

With that, Pitr and I walked down several bunks to where Jaime lived. After the standard inmate pleasantries, Jaime showed me his right arm. There was a moderate-sized reddened and raised area in his antecubital region—the inside of the elbow where it bends—where all the veins are visible, at least most of the time, when they haven't been sclerosed by previous abuse as a heroin injection site.

"So, Doc," Jaime was nervous. "Is it bad?"

"It's definitely inflamed, but it doesn't look like it's formed an abscess yet."

"So it's not that flesh-eating stuff?"

I stopped my examination and looked back and forth between Jaime and Pitr. "Where did you hear it was a flesh-eating bacteria? Or was it 'mersa' you heard? I wonder who told you that," staring at Pitr.

"I was just trying to help. Doc," Pitr turned red as I stared at him.

"Yeah, yeah," I brushed his comment off. "First of all, almost all abscesses are Staph. That's Staphylococcus aureus, a normal skin bacteria. Because of so much use of antibiotics, the bacteria have become resistant to antibiotics like methicillin. MRSA stands for _Methicillin_ _Resistant_ _Staphylococcus_ _Aureus_. You need to be on antibiotics, and if it becomes an abscess, it needs to be lanced."

"I'll lance it myself," Jaime concluded.

"Without anesthesia? And what are you going to lance it with?"

"I'm tough. I'll use a razorblade or my needle."

"Jaime, using a dirty needle or a dirty razor is a bad idea."

"Welcome to prison, Doc," Jaime laughed. "There's nothing here but bad ideas."

Later that evening, I saw Jaime with a bandage on his arm. He gave me a thumbs up, which I took to mean he'd performed his own surgical incision and drainage. What I learned early on at JRC is that there is little fear of pain, and the invincibility of youth triumphs over much adversity—medical and other.

"Did you hear about the governor?" Pitr asked a crowd one night in 2011. Everyone was shaking their heads, including me. "Some court says we're all gonna go home soon. That's what I think they said."

I didn't know for sure, but that statement didn't sound very realistic. That night I called my wife and had her do some investigating. Governor Moonstone Isadore Strange, "Izzy" to most, was one slick politician. He'd been shucking-and-jiving his way around the courts, along with his predecessors, for a couple of decades on this prison issue. This mental health problem the state has—treating inmates poorly, if at all—has been a worsening situation for decades. In the 1990s, a federal lawsuit was filed—that's a really big *602* complaining about the mental healthcare, or the lack of it, more accurately. Then another lawsuit was filed in the early 2000s. The two suits were consolidated a few years later and have been wending their way through the court system ever since.

In 2009, the federal Ninth Circuit Court of Appeals ruled that the root cause of the problem was overcrowding in the prison system, resulting specifically in poor mental health care, and poor healthcare in general. They declared the lack of care equated to "cruel and unusual punishment" and was unconstitutional. In May 2011, "The Supremes" entered the fray and ruled 5-4 to affirm the appellate court's ruling. That's the U.S. Supreme Court, and the governor was none too happy about it.

The truth was, contrary to my inmate friends' knowledge, the governor had no plans to release anyone. In fact, he claimed that he would appeal the decision—I guess he knew how to file a *602*, too—only to this day, I can't figure out how you appeal a

Supreme Court decision. I thought they were the ultimate. Over the next two years, I would be obtaining a legal education I hadn't planned on.

And then there was the great "Valley Fever Scare of 2013." This was the state's quest to rid the prison system of the dreaded fungus, *coccidioidomycosis*, also known as the *San Joaquin Valley Fever*.

It came to pass in the spring and summer of 2013, that several inmates incarcerated at two other prisons in the northern part of the state died from the disseminated form of the disease. This soil-borne fungus, first discovered in the San Joaquin Valley of California, is actually most prevalent in Arizona. There are approximately 16,500 cases annually in that state and about 10,500 in Jefferson.

Approximately 60% of those affected don't even know they've contracted it because they have no symptoms. The only way to know is if they are skin tested—like TB. The 40% who do exhibit signs of infection primarily have upper respiratory symptoms such as coughing, congestion and aches, but very self-limited and mild, like a cold. An exceptionally unfortunate few develop disseminated *coccidioidomycosis*, a potentially fatal form that spreads through the blood and commonly lands in the brain, causing meningitis.

Of this form, the bureaucracy was suddenly in a panic. Since the state's medical care is under the care of a trustee—the federal courts having ordered this prior to the 2011 decision—the trustee decreed that "susceptible" ethnic groups currently incarcerated at the two facilities must be moved immediately. The appellate court concurred and ordered the transfers to be completed within 90 days.

Ah, but there are a few problems the courts and the prison bureaucracy overlooked. First, the "susceptible" groups. *There is no scientifically proven ethnic or racial predilection* for acquiring this disease, so how does one determine who is a member of the "susceptible" group? There's the rub.

Filipinos are known to be about 150 times more susceptible to the disseminated form and Blacks about ten times so—BUT (and it's a really big but) that's only if they have the disease, which is relatively rare and hard to get in the first place. The trustee, nevertheless, ordered all Filipinos and Blacks to be transferred. Enter the ACLU, our defender of rights extraordinaire. They attempted to stop the transfers by filing for injunctive relief as well as filing a lawsuit asking the court to close both prisons completely. That suit will take several years to wend its way through the courts; by then the transfers will be long over and whatever potential damage completely done.

What should have happened is simple: perform the skin-test on anyone being considered for transfer *to* one of the two problem prisons. If positive, it means your immune system has already been exposed and if you don't have any symptoms, you're good to go. Your immune system is ready and able to fight a second contact—which would mean you could go. If, on the other hand, you were negative, it means your immune system has *not* been exposed to the fungus and you are a potential candidate for the disease—a veritable *fungus virgin*. You should *not* be transferred due to the possibility of contracting the disease.

Of course, in its rush to comply with the court order, none of this rational approach was undertaken, even if someone had considered doing that in the first place.

It's curious, however, that the state chose to comply *with this order* immediately—issued by the same court that determined the state was guilty of overcrowding in 2009—rather than fight it tooth and nail as they had the overcrowding case. No Supreme Court appeal, just immediate compliance.

Makes you think they wanted one and not the other, huh?

I was sitting on my bunk reading when CO Punkin's personal public address system went off—he screamed for the dorm to listen up. "OK, tomorrow no one goes to work. Stay in the dorm until they call you upstairs, it's flu shot time again."

With that, the next day after the obligatory three hour wait—we trekked up to the chow hall in bunk order for an annual ritual altogether similar to TB testing, but this time to be offered influenza immunizations. Anyone who has spent five minutes in any ER during the winter and spring months knows that "the flu" is no fun. Close quarters breeds epidemics and prisons are prime targets. So, I supported the concept and actually wanted to get immunized.

Unlike mandatory TB testing, however, flu shots were voluntary. Maybe it's the rebellious nature of being an inmate or whatever, but subordinating to anything the state says is resisted at all costs, even at the cost of one's own health. Many of my colleagues refused the immunizations, and did so proudly.

A month or so later when flu season was in full swing, several dorms were quarantined for two or three weeks.

Only then did I recognize the brilliance of the experienced inmate plan in refusing immunization. By getting the flu, they believed they were in control—*by golly, they really showed the state!*

In fact, most came down with only garden-variety colds as many do each winter, but the state, not being able to quickly rule influenza in or out, quarantined them to be safe. Lying on their bunks, the hacking, spewing cacophony of inmates was happy as could be—not working, not doing much of anything. Yep, they showed the state who was in charge. My dorm, and me personally did not get quarantined and did not get the flu. I was good with that.

"Damn it, Doc," Leonard fumed. "They're taking me to outside medical again."

"When?"

"Aw, you never know. Sometime in the next two weeks."

"For the hernia?"

"Yeah," Leonard sighed. "I'm getting nervous about going outside too many times."

"Why are you going so many times? What are they telling you?"

"Well, I've been seen twice by somebody who says it needs fixing," Leonard looked up, thinking. "Then there was some guy with a real cute nurse who said he'd be taking care of me during the surgery."

"Probably an anesthesiologist," I concluded. "The first two visits were to see the surgeon? Why two?"

"You tell me, Doc. Said the same thing both times. I hate getting up so damned early," my Christian friend cursed.

"Leonard?"

"Yeah?" "You said 'damn' twice," I grinned. "You're bothered by this, aren't you? Is it having surgery that has you upset'?"

"No," he said. "I want the surgery. It's just . . . well," hesitating. "I'm worried they aren't gonna fix it, but they will keep track of all the outside visits and declare me a chronic problem."

"But it isn't even a problem once they fix it, so how could it possibly be chronic when they're about to fix it'?"

"Oh, Doc," Leonard smiled back weakly, "You just don't know. I've been dealing with this hernia for two years or so. Those outside medical visits are just this year."

"You mean there's more? Why the hell don't they just fix it?"

"Yeah, why don't they?" Leonard agreed, but was wise to the JDCR ways. "They got these arrangements with the outside hospitals—a lot of money's involved so they keep looking my problem over, but not doing squat. I've probably been poked and smashed on ten or fifteen times by one doctor or another. They've even scheduled me for surgery two or three times before, but it's still there. It makes me nuts."

As Leonard wandered off, I contemplated his dilemma. When I awoke four days later, I noted Leonard was gone. They wake you up at 3:30 a.m.—you never know what day—to go to outside medical. First, they take you to the prison medical area where you are stripped, searched, and placed in the obligatory paper gown, handcuffed and shackled, and ultimately placed in a van for transport. Next, on arrival at the particular outside medical facility, you sit on a bench waiting your turn—still handcuffed and shackled. That's usually a several hour ordeal. Finally, you see your designated outside medical doctor, team, or whoever "they" have picked for you and your problem is discussed.

I say discussed, because that's mostly what happens, not much doing, only more talking. They always talk about doing, but the actual doing rarely occurs. When that brief encounter is over, the reverse process begins—sit on the bench for hours, get placed in the van, and transported back to JRC, where you're un-cuffed and un-shackled, and returned to your dorm. The entire process takes all day, which is why it always begins at 3:30 in the morning.

Many times you return with no greater degree of insight into your problem than when you left the last time—as did Leonard. Yeah, that's one helluva way to run the trains. Now I understood why it took Sigmund so long to get his "lifesaving" abdominal aortic aneurysm repaired. Based on his experience, a routine inguinal hernia shouldn't take more than a decade or two.

"Doc, they say they're gonna fix it for sure this time," Leonard seemed ecstatic on his return. "Probably in the next week or two is all."

One week later, Leonard was summoned to our counselor's office. He assumed it was to discuss his pending operation or maybe to sign papers. After sixteen years of incarceration, he was scheduled to parole in only 109 days—another reason he was eager to get his hernia repaired. When Leonard returned from his meeting his dejection was obvious.

"Leonard, you don't look happy," I queried.

"I can't believe it," shaking his head. "The bastards."

If Leonard was cursing, I knew it was serious. "OK, so what'd the counselor say?"

"I'm being transferred."

"What!" I had to know more. "Why, I mean, can't you *602* it?"

"No," more agitated than ever. "Doc, haven't you learned about *602s* yet?"

"Why not *602* it? Whaddaya mean, 'haven't I learned about *602s?*'"

Leonard just sat there shaking his head. Not another word was spoken. He had been told he was being transferred to a medical prison facility in the far northern part of the state. With only 109 days left, his hernia was deemed a chronic medical condition and he would start over at the new facility, meaning he likely wouldn't get his hernia fixed before parole.

Apparently, he was being transferred because of too many outside medical visits. *Bastards!*

Chapter 10: Armed Babysitters with Attitudes
Thy rod and thy staff they comfort me

I will admit there are a goodly number of people who genuinely deserve to be in prison. The Level Threes and Level Fours, in particular, are occupied by some pretty dysfunctional souls. However, in the Level Twos like JRC—and I'm betting the Level Ones as well—everyone is eventually supposed to be going home. It is that "eventually," however, that contributes to substantial angst. In my experience at a Level Two facility, even the gang-bangers get out—eventually. Public safety isn't the primary concern of the staff here, personal safety is—and it was my concern and well. That and keeping a lid on the games people play.

Leaving the frying pan for the fire, I want to offer some details about the correctional officers and their role in the game. COs are people, too—or should I say first? It's not kosher for an inmate to say it, but there were several I considered exceptional people in the best sense of the phrase. There were also a significant number that fell into the opposite camp, too. Both types stand out, but for obviously different reasons.

Before I could conquer the system and survive, I had to understand it. To do that meant I had to understand its assorted parts, and the COs are a large component of the system. They are, by and large, a big part of its problems, too, which translated into a very large part of my problems.

There is a group psychology that develops within any bureaucracy, including the prison bureaucracy. There is a group karma as well. Society also plays a role in this game—there is a major societal karma; the concept of "debt to society" stems from it. The societal karma divides along a "them versus us" mentality. Many COs seem to adhere this pattern of psychological separation, what I consider the "I could never be in your situation" mentality.

There is a bright line that separates inmates from staff and another bright line that separates inmates from society. The idea that those upstanding members of society and Correctional Officers cannot cross that line is folly. COs traverse that line frequently—sometimes daily. The significant difference between inmates and staff is simple: inmates got caught. "To err is human," wrote Shakespeare, "to forgive divine."

Not so, according to the state or its agents—the correctional staff. They and society relish in a *schadenfreude* sentiment—that is, a certain enjoyment in the misery of others, specifically us inmates.

There is a constant psychological competition between *schadenfreude* and sadism—another line over which some tippy-toe back-and-forth. *Schadenfreude* is enjoyment at the misery *someone else* caused, whereas sadism is being the causative agent. Several of the COs I encountered could not distinguish the difference.

Remembering that mindset, I was perhaps fortunate to work in a part of the prison world—or at least on its fringes—to which very few inmates have access. As a clerk for the correctional staff, I was allowed certain freedoms not normally afforded inmates. The staff jealously guarded their own domain and chose carefully who they let in—even at the fringe. I occupied the tenuous "no man's land" between inmates and staff. That can be good or bad . . . or both. Good for you, if the COs invite you in, but bad as far as the other inmates are concerned. It can be bad from both sides, especially when one or the other misunderstands the situation or what's happening.

CO Paver was one buff workout specimen. Lean and mean, he routinely wore a three-day growth of beard in spite of the JDCR rule against facial hair. He strutted rather than walked, chest thrust out, like male peacock parading with its tail feathers fully arrayed in search of a female companion. Some say he was looking for a fight most of the time. Let me describe one of his "finds."

"Hey, you!" from about ten feet away, Paver shouted at an inmate carrying a TV. As the facility gate officer, he was not at his station, but standing close by in the adjacent dorm hallway. "What are you doing with that TV?"

"Taking it into my dorm. The CO gave it back to me," the unknown inmate replied, struggling to hold on to the old-style television. The newer models were flat screen, light and digital. This was one of the clear plastic "bubble" televisions—heavy, very heavy, and awkward to carry. All prison electronics are clear so anyone can see through them—ostensibly to prevent storage or transportation of contraband items.

"Give it to me," Paver shouted, drawing closer.

"But . . ."

"Didn't you hear me? I said give it to me. I'm taking it back."

After struggling to carry the bulky cargo at least a hundred yards, being forced to part with it was not the expected outcome; combine that with this inmate's short-fuse made for an unhappy camper. So, in compliance, the inmate threw it to the ground. Perhaps more dropped it than threw it, but it definitely ended up on the ground.

Instantly, Paver pounced like at big cat, tackling the inmate and knocking him down. With clenched fists, he struck the inmate in the face several times. For good measure, he struck him with his baton as well. No call went out for back-up, no pepper spray, no alarm . . . and no resistance by the inmate—he was too surprised by the outburst to offer any response. A second CO, Daley, the dorm officer, was quickly on scene to help "subdue" the battered inmate. The inmate was summarily hauled away in handcuffs for an evaluation of his condition by medical.

How do I know all this? Because it was the primary topic of the inmate gossip mill *and the fact that I got to type up all the reports.* Paver was placed on paid leave pending the investigation. The inmate was admitted to a local hospital for a broken jaw and several other injuries, all of which were less serious. Several inmates who witnessed the incident were eventually called to testify at the disciplinary hearing for Inmate Strake after he was released from the hospital and transferred to solitary confinement where he spent several months following the incident.

I wish I could say this was the only such "use of force" incident I knew of. Unfortunately, it was an all-too-frequent occurrence.

If an accused inmate is no longer at an institution, he can't ask questions or perform any kind of investigation in support of his defense. He certainly can't interview witnesses or gather physical evidence. In that situation, an Investigative Employee, or IE, is appointed to act as the inmate's mouthpiece. Since the inmate in this instance was in solitary confinement, he couldn't exactly prepare his case, like asking for witnesses or interviewing others, which is why an IE was appointed to do the legwork.

The IE's questions to other witnesses, asked on behalf of the inmate and answered as part of the "investigation" into Officer Paver's need to use force, appear after Officer Paver's report.

Paver's official report of this incident read as follows:

On June 18, 2013, at approximately 1432 hours, while reporting for my duties as Alpha Gate Officer, I was carrying a television and approached Officer Daley who was standing in the 101. I asked Officer Daley if he could get Inmate Strake, A., F-000111, 101-08L, out of his dorm and have him meet me in the 101 corridor. As Inmate Strake approached me in the corridor, he asked me, "Are you going to give me the TV back?" I replied, "Yes" and handed Inmate Strake the television.

While Inmate Strake was holding the television, I informed him that I was going to write him a JDC-115 for Disobeying a Direct Order in culinary on June 17, 2013. Inmate Strake became agitated with me and said, "You know what? Fuck this TV, and fuck you! I'm a convict," I then took a couple of steps back to create distance between myself and Inmate Strake when Inmate Strake stepped toward me, throwing the TV at my face with both hands. I was able to block the TV from hitting my face by allowing it to strike my left arm.

While blocking the TV with my left arm, I was able to strike Inmate Strake in the facial area with my right closed fist to stop the attack. The TV broke when it hit the ground and Inmate Strake took off running towards Alpha Gate. I ordered Inmate Strake to stop running and to prone out as I called for a Code 1 response via institutional radio. Inmate Strake complied and proned out adjacent to the Alpha SAP Gate.

I then drew my Monadnock expandable baton and ordered Inmate Strake not to move and to place his hands behind his back. I provided coverage as Officer Daley applied handcuffs to Inmate Strake and waited for responding staff to arrive. Once responding staff arrived, Sgt. I. Whining instructed Officers Smith and Jones to take custody of Inmate Strake and transport him to Urgent Care for completion of a JDC-7219 Medical Evaluation Form.

I advised Sgt. Whining that my right hand was injured and needed medical attention. Sgt. Whining accompanied me to Urgent

Care for medical evaluation and then transported me to U.S. Healthworks for additional treatment.

Inmate Strake is in direct violation of JCR §3005(d)(1), FORCE OR VIOLENCE, specifically, BATTERY ON PEACE OFFICER WITH WEAPON. (Inmate Strake is aware of this documentation and is not a participant in the Mental Health Services Delivery System at any level of care, and has a score that is less than 4.0 on the T.A.B.E., and a Staff Assistant is required.)

What follows next was excerpted from the "Investigative Employee Report," submitted by the CO who acted as the investigator:

On 07/04/2013, at approximately 1130 hours, I met with Inmate Strake, A, F-000111, at the Jefferson Institution for Men (RCC/JIM), Administrative Segregation Unit (AD-SEG), and informed him that I had been assigned as the Investigative Employee (IE) in the matter pending against him at this time. Inmate Strake stated he had no objection to me performing as the IE and requested that I interview the following witnesses:

Inmate Strake asked the following questions for Inmate Baldwell, S., AK-1234, 101-18U about incidents on 06/17/2013 and 6/18/2013.

 Question 1: Does he recall what happened on 6/18/2013?
Answer 1: All I saw was Strake run out the gate and lay down on the ground. CO Paver had his baton out walking behind him. Baton in the left hand, right hand was free.
Question 2: Were you at the Facility A entrance at the time of the incident and where was Inmate Strake?
Answer 2: Yes. Like I said, he was lying on the ground.
Question 3: What did you see?
Answer 3: Same as A1.
Question 4: What did you see in the chow hall?
Answer 4: Upon departure from the chow hall, we all got up and went back to Dorm 101. Officer Paver then came down

from the chow hall and tore up Inmate Strake's shit and took another inmate's TV of another race (Hispanic). The following day (6/18/2013), Paver came back to Strake and asked would he give the TV back to keep him from getting rolled up. Inmate Strake stated, "No, I'm going to do my paperwork and you do yours." He told the two Hispanics when he came back to work on 6/18/2013 he was going to give them (Hispanics) their TV back, but instead he came to work and had Officer Daley call Inmate Strake to the gate. And that's all I know.

Question 5: What did you see in the dorm on 6/17/2013 concerning Inmate Strake?

Answer 5: On 6/17/2013, we were in the chow hall where Officer Paver addressed Inmate Strake as "hoover". Inmate Strake then asked him to call him by my last name and last two. Officer Paver then got pissed and told Strake, "Pick up your tray, leave the chow hall, or I'm going to tear your shit up."

Inmate Strake asked the following question for Inmate Stiley, A., T-1234, 101-01L.

Question 1: Will you be willing to testify at Inmate Strake's hearing?

Answer 1: Yes.

Question 2: Is there anything you want to add to your statement that was not included?

Answer 2: No.

Inmate Strake asked the following question for Inmate Gafney, K, V-1234, 101-44U.

Question 1: Will you be willing to testify at Inmate Strake's hearing?

Answer 1: Yes, I will go testify.

Question 2: Is there anything you want to add to your statement that was not included?

Answer 2: No, I have nothing else to add.

Inmate Strake asked the following question for Inmate

Testy, M., J-1234, 101-08U, on 08/17/2013 and 6/18/2013.

Question 1: Please give a complete statement on what happened between you and your bunkie on 6/17/2013.

Answer 1: Officer Paver just came and searched my bunk and took my TV.

Question 2: What happened on 6/18/2013?

Answer 2: I don't know what happened.

Inmate Strake asked the following question for Inmate Blyer, C., AL-1234, 101-08L on 06/17/2013 and 8/18/2013.

Question 1: What happened on 6/18/2013?

Answer 1: Yes. I saw Officer Daley call Inmate Strake to the hallway and at that time they locked the gate and Officer Paver threw the TV at Inmate Strake and it struck him in the eye and Inmate Strake ran outside the gate to the hallway, and I'm willing to go to court.

Question 2: Were you able to give any other statements to anybody else after the incident took place?

Answer 2: No!

Inmate Strake asked the following question for Inmate McSmith, J., AM-1234, 101-38U, on 08117/2013 and 13/18/2013.

Question 1: What happened on 6/18/2013, the day of the incident with Inmate Strake and Correctional Officer Paver?

Answer 1: All I know is they were calling him for 10 minutes to talk, to him. He knew something was going to happen because he gave me some stuff in keep.

Question 2: Do you recall where Inmate Strake was before he incident took place?

Answer 2: He was back at his bunk.

Question 3: Do you recall what was said to you by Inmate Strake before answering the call for Inmate Strake?

Answer 3: That they were going to try to do something to him.

Inmate Strake asked the following question for Correctional

```
Sergeant I. Whining, on 06/17/2013 and 6/18/2013.
    Question 1: Do you recall the incident that took place in
the chow hall on 6/17/2013?
    Answer 1: Sgt. Whining was not available for questioning
due to being out on military leave.
```

This report was just one example of how the system is stacked against you. Now, before you shrug this off with a "who cares?" remember that the Fourteenth Amendment to our Constitution says we all are entitled to "equal and impartial justice under the law," even incarcerated ones, according to the U.S. Supreme Court. The words "Equal Justice Under Law" are even engraved over the entrance to the U.S. Supreme Court building itself.

Yeah, having an "unbiased" correctional officer is a big help. Not in my experience. Aside from making for some bitter convicts, it jeopardizes the safety of staff, inmates and . . . me.

So what happened to the good Officer Paver? I don't know exactly, but he was back to work within the month—much sooner than Inmate Strake's fractured mandible healed. Needless to say, the inmate was found guilty of "Battery on a Peace Officer." *Schadenfreude* or sadism?

And the business about Sgt. Whining not being available for questioning because of being on military leave was particularly interesting, because she managed to be there every time I was looking for her on other matters.

On a different note, there was a most likeable CO I'll call "Bobby."

Bobby was a big man, a former Marine, and a recent college graduate with a degree in psychology. After his time in Iraq in the 1990s, he became a CO. He worked the dorm next to my Program office, so I saw a lot of him. I even helped him study a bit for some of his tests. I actually enjoyed talking psychology, current events, and "normal" stuff with him. He appeared to enjoy the conversations as well.

But he was still on the other side of the "green line." When other COs were around, he acted differently. He assumed the standard-issue, macho correctional officer psyche.

I learned he coached little league baseball and was a major sports nut—like me. One day, Bobby told me why he'd never made Sergeant after his fifteen years or so as a CO. He'd passed the requisite examination many years ago, but got caught up in an "incident."

On arriving to work several years ago, he walked into the Sergeant's office to find an inmate handcuffed sitting in a chair. Several COs, a Sergeant, and a Lieutenant were "questioning" the inmate. The questioning also involved slapping him and striking him several times with closed fists. When Bobby walked into this fracas, he was asked if he wanted in on it. He declined, and from that point on he was treated differently by the COs involved.

A few weeks later, he was informed that he was under investigation on trumped up, trivial charges . . . for which he was ultimately exonerated. However, the Lieutenant in the room during the "interrogation" Bobby refused to join was now our facility Captain.

Bobby is a well-respected CO—but his interest in rising in the ranks was squashed. I don't know what happened to the inmate, but Bobby told me this wasn't the only such incident he'd experienced.

I'll admit to my ambivalence about working in the Program Office. While it provided me an oasis, allowing time and space to get away from "normal" prison activities, I necessarily had to interact with many COs and their higher-ranked supervisors. I found a number of their behaviors repugnant, but also found many of them personally likable, and I frequently identified more with them than with my fellow inmates. This is probably some variant of the psychological "Stockholm syndrome"—having sympathy for one's captors.

Maybe it was because there were so few inmates I wanted to talk to or get to know better. Maybe it was from being alone in the Program office most of my day, working around and for the staff. Whatever the reason, eighteen months, or so after my anointment as Captain's clerk, the assignment office placed three inmates into the vacant Lieutenant's clerk positions. Not only was my refuge suddenly being violated, to add insult to injury, I was ordered to train them.

The first new clerk was an overweight, forty-something American Indian-Japanese American, who was also a former Marine. I guess his demographics were evidence we are a homogenized society and lends credence to the premise there is no such thing as race. He was friendly enough, and I hoped would come to share my belief about the office being our sanctuary. In order to maintain this retreat meant not bringing any "heat" on the office. Many an inmate couldn't grasp that concept—this new one, it turned out, was of that persuasion. He was difficult to train because he either didn't listen, or listened and ignored it, or, most likely, listened and didn't get it. Luckily for me he, after three short days of training, he was moved to the Third Watch.

Lucky? No, not exactly. Because he was so incompetent, I was frequently called by the Third Watch Lieutenant—almost every day in the first few months. That meant I worked my normal Second Watch shift, went to my dorm and ate my daily peanut butter and jelly sandwich . . . and then got called to "help" on Third Watch. Add that to the calls on First Watch—blessedly rare, since they had no clerk—and I was essentially the "go to" guy for the facility at all hours. Although that role had its perks, sleep wasn't one of them.

The second assignee was a skittish Armenian-American heroin addict—whose attention span was shorter than a gnat's and about as complex. He was transferred to Third Watch after the three days and lasted there about a week before the Lieutenant banned him permanently.

The third new clerk was a thick-haired Korean about twenty-four-years-old whose English I barely understood on his first day. Having immigrated to this country at age sixteen, his understanding of English was fairly remarkable for such a brief period; in the eight years since his arrival, Mr. Kim had completed high school and even taken some college classes. His spoken English, however, fell far short of his understanding—in particular, his pronunciation of words with the letters "R" and, in particular, "L"—not at all uncommon for most Asian-born Asians. I was charged with training him along with the other two.

Because of his limited language skills, I did not look forward to the task, especially if he lacked computer abilities. Mr. Kim—Hyun-jin Kim—it turned out, was actually a welcome breath of fresh air. Forty years my junior, there was no reason to think we would get along, let alone enjoy each other's company. But we did. He had excellent computer skills, played chess, and had a smile and positive attitude I found to be a pleasure.

Just don't get him rattled.

When he became anxious for whatever reason, he began sweeping back his jet-black hair across his forehead with both hands, over-and-over, and his English inadequacies were replaced by frequent "F-bombs" clearly articulated between utterances no one could comprehend.

And he paced. Back and forth within an invisible, self-imposed cage, like a frustrated lion in a 1950s zoo.

My first challenge with my new junior associate was language. If he was going to be proficient in creating the forms we clerks were required to complete, a more than rudimentary understanding of English was necessary. How Mr. Kim was even assigned to this clerking role was beyond my comprehension.

Since the esteemed, and frequently illiterate, correctional officers created linguistically imperfect reports—many unintelligible—it was up to the clerks to bail them out by modifying them. Mr. Kim didn't really need much improvement—just enough to stay ahead of the staff. I designed a weekly routine for Mr. Kim, having him write a paragraph or two in "present" or "past" tense and then correcting it in an effort to improve his English and writing skills.

I also required him to recite his "little Leonards." Each day, I insisted he practice and speak the following sentence as clearly as possible, "Little Leonard licked his lips and looked lovely." After a month or so his Ls were much improved. His shyness also evaporated into the haze of the prison bureaucracy.

In relatively short order, Mr. Kim became a worthy right-hand man to me. He embodied my prison *Zeitgeist*.

"LISTEN UP!" The Punkin intercom announced one morning. "Tomorrow is quarterly blanket exchange. If you want to change out a blanket, have it ready at nine a.m. Don't be late. No do-overs."

I turned to my prison resource, Sigmund, "I've been here two years, did I miss this exchange for eight quarters?"

"Hell, no," Sigmund scoffed. "I've been here five years and it's only my second. Them bastards'll tell you one thing and do another. Damn bastards."

"Let me get this straight. The 'quarterly' blanket exchange happens every *few years*?"

"Damn, Doc. You finely startin' to catch on," Sigmund wheezed. "Why the hell you see all them boys washin' blankets in buckets. Damn laundry, lyin' bastards."

"Can't you *602* the laundry?"

"Sure," Sigmund shrugged. "Doc, you know what 'useless' means?"

"Yeah, of course," I answered. Sigmund just sat there, staring at me. After a minute, I realized what he was saying.

An interesting prison phenomenon, the laundry. Not only was the blanket exchange not even remotely quarterly—not annually or even biannually for that matter—it basically occurred when they felt like it.

Like many of the internal services, the laundry was supervised by "free-staff," civilian workers on the state payroll charged with supervising inmates who do the actual service work—*or not*. Anything inmates are involved in is subject to certain "rules," such as, "if it's in my area, it's mine." Each dorm gathers its dirty laundry and sends it to the laundry department each week in those ubiquitous large plastic bags. There, inmates from this prison put it on a truck and send it to another larger prison not far away, where the laundry is washed. It is not dried and fluffed. It is thrown into large, commercial washers, still in cloth personal bags, and then drip-dried.

Before it leaves here though, our laundry inmates peruse it to see if there's anything they might want to steal. I learned this the hard way.

In my first month, I received a much-anticipated package my lovely wife sent. Included were six pairs of underwear—briefs, because I hate boxers in general and, specifically, I hated the boxers provided by the state. Not wanting to wear unwashed, new briefs, I decided to send them to the laundry. Picked over by my brethren in the laundry department, I never saw those briefs again.

Laundry Lesson #1. Committed to memory.

In addition to having their choice of our laundry, these good fellows also had a tendency to just plain lose individual bags with a maddening frequency—I'd say your chances of having the same laundry for more than six months was slim. I came to view it as a way of getting new underclothes . . . except "new" meant only now they were yours . . . and getting anything was difficult.

The laundry department rarely handed out clothes which actually were brand new, not unless you worked there. They all got to the new stuff first, which usually meant that it was all gone before anyone else might have had a chance at it. We got used undies—sometime *very used*. And all you get is boxer-shorts, T-shirts, and socks—although getting any socks was dependent on whether the laundry had any.

Ah, but there are ways around this. As in any close-ordered bureaucracy, money talks—or in this case "soups"—soups are the coin of the realm in prison. Soups, or their equivalent such as a juice card. Soups are the dry packed, ramen noodle sort.

After spending time in the system, I developed a lot of "friends," as I acquired more *juice* (not the fruit variety). Being the Captain's clerk landed me in a position of significant power, that was the *juice*. Inmate-to-inmate transactions are common, and I traded my talents for theirs. Often, it was a way around COs and free-staff; many times it was simply more expeditious.

"Damn laundry," Sigmund snorted. "Well, at least they ain't them ISU boys. Don't you get messed up with them boys, Doc."

Messed up with them—no. Having to deal with them—yes. The Investigative Services Unit, or ISU, is similar to the Internal Affairs division of a police department or the Inspector General's office in a civilian operation. No one wanted to deal with them and certainly not in here. They investigated major inmate transgressions and staff issues, too. My dealings with them consisted mostly of typing their RVRs, or other reports.

Still, each time I encountered them, they made my hair stand up.

In my time here, I typed numerous reports of heinous, inmate-instigated crimes investigated by ISU, such as excessive kissing in the visiting area, theft of state food (actually, an extra sack lunch), being out of bounds, refusing to work or failure to report for work, failure to follow a direct order (what do they expect—that's why half the people are here in the first place!), and "cheeking" medications (where you don't swallow it, but hide it in your cheek and spit it out later). There were a few serious investigations, including battery on a peace officer, battery on an inmate, conspiracy to distribute narcotics in a state prison, and being under the influence of alcohol or drugs. ISU was deeply involved in those kinds of cases.

The vast majority of the reports I generated, by far, fell into two categories—drug-related and possession of a cell phone. Occasionally, ISU was involved in these more mundane cases, but more often than not they were investigated by regular COs. Cell phone possession accounted for probably 50% of the total reports typed, and is part of a larger group of offenses—dangerous contraband. In my experience, the use of cell phones was not so much for nefarious purposes, but mostly just to be able to call family and friends, since the pay-phone system in prisons is notoriously expensive... when it's actually working.

The state contracts with a private company (which shall remain nameless) to provide fixed-line telephone service in the dorms. All calls are monitored by staff and recorded—that's probably the reason why there are so many cell phones, too. Since the company has a monopoly, and a truly captive audience, the telephone rates are exorbitant.

During my last year, the federal courts actually heard a case filed by inmates and their families over the high rates, and ruled in favor of the inmates. The company was supposed to refund monies—yeah, right.

Cell phone use kept Mr. Kim and me quite busy. One quarter, JDCR published data saying that 300 cell phones had been confiscated at JRC alone. How many do they actually find? Fifteen percent? Twenty, maybe? For the sake of argument, let's use ten percent. Since the total inmate population was about 3,400, if they confiscated some 300 phones in a quarter, according to my calculations that means there is a prohibited cell phone for every inmate! Truth is, there *are* a lot of cell phones here.

Now that "dangerous" contraband didn't just fly in here. No, it is brought in "somehow" and sold for a nice profit. It also keeps ISU busy investigating how they find their way into a secure state prison.

In addition to not being allowed to have a cell phone, it goes without saying that having one to check out the Internet—you're *Facebook* page and all—is not permitted either. Turns out ISU monitors *Facebook* and other social media looking for inmate use. I typed several RVRs against inmates for posting pictures to their Facebook accounts. Now, did they post it, or was it posted by a "civilian" loved-one? Who knows, but JDCR found them guilty anyway.

During my last two years, the state legislature passed a law making cell phone possession and/or use a mandatory 90-day forfeiture of credit. I can understand the concept of a cell phone potentially being used for illegal activity. But I also understand cell phones are a huge revenue source for the state, too, and not just the individuals providing them. You see, the state gets extra money when an inmate has credit taken back.

Then there were the drug-related RVRs, the second most common—compared to cell phones and drug-related RVRs, everything else was a distant third or even farther down the list. Of course, possession or use of any illegal drugs isn't allowed. Also not allowed is possessing drug paraphernalia like needles—real or inmate-manufactured—bindles or baggies. Whenever an inmate is found in possession of drugs or paraphernalia, they are immediately searched for additional contraband and ordered to take a "piss test"—provide a urine sample to test for the presence of controlled substances.

If you refuse to provide a specimen, you are automatically guilty. If you do provide one, it is sent to an outside laboratory for testing. Several weeks later, the test results return to JRC and, if positive, a state medical doctor confirms the inmate is not taking any legally prescribed medications that would cause a false-positive test. Next comes the write-up—an RVR for possession of a controlled substance through a positive urinalysis.

Each RVR has a life-cycle. The inmate screws up, a correctional officer or other staff member handwrites a report, a Sergeant approves it and logs it. Then a program clerk types it up and returns it to the Sergeant, who proof reads it (or not), signs it, and gives it to an "S&E officer" to take to another Lieutenant for classifying, who then passes it along to yet another S&E officer for serving. And just what is an S&E officer? Each watch has several correctional officers assigned as S&E officers—Search & Escort—they are the enforcement arm within each facility, whereas ISU is institution-wide.

The inmate is "served" (or not) within fifteen days—that is, given copies of the report—signs it (or not), and the S&E officer places the RVR in the "to be heard" box (or not) for the Lieutenant to review. The Senior Hearing Officer, a Lieutenant, hears the case and determines guilt or innocence—well, in here there are no innocents, only the guilty or not guilty—and gives the hearing report to a program clerk to type, who returns it to the Lieutenant for final review and signature.

The LT hands it off to an S&E officer to take to the Captain for final review—except it still isn't final then. Even after the Captain's review, it goes to an associate warden for final review. Assuming all the Is are dotted and the Ts crossed, the inmate is served his final copies by S&E. Can you envision the fact that there are more than just a few places where something could go wrong?

That was the workflow in an *ideal* scenario. Nothing was ever ideal. It presupposes that there will be no unusual circumstances. In reality, that was what *never* happened.

The many opportunities to lose things are obvious. There are also time constraints at each level—that is, an RVR must be served to the inmate within a limited time period. Additionally, if an inmate is CCCMS, or has a disability—like hearing or vision impairment—it may generate the need for a Staff Assistant. If an inmate has a T.A.B.E. score below 4.0, it does for sure. Supposedly, the Staff Assistant is an uninterested party who acts as an advisor to the charged inmate. All Staff Assistants are Correctional Officers—so they are hardly disinterested. Many times, it may just be to translate for a Spanish-speaker. At other times, not so benign. Remember inmate Strake?

In some cases, somebody along the chain of command decides something isn't proper and sends it back for correction. That may also precipitate restarting the time constraints requirements from the beginning. In more complicated instances, the RVR may include many different types of supplemental documents, such as photographs, medical reports, Miranda warnings, and so on. That can become a big headache for the S&E officer trying to sort it all out—if they even care or try. And those supplements can get lost, too.

On Second Watch, there are three or four S&E officers. These are whom we clerks actually interact with the most. They are quite dependent on our work, and most will freely admit it. That affords clerks ample opportunity for acquiring juice and occasionally to be on the receiving end of nice favors from the S&Es. I also liked several of them. They are the COs who enter dorms to search for contraband and generally do the prison's dirty work such as escorting inmates to and from the cages to higher custody. As such, they are not held in high regard by inmates. They are viewed with disdain, barely above ISU officers. Having to work closely with them creates a potential problem for clerks with other inmates. For clerks, there is constant friction from being in the middle.

That friction, and other day-to-day issues, tended to grate on me. I was different than most inmates—and I knew it. Maintaining that distinction became a constant vigil. The inmates wanted to pull me in their direction . . . to the dark side . . . and I struggled to prevent the prison experience from changing my essence. Prison was a huge change in my "routine," but I wanted desperately to remain "me."

While survival was my first priority, survival as the new-and-improved "me" was just as important. I was alone among many and felt a void in my life. Mr. Kim helped fill the daily work void. Leonard, before he was transferred, and a few others filled some of those empty spots in the dorm. I yearned for spiritual help.

One morning, as I arrived for work, a new inmate—to me, not to the system—was waiting for me to open the office.

"I'm Robert, the new supply clerk. I've heard about you, Doc. I'll take care of you," extending his hand.

I shook his hand, a bit leery, but offered him a chair in the program office. "Good to meet you. We do need some supplies."

"I know. This isn't my first rodeo," Robert replied. "I've been here a couple of years, but just got assigned as supply guy. Whaddaya need?"

I'd been in my position long enough to know that nothing is free in prison. Over the next year, Robert would prove to be an exception to that rule and renewed some of my faith in humanity. That day, however, we talked for a good thirty minutes, and from then on, Robert would come by to visit each morning. Along with Mr. Kim, Robert became a daily fixture in the program office. He had a great philosophy on prison life, was never rattled by the COs, and became one of the few consistencies for me. He dispensed daily observations and witticisms.

One of Robert's witticisms: "The consistent rule is, enforcement of the rule is inconsistent."

Chapter 11: *Philosophy, Spirituality, and Robert*

After moving my King's Knight from G1 to F3—my most favorite chess opening—I looked up from the board.

"Your move."

My young opponent quickly countered with his Queen's Pawn from D7 to D5.

Next, I moved my Queen's Pawn from D2 to D4 to confront his and stared into his eyes. Chess is as least as much an exercise in psychology as it is skill.

He refused to make eye contact, looking down at the board as he quickly moved again, pushing forward his King's Pawn one space, from E7 to E6. He was playing his Black pieces conservatively.

I moved my King's Bishop from G1 to G2 and he answered with King's Pawn from G7 to G6. I castled, completing the Barcza opening. The Hungarian Grandmaster, Gedeon Barcza, who lived from 1911-1986, called this his "quiet" opening. I use it almost exclusively as my opening because it reliably protects the King by castling and the Bishop *fianchetto*[2] covers the diagonal across the entire board. Protection, in chess as it is in prison, is paramount.

Robert was here checking supplies. I knew he was really here for companionship.

"You pray the same move," Mr. Kim sighed.

"Play, not *pray*! Say your 'little Leonards'," I smiled. Then I condescended ever so slightly, "I *pray* it because you don't have a good answer to it." Mr. Kim began mumbling his "little Leonards" as I listened.

Turning to Robert, Mr. Kim nodded. "I am a Christian."

"I don't know what I am," Robert barely smiled. "I just know there has to be something better than this."

---

2 *Fianchetto:* An Italian word, meaning *on the flank*, applies only to Bishops. Pronounced fyan-KET-toe, it involved placing a White Bishop on the G2 (or B2) square. Black equivalent is G7 (or B7).

As our game continued, I reflected on Robert's statement. Chess is a game that resembles life—for every move, there are consequences. Everyone in here is dealing with the consequences of their actions. Some understand that, most don't. Only a few accept the consequences, in my experience.

I looked up from the game and fixed my eyes on Robert, "Do you ever ask someone what they're here for?"

"No."

"Why not? Don't you want to know?"

"It's none of my business."

"Really? Do you not want to know because that person isn't dealing with the consequences of their actions, or maybe you aren't?"

Robert didn't answer, sitting down from inventorying supplies. I took that to mean he was prepared to engage in a discussion on consequences. Mr. Kim was relieved from pondering his next chess move. Kim listened intently—and learned.

After a few moments, Robert leaned back in his chair. "Are you dealing with your consequences, Doc?"

"Are you?"

"I asked you first," Robert grinned.

"Yeah," pausing, "I think I am dealing with the consequences of my actions, the reason I'm here. It's painful, but one thing about prison is it forces you to look inside."

"Or not," Robert demurred.

"True enough," I agreed, "but for those who want to improve their lives, it is totally necessary." I stopped focusing on the ceiling, locked onto Robert's eyes, and continued.

"I needed to find the root cause of my actions—why did I stop in my accident? Why didn't I let the cops handle it. Well, they weren't handling it and I thought I could. Why did I think that? Because my entire life I've been a problem solver."

I paused, for no apparent reason. No one else spoke either.

"I think I *thought* I could solve the issue. That's what an ER doctor does—fixes other people's problems. But there are two problems with that line of thinking: First, it wasn't my problem to fix. It was something for the police to solve, even though they weren't doing anything. And second, if you're a problem solver, your plan had better be right.

"My personality makes me one who makes errors of commission, not errors of omission. I act quickly, rather than take too much time to think about a problem. My solution to the problem was flawed. I should've thought it through more thoroughly, but I didn't. Now I'm paying the consequences for that." I faced Robert directly.

"Admitting that is hard."

Robert's eyes broke away from mine and closed as I finished. "I'm not at that stage yet. I can't say I've accepted . . . accepted . . ."

"Responsibility?"

"Yeah, I can't even say that word," Robert took a deep breath. "Isn't that the problem in here? Nobody takes responsibility for anything."

Robert had nailed a major JDCR issue—responsibility—but I think it's a larger societal one. I hear a lot of talk from inmates about mistakes the courts made, or how they beat this or that, even in-prison issues. They'll file a *602* or focus on how they've been wronged. Rarely do I hear anyone accept any blame, or take personal responsibility for why they're here. No one admits to anything. It's always someone else's fault, or society, or poverty or some excuse.

You never hear, "I screwed up."

Well, I screwed up and I was paying the price for it. You can argue that the punishment doesn't fit the crime or justice was not being served. But those are different issues. As humans, we make mistakes. To admit them requires introspection and self-examination that comes hard to most. It requires courage.

In medicine, especially during medical school and training, there are Saturday morning "M&M" conferences. That's morbidity and mortality, where someone presents a case—usually a screw up—and the professors, and even the juniors, critique the care as it was given. It can be brutal, especially if you're the one who screwed up. The purpose is to train you to take responsibility and to think critically. It's a learning technique. Because of that experience, I believe I am better equipped at self-criticism. Still, it is painful no matter how often you've done it.

Before I came to prison, I had lost my way. I was more self-absorbed than self-critical. That, too, is hard to admit. There are valid reasons rationalized for it, but the best of reasons is still an excuse. It is excuses that fill the corridors of this and every other prison.

"Check," Mr. Kim beamed.

"Check? What the. . . "

While Robert and I were engaged in our discussion about responsibility, Mr. Kim had diligently being concentrating on our chess game. I had been making moves in distraction. Now I was paying the price for that inattention. Staring at the board, I was in a hurting way. I studied my options for a few minutes, glancing at Robert on occasion, noting he was obviously still thinking about our discussion. For not paying much attention, I was essentially even in loss of pieces, down only two points. It was my positions that were inferior. To extract myself, I hit upon a strategy of sacrificing a significant piece to entice Mr. Kim. Now, will he fall for it? I moved my Knight into a vulnerable position, hoping he would take it.

"Why you give me your Knight?" Kim was dubious. And greedy. After a few seconds, he took the Knight, putting into play my plan from which he had no return. By taking my Knight, he took his Queen out of any possibility of defense against my next few moves. I made two moves, he countered, but it was over.

"Checkmate," I stood up from the board. Mr. Kim began pushing his hair back and making all types of guttural noises, standing up and pacing.

Robert remained seated and silent.

Just then, Sergeant Whining passed by the door to our office and stopped in her tracks. "Who the hell are you?" she demanded, staring directly at Robert.

"Stephenson. The supply clerk," Robert barely looked up.

"And why are you in the Program Office? Why aren't you doing supply work?"

"I am," Robert now turned his eyes in her direction as he stood. "Officer Crapulveda asked me to inventory the supplies every day, to monitor them."

"Well . . ."the Sergeant hesitated, "don't be hanging out in there," struggling to come up with a response.

"Crapulveda said it's OK to stay in the Program Office so I'm available to him when he's here," Robert volleyed. "Would you like to talk to him?"

Robert knew even Sergeants didn't want to mess with Crapulveda. He'd been a CO for longer than anyone and had the stripes to show for it, except he didn't wear stripes. Many of the COs have linear, yellow hash marks on their sleeves representing the years of service to the state, sometimes called "french fries." Each hash symbolized three years. Mostly only the testosterone or insecure types wore them.

Crapulveda, an easy-going guy, was in charge of all the supplies for the facility.

Sounds impressive and important. It isn't—the inmates do all the real work. He just supervises—and complains about it.

The Sergeant grunted as she left.

Robert snickered as he sat back down. "Have you ever noticed Ima is always going at ninety miles an hour, but she's never actually doing anything?"

"Ima?"

"Sergeant Whining. Ima Whining," Robert was not being the least respectful and knew it. "She pushes on the wall, but the wall never moves."

"Huh? What do you mean?"

"We *pray* again?"

"Not now, Kim. Robert's making a point."

"If you push on a wall all day long, you're damn tired. But is it work if the wall never moves? I don't think so. Whining's a wall-pusher. Busy all the time, but never does shit," standing up and surveying our supplies again.

"We're all pushing on the wall," I replied. "But I'd like to think I move the wall sometimes."

Robert turned back as he left our office, "I'm not ready to admit my mistakes yet."

"AaaaaRrrrrrHhhhh!" Kim groaned. "Wet's pray now."

I kidded Mr. Kim, "You don't like to lose, do you Mr. Kim?" Patting him on the shoulder, "Before we pray, you need to work on your 'Ls'. It's 'let's', not 'ret's' and 'Play', not 'Pray'. Besides, I need to do a little work." What I really needed was to think about what Robert and I had been discussing.

"I run CO-mit-TEH tomorrow?"

"What?" What was he trying to say now?

"CO-mit-TEH. I can *rearn* to run it tomorrow?"

"Ah, committee, com MIT-tee. It's where you place the accent my friend. You want to LEARN—not *rearn*—to run committee. You must LEARN to say it first," I counseled Mr. Kim.

One night in the dorm, I felt great after having another discussion with Robert, in spite of frequent interruptions by inmates in the dorm. What still gnawed at me was the loneliness. Loneliness in the midst of many.

I am blessed to have phenomenal family and friends . . . to the point of embarrassment. So many inmates in my dorm have been incarcerated for years without receiving a single letter, visit, or telephone call. My wife and I talked daily by phone, usually twice. I also had more than sixty people on my visiting list by the time I left and even more who wrote, some almost daily during the entire fifty-one months I was "down"—I was truly blessed. Still, there was a hole in my soul.

A letter from an old high school classmate suggested the answer. I had been corresponding with Reuben for a while. After high school, I lost track of him until our fortieth class reunion. After high school, he went to medical school and became of professor of family practice in the Northeast. It was his struggle with needing to fill a void that caused our mutual interest. After being in practice for several decades, he became a Christian minister and incorporated his beliefs into his practice and life. He had a void, too. I found him to have an inner peace, revealed to me through his letters with a professor's understanding of what life was all about.

As we exchanged letters, over time I came to an answer—what I call spiritual monasticism. As overcrowded as prison is, I felt alone, certainly spiritually. Rather than fight the loneliness, I decided to embrace it, make it a positive rather than a negative. Just as monastic scholars cloistered themselves physically, I resolved to seclude myself spiritually. That necessitated a kind of "walling off" of my mind, not physically, but mentally. Once I had made that decision, putting it in place required a measure of discipline unheard of in here. Remember, structure and discipline?

I'd previously not been much of a participant in normal dorm activities, so leaving that behind was easy. I dedicated myself to more reading, medical study, and television became mostly PBS. I began my daily routine at 5:30 a.m., rising and showering, then saying my morning prayers. After breakfast, most of which I didn't eat but gave away instead, I headed out for my office oasis until 2 p.m. on weekdays. In the event of not being called back for Third Watch, I read in the dorm until 4 p.m. count and then ate dinner. After dinner, I watched the PBS Newshour from six to seven and read again from seven until eight. Depending on who was on PBS's Charlie Rose at eight, I would watch that or continue reading. I watched local news at nine—usually on Channel Nine, said my evening prayers, and then lights out at ten.

That was my routine for the last few years. On weekends, I tried to sleep in a little, with inconsistent results—the noise never stopped, nor did the calls to go to work.

One scheduled variable was when yard fell on the afternoons I wasn't working. I was usually able to squeeze in an hour of yard two or three times a week. Another was during football season, my spiritual monasticism was put on pause, especially for college football.

On alternating weekends the highlight was the treat of going to visiting. My wife, being the trooper she is, missed visiting me only twice during the four years—once for surgery and once to visit her parents in Michigan. I guess I'll give her a waiver for both. She also maintained an intricate schedule of up to four additional visitors for each visiting weekend throughout my time at JRC. The schedule was typically filled two or three months in advance and required her juggling friends and family. Not a single visiting weekend passed without a visitor the entire time I was at JRC. As I said, she's a real trooper.

One Monday morning, Robert and I were alone in the office. I enjoyed those times and the discussions we were able to have. This day, I could tell something was bothering him. Robert Stephenson was about five-feet-ten-inches tall, with a large, protuberant abdomen I ascribed to the standard prison spread. He had thinning, salt-and-pepper hair, long-ago healed acne facial scars and wore glasses that made him appear academic.

"Doc, you probably know I've got problems."

"Actually I didn't, Robert. What kind of problems?"

"Medical. Geez, you're a doctor and didn't know?"

"Let's just say I'm less inquisitive in here," covering my bases. "Do you want to talk about it?"

"Yeah, you're about all I have to bounce stuff off of," settling into a rickety office chair. After a pause, Robert sighed and let it out, "I've had cancer for a couple of years now," pausing before continuing. "You may have noticed I'm not here some Mondays. It's because they take me out for chemo. Doc, I'm sick of it. I don't know if I want to go on with it."

I moved closer. "Have you talked to your family'?"

"I don't have any family. That's just it. There's no one to talk to. You're it."

"If I can ask, where's your primary?"

"Huh?"

"Where'd the cancer start?"

"Prostate," Robert understood now. "It's in the bone now."

I knew that wasn't good. How do I respond? As a doctor? An inmate? A friend? I hadn't really paid much attention, but he was pale. "Robert," I almost whispered. "You've become a friend. I don't know what to say. Do you want a friend or another doctor?"

"Both," smiling wanly. "Look, I know it's bad. I don't want to die in prison. Do you know what they do to you when you die in prison, Doc? Do you?"

I didn't and couldn't bring myself to say it, so I just shook my head.

"They cut you up, do one of those autopsies. I just hate the thought of them cutting me into little pieces." He was rocking in his non-rocking chair. "I don't want to be buried by these bastards either. Being in prison forever. I want to be cremated." He told me how the state performed autopsies on all inmates who died, and buried them in a pauper's grave on prison grounds.

"Robert, I don't know what to say. Is there anything I can do? Tell me about the chemo and why you're thinking about quitting." As I spoke, I was examining Robert externally as best I could. Now I understood his thin, wasted extremities and large abdomen. He had ascites, meaning his cancer had spread to his liver. When the liver functions deteriorate, it weeps fluid into the abdomen and the belly expands from all the fluid. The fluid is called ascites.

"Yeah," he mumbled before looking at me. "Just be my friend. Those are in short supply in here—even for the supply guy," smiling a little.

"Are you really gonna stop the chemo?"

"Maybe not. Talking to you gave me a boost. Maybe I'll go next week and see."

Just then, the door opened and Mr. Kim strolled through the door, perpetual smile on his face. "Today, I PLAY you and win."

"Very good," Robert beamed.

"And this week you can run CO-mit-TEH," I teased.

It's com-MIT-tee," Kim corrected.

Robert's situation reminded me there is always someone worse off—even in prison. My family and friends worried about me, prayed for me, wrote to me, visited, all in an effort to maintain my hope and faith. I didn't realize how important they are to me until I came here. I took them for granted. Hope and faith are what we all live on. When we lose it, we depend on others to help us find it again.

I liked to believe that I gave Robert a reason to hope. I'd work on the faith part later. His struggle also gave new meaning to surviving. He was truly trying to survive. It made me ashamed to think I was in the same league. Then again, we all have troubles. How we handle our troubles is what differentiates one person from another.

"You hear about this governor on TV?" Kim asked one morning on arriving, clearly confused. "Big mess. I *risten*, but don't know what it means."

"*Listen*, not risten. You know better," I chided.

"I know, I know. Listen. Did you listen?" Kim didn't want a language lesson right now. He wanted information. About that time, several other inmates clustered around the Program Office door. I had become a source of accurate information about all the politicking back-and-forth between the court and governor. I hadn't listened, but I knew where to find out what was up—my trusty wife, who worked at a large law firm.

Governor Moonstone Isadore ("Izzy") Strange took exception to the U.S. Supreme Court's decision several months earlier ordering him to release inmates as the solution to relieve overcrowding. The next day, he took to the podium at a well-publicized press conference to announce he was going to wait for a decision on his appeal of the appeal. I still don't understand how you can appeal a Supreme Court decision, and I don't think the governor did either. Doesn't that set up an endless chain of appeals—if you don't like the decision, you appeal it until you get a result you do like?

"I've called you today to announce my plan for dealing with this outrageous decision by the Supreme Court," Old "Izzy" was one slick politician. He could read the tea leaves with the best of them and thought the public was with him on this—another example of how wrong he was.

"We've spent millions of dollars improving the very services they say we haven't, you know, health care and mental care. So today, I announce that until we exhaust our appellate rights, we will continue to improve care on our own. If the court insists on forcing their will on this great state by saying we haven't, I will decrease the numbers of dangerous inmates by transferring them somewhere, either to county jails or other prisons. My staff will release the details at a later time. Any questions?"

The governor hoped that would quell the furor and rally the state's voters to his side. Instead, it did exactly the opposite. It increased the furor and the voters began grumbling about the delays and the money being spent on the appeals.

A reporter asked the governor, "Governor Strange, how is transferring inmates to county facilities going to improve mental and medical care? Isn't that the reason for the court order in the first place? Jails are short-term facilities and don't provide long-term care. "

The governor was testy, "Do you want an answer, or are you making a statement?"

"Sir, the Supreme Court found against the state because of inadequate care, not because of overcrowding *per se*. The overcrowding worsened the care to the point of being unconstitutional . . ."

"Well that's your opinion," the governor interrupted. "We have spent much time crafting a plan to deal with the court's order. We just need more time. Old Izzy knows how to satisfy the Supreme Court and I know what the *people* . . ." he paused for dramatic effect, "what the *people* want. "

Another reporter interjected, "But governor, where is somewhere? You said you would transfer inmates, and I quote, 'somewhere—either to county jails or other prisons.' Just where are these 'other prisons' you refer to? There are no available beds anywhere, so where is 'somewhere'?"

The governor turned away from the reporter's query and looked directly into the cameras, "Any other questions? Well then, that will be all," leaving the podium to a hail of reporters shouting more questions.

I'd watched this performance on the small TV in the Program Office and hadn't noticed Robert slip in. As I rotated my chair back to the desk, I saw him sitting behind me, watching the screen.

"Won't help me," Robert shrugged.

"I'm not sure it helps anyone. Why not you? Have you looked into getting a medical release?"

"Naw," Robert shook his head. "I filled out paperwork a few years ago. Even *602d* it. Never heard a thing. They didn't even tell me they'd gotten the forms."

"Send them in again," I advised. "Did you go to outside medical last Monday?"

"Yeah. It wasn't so bad. I feel tired more than anything."

"Do they check your blood counts?"

"Yeah, sometimes, not lately."

"Might be a good time to ask them to do it. Have 'em check your liver and kidney functions." I started working on a *115* hearing for Lieutenant Croquet while Robert loitered in the office. That meant he wanted to talk more. I stopped what I was doing.

"So what's up with you, Robert?"

"Doc, I've been thinking. What are we here for? What's it all about?"

"Sounds like a song," I kidded him. "I'm not sure I understand where you're coming from. Wanna explain?"

"When you die, Doc, how do you want to be remembered? How do you want to make your mark? That's what I'm talking about."

"Whoa, that's pretty heavy," I observed. It took me a while to respond to his question. "I want to be remembered for good things I did, not for this."

"By this, you mean prison?"

"Yeah. I don't want 'he went to prison' as my epitaph. I guess I want to leave this earth a better place. To feel like I made a difference."

"Do you think anybody in here has even thought about that? You know, making a difference? "

"Probably not. Why?"

"Well, I have," Robert explained. "I've thought about it, but I can't think of a way to escape just being an inmate. How do I make a difference?"

Tough question and one I couldn't answer at the moment. I sat there without speaking.

Bounding through the door, Mr. Kim was all energy. "Committee today."

"Yes, Mr. Kim. Committee today. And you can run it," I let him know. Right now, Robert had given me something more important to think about.

That weekend, I was off to visiting to see my wife and four friends. The visiting area is about a mile's walk from my dorm. The walk gave me time to collect my thoughts and gather subjects to talk about with my visitors. Robert's questions about why we're here and how or whether he could make a difference had been weighing on me for a few days. After the ten-minute walk, on entering the visiting area an officer pats you down and you list any non-prison-issue items, like glasses before going into the main visiting area. There are about sixty tables of various sizes in visiting, about half inside and the other half outside under a shaded tarp. There are plenty of COs lurking around and video cameras throughout.

There's also a gaggle of inmate porters who clean up and generally act as help to visitors and inmates alike. Several of the porters became friends over the years. One in particular, took care of my wife and me each time. John became a part of our family. My dad even "adopted" him on one visit—although I'm not sure an eighty-five year old can adopt a fifty-year-old—then subscribed to a newspaper for him, and my wife began sending him various materials—all legal. He was a Christian and a saint—especially to the two of us. I asked him Robert's question this day, hoping he might give me some insight.

"Remember the movie, *Pay it Forward*, where the guy does a good deed for someone and all he asks is for the recipient to do the same thing for someone else down the road? That's kind of how I feel about what an inmate can do to make a difference. All any of us can do to make this world a better place is to pass on a little human kindness. Like the Good Book says, 'Do unto others as you would have them do to you.' You don't have to do big things. It's the little things." —

Simple. That advice started this visit. It kept getting better.

The visiting area has multiple vending machines holding varieties of food unavailable to inmates in the chow hall. For the first year or so, there was even an outside vendor that sold fresh foods from his restaurant, including fruit. The strawberries made my day. Their contract wasn't renewed, so that stopped. Still, even the packaged food did the trick. Who'd have thought vending machine offerings were better than prison food?

Normal visits lasted from forty-five minutes to several hours, depending on space availability. Thanks to our friend, John, we rarely had visits less than three or four hours—thank you, John. Somehow, he pulled my ticket. I lived for these small slices of normal—and for the small slices of real food.

The next day, I talked more to Robert about what John had to say. Over that next year or so, we both grew in our effort to define what making a difference meant.

Mr. Kim joined in the discussion, adding his unique Korean perspective. The power of positivism, along with hope and faith are strong medicines. The spiritual monasticism I embraced helped me explore how and where I needed to improve. Unfortunately, that need to improve is sadly lacking in prison.

Sometimes we need a crisis to precipitate change. Coming to prison was certainly a crisis for me, my wife and my family, even for my friends. However, it was not the end of the world. Adopting a positive attitude changed my view on everything. Working for so many years in the ER made me cynical—everyone appeared to be a drug-seeking patient there.

Strangely, prison renewed my faith in humankind and gave me reason for hope—for myself, my family and friends, and all of humankind. It took me a while to figure that out. This place, JRC, is not Siberia and, despite the food criticism, in the state's own benevolent way, we are fed, clothed, and cared for. As in life, there are negative aspects—drugs, gangs, violence—but all can be overcome. As bad as the health care is, I was able to work around it and help others do the same. I'm reminded again that everyone in here will be going home. My goal of survival gradually changed from just surviving to thriving. In order to survive I needed to thrive. To thrive, I needed challenges and the discipline to improve myself.

I read and completed continuing medical education articles to stay current—provided to me by a long-time physician friend. To what end? Self-improvement was an end in itself. I also hoped it would demonstrate my interest in medicine on release, when I would apply to get my medical license back.

I tutored other inmates, not just to help them, but also to help me. It allowed me to relearn basic math and language. Teaching Mr. Kim better linguistic skills retaught those same rules to me. Having to defend the English language is not easy. I stayed up on current events, having decided getting my civil rights back on release was also a priority. Thriving, not just surviving.

The next Monday, Robert slowly entered the office. He looked more pale than usual, his abdomen more distended, too..

"Not doing well today, Doc. Didn't sleep well either. But I wanted to talk to you."

"Yeah, you don't look good today." Robert and I had both come to an understanding about being truthful about his condition. We were both at peace with that decision. "What's the subject today?"

"If someone improves their life and tries to make things better for society, does society care? Like a tree falling in a forest, does anyone hear it?"

"Does it matter, Robert? Don't we do it for ourselves? Isn't it enough that one knows they left the world a better place?"

"But does society remember that we made it better?"

"I dunno," I confessed.

"Because if society doesn't care, why would they remember?"

"I think it's reward enough to know in your heart you've done the best you can do. If society notices, all the better. However, it is not a contest to get society's blessing. Knowing in your heart is enough. God knows."

The next day, Tuesday, September 11, 2012, at age 43, Robert Stevenson died at a local hospital. Sleep well, Robert. God knows. You are remembered.

And everyone eventually goes home.

Chapter 12: *Day by Day*

Time can be warped, according to Albert Einstein, by modifying the space-time continuum. Warped? As in twisted, turned, bent, distorted, misshaped and perverted, corrupted, debased, misguided, even infected? Humans mark the times of their lives by events, people and places—not necessarily all significant. Even the insignificant are important as markers. Think about time not only as a physicist does, but also as a prisoner must.

My explanation is more simplistic. Traditionally, time may be examined in many ways—looking forward or back, to the past, present or the future; by seasons; by years or months. In here, time is measured differently—by cheap wall-clock or cheaper plastic watch, by number of soups or other forms of indebtedness, from phone call to phone call, letter to letter, by kiss to kiss, and visit to visit. Time is also a measure of all we endure by counting the terror of a long night and the relief of a new day.

Without hope or with no faith, time does warp, becoming distorted and corrupted. It slows to such a glacial pace as to be almost beyond measure. An inmate without hope or faith finds himself counting the holes in the ceiling, the ants in his locker, the steps to the yard and back, or the threads hanging from his threadbare underwear. All-in-all, it is a wasted existence where time is of no consequence—it doesn't matter anymore.

Once I accepted the concept of a spiritual monasticism, time became irrelevant. Faith and hope were my measure, not the trivial theories of humankind. "Time is on my side," the *Rolling Stones* sang. And so it is. Time is mine, not the state's. What I do with it is my decision.

The state's agents—guards, counselors, and others—reminded everyone frequently to remember where we were. While most would be repelled by the intentional put-downs, once I realized I was alive, healthy, fortunate, and in charge of "me," time flew. Yes, I marked the days off the calendar like everyone else. However, I occasionally surprised myself when i realized I had skipped one ore more days when I next looked at my calendar. That empowerment of faith and hope is infinite.

Rather than living and marking time using an artificial gauge—such as an hourglass—I concentrated on the individual grains of sand. Not so much as they reached their end, but I cherished each day, hour, minute, and second as they occurred, saddened as they slipped away. Even in prison, life must be savored, embraced, and held close. That changed my day-to-day perspective in the dorm, at work, at night and every moment.

"Are you going to yard today," Kim asked on most afternoon yard days.

"I'm planning on it, if we get out of here on time."

The length of our office days depended on who was working and how hard they wanted to work. Many COs were conscientious, others adhered to Crapulveda's law: "It's prison, there's nothing but time. We always have tomorrow and the day after, and the day after that." He believed in putting off anything and everything he could get away with because, after all, "it's prison." I, on the other hand, operated by the rule of the emergency department—"always hurry to finish what you're doing before the door opens for the next train wreck." The two approaches were not only diametrically opposed philosophically and practically, they tended to create significant friction on occasion.

"I'm going, too," Kim beamed.

"Yeah? That's if we don't get work here at the end."

Several staff found it humorous to sit around all shift doing little or nothing only to hand us a load of work as they were leaving. The Crapulveda rule didn't apply to them, I guess. Interfering with our time on the yard was the one circumstance where leaving us work to do bothered me. Yard for me was infrequent, welcome, and a time of peace and tranquility in the midst of chaos.

On this day, Kim and I left on time and headed for the yard. The yard was about half a mile from Facility A. There was the quarter-mile track—the one that wasn't a quarter mile but ten yards longer—surrounded by fixed-in-place bars, two handball courts, several horseshoe pits, and two softball fields, one at each end. In the center of the track was a field of nightmares . . . a soccer/football playground, but with , no grass, just hard-packed dirt, rocks, and numerous potholes.

Yard was a multi-purpose arena for our one or two hours there. It was not used exclusively for athleticism, but dispute resolution and other score-settling as well. The latter was a diversion and inconvenient interruption to me, the former a necessity for my health, both physical and mental. Around this track I walked and ran on my own "program." I relished the alone time—time that passed too quickly. It was a time for reflection, thought, and summary.

When I first came to JRC, I could barely walk a single lap around the track without becoming short of breath. Now well into my stay, I ran laps against time. I found the sweaty, heart-pounding activity cleared my head and prepared me for the rest of the day, week, or however long it would be until my next yard session. I truly looked forward to the solitude of the yard. Only my knees complained. I found that if I ran more than two laps—half a mile at any one time, they ached. Ah, the joys of aging. However, I found that if I walked a lap between my running, my knees did just fine. Consequently, I ran two, walked one, and repeated the process.

During the one hour, I walked and ran for about thirty or forty minutes. My goal was to run a total of one or one-and-a-half miles interspersed with the additional walking laps. Rising above one of the softball fields was a small, concrete stadium. I frequently ran the stadium steps in sets of two after the flat track work.

As much as I needed and enjoyed the physical release of running and walking—something unheard of in my former life of being too busy for it—the spiritual time was what I savored. After a few months, others on the yard knew my routine and let me have my time to myself. There were occasional disruptions from other inmates asking me questions, but for the most part, this was my time.

As I meditated and contemplated, time stood still. Intermingled with present-tense thoughts were past-tense reflections. I faced my toughest jury—*me*. Whatever else prison is, if one avails himself of the opportunity, incarceration offers copious time for self-criticism and improvement. Admitting the problem truly is the first step in fixing it. In the "real world," we're usually too busy to consider our frailties . . . our egos tend to get in the way. Not so in prison. In this situation, the Crapulveda rule is applicable—time is all we have, and it affords the opportunity to find solutions.

Of course, that depends on whether we can get our egos out of the way. Time helps you do that. Prison strips away all your excuses and leaves you alone with your naked truths—about who and what you are, where you've been, and what you've done—if you allow it. If so inclined, it is an ideal situation for engaging in self-reflection and self-criticism—the important first steps to redemption.

Upon leaving the yard, there is a scramble to get back to the dorm as fast as possible because of the competition for the six showers. When it was my turn, I rinsed off the dirt and grime, the thoughts and cares, and the guilt and blame, hoping to leave a few of the hopes and dreams intact.

As I toweled off from the shower, I heard the distinctive voice of Punkin calling me to the office. As I returned to my bunk, I was met by another now-familiar character.

"Doesn't anyone play cards anymore?"

Stinky wanted a game, which really meant he wanted conversation or companionship or something, but not just any card game. Stinky was now the White's leader—our dorm rep—after Doper paroled. I was relieved Doper and all his drama was gone. During his tenure, there was a constant tension in the dorm, mostly related to his mood swings stemming from his sleep deprivation induced drug habits.

Time is also calculated according to when someone comes or goes. Doper had been a big part of my universe each day, as White rep. He determined whether my day would be easy, a hassle, or somewhere in between. Then one day he was gone . . . paroled in his case. This guy, who structured the main dorm rules I lived by was, in an instant, gone.

The new rep would have his own rules.

When a new regime comes into power—following an election or preceding a coup—it's usually foreseeable when and how they'll arrive. With inmates, they come and go like night and day. There were other reasons inmates leave and arrive. Parole is scheduled, but inmates typically keep that date close, lest other inmates find out and try to collect any outstanding debts before the parolee scoots out the door.

Just as quickly as inmates leave, others arrive. The buses never stop. It is rare for a bunk to stay empty more than a day or two—one inmate falls out of your life and another falls in. Some become "important" to you, but none are ever close.

I am amazed at how rapidly I forgot nicknames and real names when someone left. Some remained for years, others for days. There is a constant movement of inmates within and between facilities—that's simply "routine" comings and goings. Stir in a pinch of turmoil, and movement becomes less predictable—with lock-downs, prison-politics, fights, and disciplinary actions causing unexpected moves.

"Sorry, Stinky. Punkin told me I just got called back to work. Don't know for how long." I still played cards on occasion, but I found my alone time more valuable. My spiritual monasticism offered me more peace.

Time is measured in "LT units" as well.

An LT unit was a measure of time Einstein did not comprehend. My day-to-day routine was settled, punctuated by staff changes as common and frequent as leaves falling from an autumn oak. During my tenure in the Program Office, I passed through Lieutenants Botelo, Tilkerson, Zaponte, Baris, Croquet, Talexi, Malarkcum, Sejia, Stroopplewell, Sterrera, and a few floaters, before Croquet returned. Each "LT season" was marked by idiosyncrasies, inconsistencies, eccentricities, and quirks—standard human foibles— some more enjoyable and interesting than others.

And that was just Second Watch.

There were also "Sergeant units." I endured a nearly equal number of Sergeant changes. The Sergeants, however, run prisons—they determine day-to-day discipline, such as inspections or dorm tear-ups, approve disciplinary write-ups, and supervise most everything else. The LTs stay out of their hair most of the time, but make no mistake, the Lieutenants are still in charge. Though rare, I saw several instances of a Lieutenant overruling a Sergeant.

For the most part, however, it is a team concept. As clerks, we were definitely the lowest member of the team—but still a part of it. Most of the staff abided by the concept of team. There were, naturally, a few who didn't and ruined it for all.

"Doc, I need your help." Lieutenant Stronzales was the second-most senior Lieutenant at JRC and the Third Watch Lieutenant during my last few years. He was great guy, even though I'm not supposed to say that.

Saddled with Third Watch clerks, he all too frequently called on me for "help" with something, which usually meant he wanted me to "do" the something. I didn't mind much, since the work was actually easy, and I enjoyed the opportunity to talk with Stronzales. He was different from most JRC types. Of Hispanic heritage, overweight, myopic to the point of needing to remove his glasses in order to read his reports, he always had a smile for me. A diabetic, he also had several challenging medical issues about which I was happy to offer advice. Tonight, I was "helping" to complete a relatively simple "roll-up"—from start to finish—while the Third Watch clerks watched TV.

Time, for me, was also measured by the number of visits to work during what were supposed to be my off-hours. The inmate subject of the roll-up this night would soon measure his time by a new clock—in a new facility, in a new cell, with new fellow inmates. Time like this starts and stops suddenly.

After I finished the report, I took the *114-D* to Lt. Stronzales for his review, which gave me an opening for a moment of normalcy—an opportunity to discuss life. I treasured this kind of time—ordinary, natural, comfortable—real time, not prison time. That he allowed me the liberty is what made him different from the others. Timeless, infinite, perpetual, lasting periods that validated me as alive. These were the flashes when time stood still for me in a good way. This night we discussed several philosophical issues and exchanged opinions on current events—rational topics, certainly not prison ones.

Was our discussion significant? That depends on your outlook. Did we change the world? No, but that wasn't the intent. Normalcy was—which changed my world. When I think about what demarcates my life—the good and the bad—I realize it takes both to create bookmarks. It takes hills and valleys, highs and lows. If life were all peaks, it would be routine, mundane, boring. Isn't that what most of us try to guard against—the boring?

"What are you gonna do when you get out?"

I felt the LT was not asking as a correctional officer, but as colleague.

"You know, I haven't really thought much about it," I reflected.

I hadn't. In my effort to avoid counting time, I'd sort of forgotten that I, too, was leaving someday, and that day was drawing closer.

"You're well past the halfway point," Stronzales pointed out. "Once you get past halfway, things tend to go much quicker. You've got lots of options. It's time to start thinking about the future."

The good Lieutenant reminded me there was an end coming to this chapter of my life. He caused me to be more enlightened about my survival . . . not just how to survive, but to thrive. I did have a lot to consider about the future. What was I going to do? Where were we going to live? How were my wife and I going to reclaim our lives?

Upon returning to my dorm that night, I was met by several inmates. That usually meant some kind of crisis or the need for an explanation about some pressing issue.

"It's bad, Doc," Stinky confided, breathing heavily. "I couldn't get to Punkin in time."

"What's bad? Slow down and back up."

"Patrick," Stinky replied. "They beat him up pretty bad. Just hauled him outta here on a stretcher."

"Patrick? The new old guy? Who the hell would beat him up?" I really wasn't sure I wanted to know.

Violence, and deliverance from it, occupied a significant portion of my nightly prayers. As the preferred method of dispute resolution, I took issue with it on several levels.

Patrick was a fifty-something, gray-haired man who looked much older than his years. He acted older as well. He had only been in this prison, and in our dorm, for about a week, so no one really knew him. In my brief study of him, he seemed to be confused about the simplest of things, causing me to suspect he might even have Alzheimer's disease or some other form of dementia. He couldn't find the medical area, the chow hall, or even the bathroom. I found him wandering in the staircase one day—not a good place to hang out, since it is one of several favorite dispute resolution areas. He wasn't sure where he was going. Thin and underweight, Patrick met all the criteria for someone in need of assistance.

"I don't know exactly who beat him up, but I do know why," Stinky continued, clearly upset. "That's why I was going to Punkin when it happened."

"Huh?"

Stinky let out a long sigh. "I asked him for his paperwork a few days ago. Course he couldn't find it—something's wrong with that guy, Doc. Have you noticed that?"

"Yeah, I think he's got dementia or something. He needs a medical evaluation."

"Well, he'll get one now. He was out cold," our new rep advised.

"Unconscious? Are you kidding me? Somebody beat that old man unconscious? You know I hate violence, but that makes me wanna beat the crap out of someone."

"Yeah, well, he finally found his paperwork, that's the problem. He gave it to me and waved it in front of a few other guys, too."

"So what? Why's that enough to beat him up?"

"He's a *Chester*, Doc," Stinky sighed again. "Well not exactly a *Chester*, but, well, anyway . . ."

"Dammit, Stinky. What the hell are you talking about?"

"His papers say he had a case—a long time ago but it's still on his record—a case of molestation. He slapped some girl's ass and picked up a case for it. Wasn't convicted of anything, but it's on his record. That's why he got beat up. Someone must've overheard him or he showed them his paperwork, I don't know. That's why I was going to Punkin the second I found out."

"What's Punkin gonna do to help?"

"He coulda moved him," pausing. "Nothing now. He's off to the hospital," Stinky sat down on my bunk, clearly needing to get this off his chest. "I tried to get to Punkin. I just missed by a few seconds. He'd've gotten him transferred out."

"Where to?"

"To the SNY yard. I can't believe JDC sent him here in the first place. They're supposed to send him there from Reception. That's what they're supposed to do with them molesters."

"But you said he wasn't convicted and that it was only a slap on some girl's behind."

"Yeah, but nobody looks at the details, only the Penal Code charge. It's the charge that gets him labeled as a molester even though it was twenty years ago," my rep spoke quietly.

Stinky didn't need to tell me more, I could guess. "So this old guy got beat up because twenty years ago he slapped some chick on the butt and the cops charged him with being a molester? Can't you get that kinda thing off your record? Once he got in the prison system, can't he *602* it or something?"

"Never should've happened in the first place, but Doc. You've been here long enough to know once it's on your record, it's there forever. Just like that damned debt to society."

The frustration in my companion was obvious. Lots of things shouldn't happen, but they do. It's the nature of humanity to be egocentric—to care only about oneself. Many are also vindictive or hateful. In a way, it is a form of superiority.

Judging others . . . I'll plead guilty to that charge in my past. That is one of the lessons I hope I've learned—to not be so judgmental, to be more humble, patient, and tolerant of many things. Society could use a dose of that kind of medicine, though it is unlikely to swallow the pill.

For a convicted felon, however, one's "debt to society" is never repaid in full. That's a lesson I've also learned.

"What happens now?"

"You're the doctor, you tell me," Stinky almost moaned. "It's my fault. I should've gotten to Punkin sooner. You know, bugged him more to get me his paperwork."

I put my arm around Stinky's shoulders.

"The guy has Alzheimer's. How can you speed up someone that doesn't know? You got to Punkin as soon as you knew," I consoled. "I can't tell you what happens next. It depends on how bad he's hurt. At least maybe they'll look into his dementia now. Helluva way to get a diagnosis. Helluva way to out of this place early, too."

"Oh he won't get out early," Stinky corrected. "They'll patch him up and ship him back here."

"Here?"

"Well not here. To SNY."

"Geez," I muttered. "What's it take to get outta this place."

"More than a stretcher. Takes a damn morgue wagon. Like Robert."

Stinky reminded me of Robert and all his fears about this place.

"Yeah, like Robert," pausing briefly to honor him.

An interesting notion, getting out early. Every inmate thinks about it, some even become obsessed with it. As it turns out, there *is* a way to get out early—you save a staff member. Should one collapse and require emergency life-saving measures and an inmate is in a position to provide them, in most circumstances the inmate will be sent home. Save another inmate and all you get is a pat on the back, or maybe a few months off your sentence—*if* you submit reams of paperwork and are approved. Gives you a sense of what life is worth to the prison system. Robert knew about that.

Chester the molester.

There has to be a better way of dealing with inmates was all I could think about for the next few days. Inmates are still people, even molesters who aren't really anyone's favorites. Patrick marks his time now on the D Yard, recovered from the acute head trauma. I'm not sure about his underlying and pre-existent neurological condition. Would he survive? Would he thrive?

As time marched on, it became less of an issue for me. I was at peace for the most part.

Not so my wife. God love her, she was determined to find a way to get me released early. The Supremes might come through, but with the governor resisting, who knew when or if that would even happen. She wanted another avenue and she thought she'd found it. About a year or so before my scheduled release, she crafted a letter to the state's Bureau of Parole Hearings, or BPH.

So began a circular process whose results resembled a circular firing squad.

Her concise, two-page letter was sent to the BPH, along with 183 letters of support from friends and family, including two sitting federal judges, one U.S. attorney, one former governor of Oklahoma and various lawyers, doctors and other upstanding citizen-friends—many of them the same letters never read by the judge who presided over my trial. This cumbersome package arrived at the BPH offices in the state capital about fifteen months prior to my scheduled release date.

And there it sat for two months, until my wife called on the telephone. She was told that the packet had arrived, but needed to be sent to the local institution's warden. They said it had been forwarded.

Another call—this time to the JRC Warden's office—revealed no such package was in their possession. Therefore, another cover letter and copies of the supporting documents were sent directly to the JRC Warden—where it, too, sat for another two months. When my wife called again, an underling admitted they had received her package, but they didn't know what to do with it, so it was just sitting there. When asked what would happen next, she was essentially told nothing would happen because they didn't know what to do with it.

"They" again. A case of time standing still?

"Mr. Bendington, do you have a minute," I was determined he did.

Davis Bendington was the Facility A CC-II, the equivalent of a Lieutenant, and in charge of the five CC-Is. Tall, lean, and always immaculately dressed—a rarity in JDCR—this late-thirty-something guy was clearly an up-and-comer in the prison system.

He was also an extremely likable man—articulate, intelligent and one of the group who treated me well. As Captain's clerk, I worked closely with Mr. Bendington and I considered him one of the small cluster of JDCR employees with integrity, one who tried to do the right thing, although not always the most expeditious.

"Yeah. Can you give me about five minutes," Bendington asked.

"I won't even ask why." I responded to his chuckle.

I knew what he was doing that morning—renewals of previous *114-Ds*, a chore that had time constraints and was generally a pain for the Facility CC-II. I gave him fifteen minutes to be on the safe side.

When he called me in, I sat down in his less-than-plush, standard-issue small office and told him what my wife had submitted and the utter lack of response or interest.

He shook his head and said, "I'm not surprised. They probably don't get a lot of these. What do you want me to do?"

"Just tell me what to do, or even who to send a complaint to. We just want to pursue this in the right way."

"Let me call the capital, I've got a friend," Bendington sounded hopeful.

Several weeks passed without word, although he stopped me at least twice to say he hadn't forgotten about me. Just that moment of kindness was appreciated and more than most staffers did in JDCR. After a few more weeks passed, he called me into his office again.

"I'm really embarrassed," he frowned.

"I don't understand."

"I called my friend, who referred me to several other people, and basically all I got was the run around for the last few weeks . . ."

"A month."

"That long? Geez, sorry. Anyway, I can't find anyone who has ever dealt with a petition like this," Bendington confessed.

"So what do I do?"

"I wish I could tell you. But I don't know."

Here was the go-to guy telling me he doesn't have answers—and I know he tried to get them.

"This is ridiculous. I can't even find anyone to complain about it."

"That's why I'm embarrassed. Even I couldn't get help. I guess you could write the governor."

I didn't want to add to his embarrassment by telling him we'd done that first and were told to send it to JDCR.

"Well, I appreciate your trying to help. I'm not giving up."

"Maybe 'old Izzy' will stop fighting the court," Bendington suggested, more out of desperation than really believing it possible.

"Yeah . . . right."

That night during my phone call to my wife, I related the story and could hear her tears.

I wrote a *602*, but still didn't know exactly where to send it. The day I was released, we were still waiting for a reply—anything—from a bureaucracy with no checks and balances. "They" are an entity without supervision.

> *Time is a measure of all we endure—time is also the cure.*
> —*Having To Learn How To Dance Again*
> Thompson

Chapter 13: *The Enemy Within*

> *A pessimist sees the difficulty in every opportunity;*
> *an optimist sees the opportunity in every difficulty*
>
> — WINSTON CHURCHILL

Prior to incarceration, I considered myself an optimist. The first few months of prison sorely tested that—even converted me to pessimism temporarily. Dying will do that. Depression will do that. Did I think of suicide? Absolutely. Had they not arrested me immediately in the courtroom, I'm not sure I wouldn't have taken that easy way out. Now, in prison, there simply was no easy way to accomplish it.

I'm proud to say I never attempted it.

Those early days were the most difficult, primarily because I saw no way out, no future—be it tomorrow or a year down the road. That inability to see the future is my definition of depression. I felt as if the world had conspired against me—and against my wife—and the world won.

In many ways, she had it worse than me. We just couldn't catch a break. Not only were things bad, beginning with the judicial system, but each new decision point heaped more on our shoulders, truly adding insult to injury. The fact that *I* couldn't see my future didn't matter—the state had that covered. My poor wife had no such safety net. She was just as scared of the future, but was suddenly living without the safety net of our marriage. She had to build a new security blanket on her own.

After my conviction, my wife and I lost pretty much every earthly thing we owned. I say *we*, but my wife was the one who was really affected the most. Not only did she experience the loss of everything personally and up close, she had to live with the uncertainty it brought. I had the "luxury" of being away from the direct insult, she was left alone to deal with the consequences in the aftermath of those losses.

Our home of twenty-plus years, my retirement savings, and our personal possessions were soon gone—our home repossessed, legal fees, and other bills consumed virtually all the rest. Without my income, even before the trial began, we were suddenly confronted with mounting bills and had no way to pay them. Add to that the fact that my wife and I had been living fifteen hundred miles away because of the bad publicity about my case.

We had moved away to escape the bad taste the city left in our mouths after the incident, not to mention the death threats and harassing phone calls, the e-mail and social media attacks, and the highly biased newspaper and television reports. We had to come back for the trial, but never considered the possibility of conviction; we didn't even make any contingency plans relative to the possibility. When I was whisked away following the reading of the verdict; my wife was left alone with only my wallet and wedding ring.

After my conviction, she returned to the arms of my family and our friends. After a month, she packed up what we had left—following a garage sale to raise funds to pay bills—and moved back to the West Coast, initially living with one of her brothers. How she survived is a story unto itself.

But survive, she did. She eventually found work as a legal secretary, an occupation in which she had over thirty years' experience. First working down south near her two brothers, she later moved back to the "big city" to work for a large international law firm. She was starting all over at the bottom of the work ladder, needing to find a place to live, cataloging and moving what little was left of our stuff, trying to figure out what truly was important and what was not. Tough at fifty—tough at any age.

Dealing with her fears from afar was one of the hardest things I've ever had to do. I felt so helpless. I guess I'm old-school. A man's responsibility is to take care of his wife, and I was failing miserably in that responsibility. Moreover, I was trying to cope with her problems while in the throes of my own depression. In addition to being separated by distance and isolated from communicating, my wife and I couldn't even share the pain together. In much the same manner as when someone dies or becomes critically ill, there is a grieving process you must go through. Elizabeth Kubler-Ross defined the emotions as *denial, anger, bargaining, depression, and acceptance.* You run the risk of getting hung up in one of those stages especially when you have no support mechanism.

We both denied what had happened and became angry because we were viewing it selfishly, in the context of *"Why us?"* What had *we* done to deserve this?

We cried, prayed, and wept to the heavens, trying to bargain our way out of this with every "what if" and "couldn't we just" imaginable. Depressed? Naw, neither of us were depressed—*how I lie!* We were both incapacitated by it. Numbed, immobilized, frozen by it. Unlike the other characteristics of emotion, depression to me is more a complete state of mind, not just a characteristic. It encompasses all emotions in time. Eventually, we both came to accept what had happened and came to grips with the consequences, developing our survival instincts, each in our own time.

As in any crisis, the objective is to experience each of the five stages and pass through them successfully—but without getting hung up in any one stage. Pathological reactions to crises occur when someone doesn't get past one of the phases. Unfortunately, it is an all too common occurrence. Think of the person who is still angry at the world five years after the death of a close relative, or someone who can't get out of bed three years after the death of a spouse, destroyed by depression.

"Don't get hung up on the unfairness of this place," John counseled. He became another mentor, confidante, psychologist, pastor, and tour guide of the penal sights. "There is no justice. Not the way you thought. Don't question too much."

Good advice in the beginning, but not questioning just wasn't my style. Medicine teaches you to question everything and not to accept the obvious, constantly looking for another explanation. The scientific method says to verify a hypothesis, and if it can't be validated over and over, you must question the hypothesis itself.

"But John," I begged, "I can't do this. I can't see past tomorrow."

John smiled and put his hand on my shoulder, "Tomorrow is all you need to see. Live for the day, plan your tomorrow, but *live* for today."

"I can't . . ."

"Yes," he interrupted, "you can." His eyes at once brightening. "You'll see that once you get in the habit of living for today, all of a sudden it's tomorrow. And tomorrow is a month later, and soon tomorrow is a year down the road."

"Believe me," he chuckled, "even in here, life can pass by too quickly."

Close enough in age to me, John had the wisdom of experience, both of life in the real world *and* in prison, having been here for more than ten years. He had been a stuntman in the movie industry for several decades, before being convicted of manslaughter in the accidental death of a fellow stuntman. I knew he had gone through the same questions about unfairness and excess I was experiencing.

Once I thought about it, John and I were on the same track. His train had left the station a few years ahead of me. I smiled at his "life passes too quickly" statement. But would I feel the same way in a few years?

Your spouse, your family, and your friends serve time with you. They may not experience the bars and fences, but they endure the pain and isolation. Because they feel so helpless, their guilt is worsened by their life of normalcy. While the prisoner suffers, his family and friends ache, fret, and compensate in peculiar ways. Some become angry—they can go through the five emotions, too—others become activists.

Many of my friends and family became activists in some way. I feel like it was a positive for them and for me. It gave them a way to demonstrate their support. It gives your partisans an outlet for their emotions—a way to do something. For that, I am most appreciative—also for their letters, their phone calls to me or my wife and family, and for their advocacy with the court and state government.

My wife became a model inmate's wife—diving right into organizing visits with my friends and family. Every two weeks she and others trekked to JRC. It was more than a one-hour trip from the city for her, and about half of my sixty-five or so visitors were from out of state. She kept a separate calendar dedicated to my visiting schedule, sent out frequent e-mail updates, and coordinated airport flights and pick-ups. She became an advocate for prison wives and inmates, organizing donations to the family visiting area.

I'm embarrassed by the richness of comfort, hope, and strength bestowed on me. It held me up—the Bible calls it "being uplifted." My family and friends are my champions, defenders, and allies. Every two weeks, when my visiting day came around, for most visits the maximum number of five visitors queued up at the dreary state prison entrance and at least a forty-five minute wait in line to be admitted . . . and not without being searched, hassled in general, and read the rules over-and-over . . . until allowed to meet with me at a small table with uncomfortable chairs—exactly the right size for children in kindergarten or first grade—for a visit that might last as little as forty-five minutes. My wife ensured that I never missed a visiting day throughout my fifty-one months.

"You are so blessed," John hugged both my wife and me one day in visiting. "Do you know how many guys here have never had a single visit? Or even a phone call?" as he quickly terminated his embrace.

"Most inmates don't get any visits and the few who do often have just one or two visitors," John said, smiling broadly as he separated from us and looked to see if any of the COs were paying attention to us. "Don't want them yelling at me for hugging you too long." Inmates aren't supposed to touch much in visiting because of the possibility of exchanging contraband.

"Thank you, John," my wife squeezed him for longer than she should—in an act of love as well as defiance. "We'll get through this. Get through it because of you."

Both my wife and I introduced our four visitors to John. Each of my every-two-week visits, John was there to meet and greet. He remembered each of my more than sixty-five friends and family who made the trip—at least by sight, if not by name. If nothing else, John became an honorary member of my family. Strange how it takes a crisis to make you appreciate what you have and its importance.

"Find something useful to do," was John's advice. "It'll keep you busy and keep your mind off things you can't change anyway. One other thing," he confided. "Learn the *Serenity Prayer*. Learn it and live it."

"But I thought it was for alcoholics. I'm not . . ."

"It's for everyone," John whispered. "Learn it," as he went back to his visiting duties.

I confronted my depression with activity. It took me several months to get out of my funk. Fear paralyzes; so does depression. I have never done well sitting still and for the first three months, while I was held in Reception, I was forced to sit, or lie down, or just do nothing. That leaves you nothing to do but think.

There is nothing about my case I haven't thought about. Let me say it clearly: ***I accept responsibility for my actions that led to my accident and conviction.*** Arguing the details and legal fine points—I'll leave that to others for the most part. I have spent endless hours digesting the reasons, rationales, and excuses for my behavior, and can only ask forgiveness from my family, my friends, my God, and from myself. I am comfortable in my own skin again, though it took a while.

"DOC!" Sergeant Whining shouted one morning. "I'm bored. Think I'll go tear up a dorm." Staring right at me, she continued, "Got any ideas which one I'm heading to?" I assumed she meant mine. *Why was she becoming friendly to me now?*

"Before I go, here," tossing me five or six *115s* to type. "Have 'em done by the time I come back," turning to leave. "Don't worry. I'll leave your space alone."

Tearing up a dorm is supposed to be about finding contraband—weapons, drugs, that kind of stuff. In my experience, it's more about staff payback or general hassling of inmates. Depending on the officer, it can also be about plain old meanness—not *schadenfreude* but sadism—intended to get an inmate pissed off enough to do something stupid in response.

Many an inmate gets suckered into that, not realizing they're being set up. Payback might be the result of an inmate "disrespecting" an officer, whatever that means, sometimes righteous, but more often not. The COs tend to go where there's smoke in order to stoke the embers into a fire. If a troublemaker has a history of drug abuse or fighting, chances are there's paraphernalia or a weapon to go along with that behavior. On other occasions, it's based only on a hunch or an unsolicited "kite"—a clandestine note sent by an inmate to staff implicating another inmate. The motives of an inmate tattling on another are always suspect.

Regardless, I was amazed by the amount of contraband a single tearing up actually uncovered.

A tear-up comes unannounced, always by more than one officer entering the dorm and walking immediately to the targeted bunk area. The inmate is called out of the bunk area, a clothed body search is performed by one officer while others "cover" him (and it usually is a "him" rather than a "her" despite the fact that there are no prohibitions against female COs searching male prisoners), then the inmate is handcuffed and escorted out of the area. Sometimes the prisoner is just asked to step away from the area rather than cuffed, but there is a certain flair for the dramatic.

Depending on whether they are looking for something specific, the officers proceed to search the selected bunk area. If it is for general purposes or vindictiveness, most possessions end up on the floor, scattered about in as disruptive a fashion as possible. The bedding is turned over, or bedding is removed and thrown to the floor, mattresses sometimes cut open in search of contraband. One's locker contents might also be strewn around the bunk area indiscriminately. This can go on for several bunks and inmates, lasting from a few minutes to more than an hour. Meanwhile, the other dorm occupants stand or lie around, tense, angry, and upset—the John Bradford idiom, *there but for the grace of God go I*, comes to mind.

One of the perks of working in the Program Office and getting to know the staff—or, more accurately, them getting familiar with me—was that they tended to leave the clerks alone. That spilled over to my dorm in general, something that didn't go unnoticed by my dorm mates. A few commented to me that our dorm didn't seem to get "hit" as often as the others. That is not the same as any of them saying, "Thank you."

No, prison isn't much about thank you at all.

"That crazy bitch," Stinky met me at the dorm entrance. "She tore the hell out of 103." He was referring to Dorm 103.

"Did they hit us?"

"No," he frowned. "But we're probably next. At least they didn't bring the dogs in on those poor guys in 103," Stinky sympathized.

"*Jes, pero nest* time they *weel*," Face concluded, based on no evidence.

Everyone got nervous when the dogs came into the dorm. This time, Sergeant Whining and the COs were tearing the place up because of some "confidential" information.

When the dogs came, however, that meant ISU and a serious problem.

ISU, the Investigative Services Unit, brought in dogs when they were suspicious of drugs or other contraband—and sometimes it was just for practice for the dogs. Inmates were stripped down to their undies and marched out into the hall, irrespective of temperature. I especially hated that in winter.

Before that march, you passed by a dog, or they passed by you. Either way, having a police dog stick his nose where the sun don't shine, or near the family jewels was not my idea of a day at the beach. As I looked around my Dorm 104, there were more sleeping inmates than active ones. We'd escaped the wrath of Sergeant Whining today—and did most other days, too. No thanks needed, boys.

Boredom is the greatest challenge in prison—for staff and inmates. The staff dealt with it in different ways—some sleep, some talk on the phone, others tear up the dorms, or delight in hassling inmates in various ways. Others walk a lot, not so much to catch inmates in some nefarious activity but, simply, to pass the time. That walking creates more hostility, more animosity between the greens and blues. Inmates tense up and stop what they're doing, even when what they're doing is legit. The green-blue line causes stress, nervousness, and apprehension. One of my goals was to decrease that for my own peace of mind and that of my dorm's.

How an inmate deals with the boredom determines their success or failure in the system. Most don't care what the system thinks about them. The system either doesn't care that they don't care, or doesn't recognize that the inmate doesn't care. Either way, it's a lost opportunity to modify behavior. What little modifying they do is done by using the stick, not the carrot—disciplinary actions, intimidation, sanctioned assaults. That indifference and supposed superiority is manifested in a variety of ways. But I cared. I was determined not to be a typical inmate. An idle mind is as bad as an idle body.

We all confront our demons differently. The last two years were a period of success for me. Internally, and early on, my dark thoughts frequently would become pervasive during the long, sometimes sleepless nights, and often in the daytime when I wasn't choosing the reprieve of distractions. You can't avoid thinking about why you are in here, rehashing every decision point that led to your incarceration. Some are consumed by the thoughts, others learn from those reflections, still others avoid them like the plague. Externally, you can bury yourself in exercise, study, or escapism, like playing games. Of course, these are mostly positive or at least neutral endeavors. You can also choose the negative anger, continued criminal activity, gang behavior, or substance abuse. You can choose to be negative or positive. I chose positive, but with a touch of deviousness. John may not want me to joust at windmills, but that didn't mean I couldn't have a little fun, a passive-aggressive way of saying "no" to the system.

While my spiritual monasticism put my mind at peace, I was still full of energy. My work time became like a game to me. After I realized a couple of basic facts, life became much easier. First, the obvious—JDCR is a big bureaucracy and JRC merely a cog in that large, cumbersome wheel. Each of the staff play a role, but a role the other players don't have much knowledge of or interest in—typical of any bureaucratic organization, and much like the proverbial *left hand that doesn't know what the right hand is doing*. The best way to overcome this bureaucracy, I decided, was to confuse it.

Think about history or the movies. The great movies work, where the good guys confuse or trick the bad guys, because they take advantage and exploit the vulnerabilities of their antagonists. From the Trojan horse, to every World War II movie, the guys in white hats capitalize on the inefficiencies and incompetence, rigidity and inflexibilities, on the laziness and boredom of large institutions—think army, Nazis, government and more.

"Sergeant, did you get those work orders I put on your desk?" I knew she didn't because the Lieutenant had given them to an S&E officer to take to the Captain for his signature.

"What?" She seemed startled, shuffling through papers on her desk. "There are work orders? Any I need to know about?"

"I don't remember seeing details, Sergeant," I replied, I did know, but why tell her, then pausing. "I didn't look at them closely. I think they were mostly plumbing issues in the dorms."

"Well, next time remember them. I need to know about them."

How I tried to hide my smile. "Yes, of course. My fault."

"Not fault, just carelessness. Where are they now, ya think?"

Carelessness? Really? "They have them."

"They do?"

"Yes, Sergeant. They do."

"Well . . ." she thought for a moment, now feeling better about it all. "Good. I'd have taken them to 'em anyway," walking back and sitting down, focusing on her computer. "Let me know if they come back with any problems."

"Do you want to call them?"

"No, I'll wait for them to call me if there are problems."

The legions of pen pushers and rubber stampers hide behind the anonymity of pronouns, *they, them, us,* or *we*. Each is, or becomes, a fiefdom unto itself—apparatchiks all, dwellers in apathy, insensitivity, insouciance, and callousness. Wanton nonchalance and indifference. To know their weaknesses is to be able to use those weaknesses against them, to use the bureaucracy rather than to be beaten by it. The correctional officers, free-staff, and non-custody employees from top to bottom fit the bill perfectly.

I could exploit their air of superiority to my advantage. When I knew something or found out something the staff didn't know about, it drove them crazy. Making myself the center of the facility accomplished that purpose. I ensured that everything came through the Program Office so I knew about it. Things like inmate assignments to the kitchen or dorm porter lists. Who was on the suspension list or who had been rolled up last night. While these were responsibilities of the supervising CO, using their indifference and laziness to take over those tasks gave me control. Control is power. Taking over more and more functions didn't take long—staff idleness worked in my favor. Sure they could take it back, but after a month or so, they forgot how to do the chore, or the CO changed, leaving my office-mates and me in command. Control is a powerful tool even for an inmate.

Survival in a hostile environment, but to what end? Since I wanted not to only survive, but now to thrive, that meant finding my way around this monstrosity. I would work to confuse it. As a child of the 1960s Vietnam War protest era, I was not unfamiliar with a bit of civil disobedience—nothing radical, but serious defiance. So while I was at it, I figured I might as well add a few creature comforts to my penal existence. And maybe have a little fun, too.

What creature comforts? Well, a hard metal bunk combined with a thin, under-stuffed mattress made restful sleep difficult. A double mattress eased the problem and the assault on my back. Doing favors for the laundry inmates allowed me the luxury of extra clothes—and new ones, too. That might not seem important, but extras like that meant not having to wear out the skimpy few pieces we were normally allotted. By taking care of the chow hall CO's scheduling needs, I made his life easier—and in return, we in the Program Office were afforded the privilege of ice at noon each day. Since there was no air conditioning, ice was a welcome extravagance in the hot, desert summers. When the quantities exceeded my needs, I apportioned out the leftover ice to those in my dorm—a perk that generated a significant amount of goodwill. There were many other comforts which came my way—too many to list now.

Defining who the pronouns are is a high priority—the *theys* and *thems* of this "enemy" amalgamation. I say enemy, because if one imagines it that way, it makes playing the game much easier. I've already admitted there were several custody staff I *didn't* consider the enemy. The enemy is really the system itself, more so than the any of its individual players.

Among many other gems of war-making strategy, the pre-Christian era Chinese military genius Sun Tzu wrote in *The Art of War*: *"The supreme art of war is to subdue the enemy without fighting,"* and also, *"In the midst of chaos, there is also opportunity."* That means figuring out how to outsmart, outmaneuver, and outfox them—waging a form of prison guerrilla warfare—exploiting the right opportunities meant they wouldn't even know we were at war.

Given the pervasive indifference within the institution, I didn't think that would be a problem. The various, unwieldy systems of the state bureaucracy are drowning in the complexity of their own rules and regulations, especially this prison system in particular. I suspect these rules are intended to combat the indifference—guidance for those who can't, or won't, think on their own. So I learned the rules—*"To know your Enemy, you must become your Enemy"*—better than most of the staff, and figured how and when to use them to my advantage—*"The greatest victory is that which requires no battle."*

Make no mistake. I did not do anything illegal—unlike others—I simply *used* the system to my own advantage, in much the same way that some of the senior custody staff had learned to do. Shakespeare wrote of *"vast sins concealing chaos."* If that wasn't a near perfect description of this place, I don't know what is. Perhaps is was *vast chaos concealing sins*. Either way, identifying the sins and the chaos became my obsession, not so much for the gain but for the game.

There is a definite hierarchy for *them, those* and *they*—some might argue, and not without good reason, it's like a big cesspool. The *them* at the top of our heap is the Warden, accompanied by *those* Assistant Wardens, all of whom report to the *theys* in the Jefferson Department of Corrections and Rehabilitation at the state capital. These *theys* are the top *thems. They* are the truly anonymous ones, and *they* pump out dicta and regulations from on high. Those dicta eventually trickle down to the lesser *theys* who manage distant bureaucracies, like prisons.

These subservient *theys* pass these pronouncements on down to their own subordinate *thems*—the Captains, Lieutenants, and Sergeants—who inform the staff COs, whose responsibility it becomes to inform the inmates—all of it, taken as a whole, is the epitome of the expression, *"Shit rolls downhill."* I don't think Sun Tzu wrote that, but my guess is that he understood it.

As with any cesspool or sewer system, what goes down may cause a back-up . . . or at least some degree of serious constipation. Assuming the information is even passed on correctly—if it is passed on at all—there may be push back at any level. That results in the lower *thems* telling the higher *thems* about it in a reverse flow of nonsensical paperwork. Of course, *they* may not like that, which, in turn, causes the higher *thems* to re-issue the original order, or demand the lower *thems* comply.

With all this back-and-forth flow, it's a wonder anything ever gets done.

Oh, wait! There much that doesn't get done. There's a similar hierarchy for the free staff, with the real work being done by the inmates. At least the free staff are somewhat more appreciative of the cheap (damn-near free) labor. But not much.

Each step along the path is an *opportunity* for a Program Office clerk to get involved, especially if it is a "public" transaction. There are, of course, confidential matters we aren't supposed to be involved in—except when we are—which afford *opportunities* for intervention. *They* were just as careless when it came to handling confidential memoranda and other documents as they were with the nonclassified ones.

You've heard it before: *indifference breeds contempt.* The difference, of course, is that confidential information could get someone implicated in a heap of hurt. While I never did that, or even remotely considered doing it, I have no doubt that this kind of carelessness around others surely did. I'm reminded of the news media bending over backwards to protect their sources on a sensitive story. Not so in here. The weak become confidential informants, who are frequently pressured into giving up information, only to have their safety jeopardized by staff carelessness that exposes an informant.

I learned to be resourceful at an early age; a skill that only improves with age. I realized that being part of the "chain of command" allowed me to intercept potentially useful information and occasionally "modify" it to meet my needs or the needs of others. It's the kind of stuff that TV sitcoms are made of, now that I think about it.

Nevertheless, I never crossed the line that meant giving up an individual, just information. As I said, learning who the *thems* and *theys* are is essential to good sleuthing and interception, and learning where *their* weaknesses and vulnerabilities lie—the fourth of Sun Tzu's five essentials for victory: *"He will win who, prepared himself, waits to take the enemy unprepared."*

If there is a problem with giving up your anonymity, it is one of forcing you to take ownership of your work—your memos, your reports, or whatever. Bureaucracies and bureaucrats abhor ownership. With ownership comes responsibility . . . and a track record. Bureaucrats detest a track record *they* must later defend. So forcing that anonymity into the light became my objective—exposing the *thems* and *theys* out of the shadows and into the brilliance of responsibility for their poor grammar, arbitrary decisions, lack of consistency, and circular logic, if there were any logic at all.

Most Program Office clerks simply typed the reports exactly as they had been written, with that bad grammar, syntax, and sentence structure. For the COs I liked, I fixed their errors. For those I didn't, I left their obvious mistakes uncorrected for the Sergeants and Lieutenants to find. The only flaw in that plan was that, with considerable frequency, the mistakes weren't identified by the higher-ups either.

Being privy to what happens throughout the facility sheds light on the blatant ignorance about the rules and regulations and highlights the inconsistencies of their enforcement. That knowledge can be successfully exploited—the secret being when and to whom to let it be known—a most powerful tool. Keeping my thoughts to myself concerning the irrational and illogical conclusions arrived at during disciplinary hearings became increasingly difficult. Arbitrary and capricious, these proceedings were a kangaroo court rather than a judicial hearing. Unfortunately, for the accused, they had little recourse and the conviction rate was easily in excess of 95%.

"He who is prudent and lies in wait for an enemy who is not, will be victorious."

Bureaucracies protect mediocrity, and suppress the extraordinary. They provide a sanctuary for the unexceptional. Have you ever heard of a bureaucrat advancing his career by saying, "Yes"? Yes requires taking risks, sticking your neck out—not a career advancement strategy.

On the other hand, "No" is the path of least resistance to promotion. Saying, "No" buries the question along with the answer. (Note: this is not the same concept as being a superior's "yes man," which is an alternate route to career advancement.)

The average inmate was unaware of most of what I was up to, and even if they knew, were clueless as to my game. Subtlety allowed me the fun of knowing *they* had been caught without *them* even knowing it.

"All warfare is based on deception. Hence, when we are able to attack, we must seem unable; when using our forces, we must appear inactive; when we are near, we must make the enemy believe we are far away; when far away, we must make him believe we are near."

Watching various COs, Sergeants, and Lieutenants as they were duped by their own rules gave me a perverse satisfaction—not illegal, or immoral—I simply found it amusing, something to help me evade the boredom. The techniques involve thinking three steps ahead, triangulation—gathering info from one in order to leverage another—and knowing I'd be catching *them* in their fraud and abuse, whether *they* recognized it or not. As entertaining as this was to me, *they* really didn't care enough to notice or bother to contemplate the consequences.

Why not? Because *they* knew there were no consequences. *They* are also a system without supervision from the outside world, because the outside world likes it that way. The less the public knows about the prison system, the less the public has to confront the truth or pay for the solutions.

Remember, bureaucracies flourish in anonymity. Terrorism, Ted Koppel once wrote, "is the means by which the weak induce the powerful to inflict damage upon themselves." I guess this was my form of penal activism and a gentle form of terroristic protest.

"Appear weak when you are strong, and strong when you are weak."

"Doc, don't tell anybody, but there's gonna be a fire drill tomorrow," Sergeant Whining confided.

"OK," I was confused. Why is she telling me this? The next morning, all dorms in Facility A were rousted up and out of the building without warning to the mini-yard adjoining the structure—a small dirt patch on a hill, with no shade or real exercise equipment. I was surprised *they* cared enough to even conduct fire drills. Of course, in the event of a real fire, the inmates would confront that crisis from behind locked dorm gates, hopefully, a dorm officer would unlock the gate and evacuate in a timely manner.

I was relieved to know they actually planned for and practiced a fire drill. Or so I thought. As I started to leave the building from the Program Office, Sergeant Whining stopped me and gestured to me to sit down.

"You don't have to go. A few officers will cover the mini-yard. All the dorm officers are coming up after getting everyone to the yard. You stay and work."

"But it's over ninety degrees . . ."

"It's not really a fire drill," my supervisor smiled.

"Shouldn't I . . ."

"The inmates will be fine for an hour. All the COs are coming to the Lieutenant's office. I need the inmates out of the facility for a while."

"Do you need me to . . ."

"No," Sgt. Whining turned to leave. "Just do your typing and don't come out of the office. We're having a little going-away party for a retiring officer."

So much for planning and practice. The enemy within.

> *God, grant me the serenity*
> *to accept the things I cannot change,*
> *the courage to change the things I can,*
> *and the wisdom to know the difference.*
> — SERENITY PRAYER
> REINHOLD NIEBUHR

Chapter 14: It's the Little Things...

I remember what John once told me in visiting when discussing Robert Stephenson's dilemma, that it's *"the little things"* which are important. It's the *good* little things and the *bad* little things that punctuate each day. They aren't the verbs and nouns—the body of life—but the little things that add context and texture, the hills and valleys, the annoyances and pleasures. Without them, the landscape of life is flat, gray, and plain vanilla. The little things offer spice and seasoning, pastels and topography to life.

"TWENTY-FIVE LOW!" Punkin bellowed out to the dorm.

I'd been waiting for the call and excitedly headed to the office. "Here, Punkin."

"Piss test," with a big smile on his face.

"Huh?"

"I need a piss test. You gotta give me a urine. You ready?" Punkin was another good thing over the years. He didn't have to, but when I was a rookie to family visiting—and everything else I asked him about—he solved my problem. He called an inmate from another dorm to come over and answer my family visiting questions.

"Yeah. In the bathroom?"

"Yep. Let's go," Punkin got up and followed me back into the dorm.

"WALKING!" someone shouted to the dorm as we walked to the inmate bathroom. The COs hate it, but anytime they walk through the dorm someone yells out to the let everyone know—especially anyone busy talking on their contraband cell phone—a sort of early warning system.

There are *good* piss tests and *bad* piss tests. A piss test is giving a urine sample for drug screening. Providing it in here is the same as in a doctor's office—but the stakes here are quite different. Oh, and you give it up with a CO standing there watching to make sure it's *your* sample. Apparently, those who know they're positive try to switch with someone who isn't.

The samples are then sent to an outside reference laboratory to test for the presence of controlled substances, such as marijuana, heroin, methamphetamine, and others—all the stuff that's not supposed to be in here. The testing takes a few days, but the reports literally take several weeks to find their way back to the Program Office. If negative, nothing happens. If positive, a *115* usually ensues.

A *bad* piss test is when an inmate is required to provide a urine sample because they are suspected of using or if they were involved in an "incident." There are literally tens of pages detailing the *who, when,* and *where* of the legal urine gathering process. An inmate can refuse, but it is automatically considered a positive test when they do, and that, like any other "choice," has consequences.

Today, I was being asked to provide a sample for a *good* piss test. I was about to have a "family visit." When that occurs, an inmate gives a urine sample before *and* after the visit. I call it a *good* piss test, but I guess if the result is positive you could say it's a *bad* piss test. If you test positive, no more family visits are in your future. In my case, it was a good one.

That's because the *biggest and best* little thing for me, and many others, is a family visit. Conjugal, connubial, marital—whatever you want to call it—family visits for us married types were a measure of time unlike any other. I marked my four years from family visit to family visit. Once approved, you are supposed to get one every 90 days. I had visits with as little time in between as 58 days and waited as long as 140 days during my stay. Doing favors for the family visiting officer can get you a place high on the standby list for cancellations. Getting to know him well almost guarantees it. My wife brought supplies and donations for the units and helped Officer Stuhrman keep them spiffed up—and that certainly helped with my access to future placement on the standby list.

These visits lasted nearly forty hours, from about 11 a.m. on a Saturday morning until 8 a.m. the following Monday. Alternatively, the visit could be from Thursday to Saturday. The visits take place in one of four double-wide trailers located behind the main Administration building at JRC. The units are separated from the rest of the prison and topped with barbed wire—as if I'd try to escape from my wife. They are air conditioned and heated—a Godsend during times of inclement desert weather—sparsely furnished, but clean. Off the entrance, there is one large main room with a couch and loveseat facing a cabinet with a TV, a Wii gaming computer, and a DVD player. At the back of the room is a dinette table and kitchen with a refrigerator, George Foreman grill, toaster oven, Microwave, stovetop and sink. The kitchen is stocked with normal utensils—something a dorm isn't allowed to have. Off the main area, there are two bedrooms separated by a bathroom, one with a double bed and the other with two single beds.

Food is ordered in advance from a long list of items purchased the week of your visit from a reputable grocery chain store—it definitely isn't prison food. Unlike our "regular cuisine," this list included fresh fruits and vegetables and real meat which was available for purchase. Everyone I knew who ever had a family visit went crazy ordering food on their first one and ended up with a significant amount of food that had to be thrown away—because inmates can't take it back to the dorm, and family members are prohibited from leaving with most items, too. In the future, you learn to be more particular when ordering after experiencing a twenty-dollar waste.

Not having funds on your books was the prime reason for having a family visit cancelled. The money was needed in advance to pay for whatever groceries you wanted to order at the usurious prices the vendor charged; it had to be in your account at least 35 days ahead of the scheduled visit. Cancellation was not entirely a *bad* thing, it simply meant someone else on the standby list would move up.

The approval process for family visits can also be arduous, depending on how you get along with your counselor. After completing a routine three-page application, an inmate turns it in to his counselor who is supposed to investigate the potential family members for the visit, certifies that married couples really are married, and sends it on to the facility Captain for approval. After being stamped and shuffled around, it finally makes it to the family visiting officer who schedules your visiting date. That's how it's supposed to go—smoothly and quickly.

It didn't always go smoothly or quickly.

Knowing the JDCR, there are numerous bottlenecks and other points for disaster to occur. In my case, after I turned it in to the counselor, the counselor subsequently accepted another position, causing my application, and those of others, to sit on his desk, untouched, during his last four weeks prior to leaving.

The new counselor started by cleaning his desk—which meant everything on it went into the trash. Of course, I didn't know about any of this. Some six weeks after submission, I inquired as to the status of my application, and was told by my new counselor that he knew nothing about it. Resubmit time. To his credit, the new counselor "expedited" my application.

It took just four more weeks—relatively rapid processing time—to get it validated and approved by the Captain. But then it sat for another few weeks on the family visiting officer's desk until, lo and behold, I received my first family visiting date—about fifteen weeks after first applying. The date was set for two months in the future.

When the day finally arrived almost six months after starting the process, I could hardly sleep the night before. Oh what a mistake not sleeping was.

Unlike beauty sleep in the real world each night, there's great potential for sleep deprivation in prison. Prisons count things. They especially count inmates—and they count inmates a lot. The purpose is obvious—to assure the entire state bureaucracy no one has escaped and everyone is where he or she is supposed to be.

Normal counts happen each day at 4 p.m., 9 p.m., midnight, 2 a.m. and 4 a.m. There are also "emergency counts" when someone thinks an inmate is missing. Emergency counts occur with some regularity: when there's fog, when an incident occurs, and when someone simply gets a wild hair out of place. When a count happens, all inmates must be on their bunks, quiet, and no roaming around the dorm until count clears, which usually takes thirty to forty-five minutes—*unless there is a recount.*

In that case, the process starts over from the beginning.

You'd think counting a dorm of 75 to 100 men would be a piece of cake. That cake must taste pretty good, because it gets eaten over and over with frequent mistakes and recounts. I always found it curious that there were five counts during the twelve hours at night and none during the day. I guess we're more trustworthy during the day?

The midnight, 2 a.m. and 4 a.m. counts happen when most are sleeping—you never know they even happen unless you're up from too much meth. I always was surprised the COs didn't make that connection. Maybe they didn't care? When the counter comes by your bunk, they may shine a flashlight in your face, especially if they're the sadistic type. Leonard made me eye-blinders that took care of that problem.

Except when on a family visit—I couldn't take my blinders and counts were different. One of the *bad* little things is count on family visits because they don't come in, you go out—at midnight, 2 a.m., and 4 a.m.—and stand outside your unit just long enough to have your REM sleep interrupted while calling out your "last two"—the last two numbers of your inmate ID—to the counting CO. Some inmates simply stay up until count is completed at 4 a.m. Others stay up all night and nap during the twelve-hour part of the day when they aren't counting. Being O.G.s, my wife and I never mastered the staying up all night concept. Bleary-eyed, after your forty hours of bliss, you wander back to your dorm to catch up on two days of missed sleep—at least until the next count—but only after giving your comeback piss test. All-in-all, a very *good* little thing.

The reason for the piss test should be obvious. These less rigidly supervised visits were an obvious route into the prison for contraband. And I had first-hand knowledge of just how that could happen.

There are many, many *good* little things about family visits; things we take for granted in the outside world. I'll re-mention good food—food prepared lovingly with your spouse. The opportunity to talk unencumbered by guards and time constraints is a huge plus.

But "good food" did not include great steaks. My wife solved that dilemma with a larger bra and ziplock bags. The magnetic wands the COs passed over every visitor prior to entering the prison could detect the underwire in a bra—something which could be weaponized, and the reason underwire bras were prohibited—or a cell phone, but they could not detect a choice top sirloin tucked beneath a breast (or two breasts). It wasn't exactly contraband, but it was certainly smuggled into the prison on numerous family visits. And it cooked up nicely on that George Foreman grill.

Other little things my wife brought, legitimately, included my electric toothbrush—I think I brushed my teeth twenty times during those forty hours. Sleeping on a real mattress—with real pillows and a comforter brought from home—was practically the next best thing to heaven. The back pain I experienced in here went away during those two nights. A good sleep is often taken for granted. Being able to eat our meals together, when you want and without a guard rushing us to finish, is paradise, especially when you throw in a real knife and fork. It seems silly to me, but in prison, as on airliners these days, we aren't allowed knives and forks—weapons, you know—but on family visits, we are. Inconsistency? Of course, the knives and forks are counted and each inmate signs for them and all the other utensils.

On one of our visits, a utensil was missing—on our arrival. The substitute family visiting CO duly noted it on the proper paperwork. When it was time to check out, however, a different CO had a different set of paperwork, one which did not indicate the missing utensil.

You would think a world war had started. My wife was accused of taking the knife—like she needed to take one from a prison—and given the third degree. I was strip-searched again and interrogated by the family visiting Sergeant and, for a while, I thought I was going to be executed, or something else perhaps even more horrible, until they called the original CO at home, who confirmed my story that the utensil had been missing from the beginning. A big relief—turn off the electric chair.

Other family visiting luxuries taken for granted are long, hot showers without twenty other guys staring at me, the quiet, porcelain toilets rather than cold metal ones without seats and out in the open, real orange juice—lots of orange juice, not some orange tasting liquid like we sometimes got at breakfast—and did I mention the quiet? Bacon, probably one of the *bad* little things, but I liked it. And did I mention the quiet? Romaine lettuce and tomatoes—only cheap, iceberg lettuce was served in the chow hall—for salads, along with real Hidden Valley Ranch® dressing. Croutons would have been great, but I'm not complaining.

And did I mention the persistent quiet?

Fresh corn on the cob with actual butter, salt, and pepper, was another food treat. Au jus and twice-baked potatoes added familiar indulgences for my palate, topped off with real chocolate ice cream, not the low-fat, melted variety served in our chow hall.

Add those tender, smuggled-in steaks, not tough, third world meat, eaten over loving conversation with my wife. Try cutting tough meat with a plastic spork—our only eating utensil in the chow hall—a spoon with one quarter- to one half-inch teeth at the end. Or, attempt to take meat off the bone of P.I.A. chicken, which is certainly not of the Foster Farms® or Tyson's® variety.

P.I.A. is *Prison Industries Authority*, a state-sponsored farming and manufacturing operation run at various prisons, and required by law not to lose money. They sell their products only to state prisons and the quality is suspect. Since the only customers are contracted states, if they are mandated to not lose money and they don't sell enough to make a profit, they have to cut back on quantity and quality to stay in the black—a vicious, and downward, cycle. They grow vegetables and fruits and raise chickens and cows.

P.I.A. also makes most of the clothing prisoners wear. Mislabeled, uneven, poorly stitched, and sloppy workmanship characterize the garments. I can't say I blame them—criminals making other criminal's clothes—why should they give a damn? That said, if the attention to detail of the P.I.A. tailors was any guide, you can imagine what the food was like.

There was hot water and actual kitchen detergent to clean our real knives and forks. On arrival at JRC, you are issued one disposable spork for the duration of your stay. You are also issued one disposable eight ounce brown cup to go with your spork. Lose or break them, and you either go without or you buy new ones in the canteen. You clean them the best you can in the sink with cold water—trust me, I will not miss my spork.

Catching up on recently released movies on DVD is another perk of family visiting. Your family members can bring them in as long as they are sealed in the original shrink-wrap and not "R" or "X" rated. The family visiting officer reviews the DVDs before allowing them into the prison. Once inside, however, they can't be taken back out—I never quite figured out the reasoning behind that, but it does create a nice library of DVDs for viewing in the dorms or dayrooms. I think it was intended to work a financial hardship on some families.

Everyone assumes you spend the entire visit in bed. Yes, all stories need sex to spice things up, and I won't deny those pleasures. It's also a real bed—not a hard metal, single bed frame holding up an emaciated mattress for our skeletal frames. No, in family visiting, we recline on a double bed, with clean sheets, pillows, and pillowcases. The best time in bed for me was the gentle touch of my wife—the holding hands, a light kiss and caress, the rubbing up against each other in the night. Those with children say they relish the time spent with them without penal supervision. Never take your family for granted—that's a *good* and *big* little thing.

The hardest part of a family visit is leaving. That last breakfast meal together, the last touch, the last electric tooth brushing, the last laugh, the last tear. Yeah, you get strip-searched—routine by now. It's the lingering kisses and hugs before having to watch your loved ones walk away. Like regular visiting, I couldn't watch the leaving. I had to turn away and not look. That's a *bad* little thing.

"Check," Mr. Kim parried one day.

"Ah, my young friend, I studied the board for at least five minutes. "How about this?" I offered in riposte. I moved my guarded Bishop into a position that blocked my King while threatening his Queen positioned in front of his King on the same diagonal—there would be no escape. The best he could do was trade his Queen for my Bishop. The lesson—what initially looks like a great decision may not be on further review. Mr. Kim squirmed in his chair. He now recognizing his predicament, but didn't need to say a word—in English or Korean.

"We have to finish. Governor Izzy is talking today," tipping over his King in defeat.

"You mean our esteemed Governor Strange is speaking on television again?"

What a surprise. The court recently issued a demand to comply with their previous orders to decrease the prison population without further delay. The Supreme Court also issued another ruling denying the governor's latest appeal of the governor's previous lost appeal.

"Maybe we go home?" Kim was hopeful.

"Don't think so," I dashed his hopes. "I'll bet it's another delay. He's Mister Shuck and Jive."

"What does that mean?"

"Never mind," I shook my head. "Just turn on the TV."

"I've called in the press to announce several agreements we've concluded with two private prison contractors. We've secured three private prisons and intend to begin transferring inmates immediately," the governor proclaimed triumphantly, staring into the camera, flanked by several official-looking plainclothes and three uniformed guards-union members.

"Uh, oh. Look at those uniform guys," I pointed to Kim. "He sold out to the guards."

"These new facilities will be leased for the next ten years and staffed by our JDCR guards. We've also petitioned the court for a delay until we can get all the transfers completed. Incidentally, we also signed a new contract with the guards union last night. Any questions?"

Reporters began shouting out a slew of questions. From one, "Governor, is the new contract for the guards the price you had to pay for their support on prison lease agreement?"

The governor scoffed, "Does everything have to be sleazy tit-for-tat with you? Can't I announce two unrelated things at the same time without confusing you in the press?"

"Oh, they're not confused, Governor!" I lashed out at the TV.

"Sir," another reporter continued, "How does contracting with private prisons solve the overcrowding issue? Private prisons won't take inmates that have mental health problems or medical afflictions."

"There you go again, drawing conclusions without the facts," Governor Strange snapped. "We'll address your question—or is that questions—in our response to the court. That's who we have to satisfy, not you."

The first reporter interjected, "I thought it was the people of the state you were obligated to satisfy?"

"Now you're splitting hairs," waving off the reporters, old, bald Izzy was not going to answer their questions, only give his canned talking points instead. "You in the press don't see the big picture. You just want to ask about little things. Get with it, people." With that, the governor of the Great State of Jefferson turned and left the podium.

Mr. Kim looked at me for an explanation without saying anything.

"Don't look at me," I shook my head. "What he just did was ignore the court's order while making it look like it's a good idea."

"I don't understand," Kim frowned. "Am I going home soon or not?"

"Not," I sighed. "Not unless the court suddenly gets *huevos*. Our fine governor is playing a version of the old shell game."

"Huh?"

"He's moving inmates around, to a prison here, or a prison there. Regardless, it's the same number of inmates. He's gonna send some healthy ones who aren't crazy to private prisons. So that means the ones left behind will have a higher concentration of sick and mentally ill prisoners. Yeah, that solves a lot. And did you hear? He wants another delay."

"*Huevos?*"

"Never mind, Mr. Kim," I stood up and turned off the TV. "It definitely loses something in the translation." The next day, buried deep inside the morning edition of the local papers were the details. The state bought off the guards' union by giving them a huge raise and the right to the first bid on staffing the newly contracted private prisons. That's why they appeared on the dais with him. Izzy Strange was one smart politician. He was trying to kill two birds with one stone—quieting down the guards' union and fixing the overcrowding issue. All he had left to do was persuade the supervising court of the wisdom of his plan—and get the precious delay he needed to make it all happen.

"Another game?"

"It's all a game, Mr. Kim."

"I don't under . . ."

"Another time." I gathered up my belongings and went to lie down in my dorm. "I'm leaving for the day. Yeah, I know. It's not time. The office is all yours, Kim." I'd had enough of the governor's little things speech for one day.

As I slid onto my bed, I knew what the governor was doing—he was trying to kill any chance I had at early release. Aside from staying positive, what else could I do to help along the possibility of getting out early—even if by only a month or so?

"Mail list up!" The shout out to the dorm suspended my thoughts. Incoming mail in prison is celebrated like a holiday; celebrated, at least, by those who get it. I was one of the fortunate ones. Throughout my four years plus, I received mail daily from my loyal family and friends. That list brought letters and *The Wall Street Journal* and magazines. My family and friends subscribed to the newspaper and several magazines—*Discover, Businessweek, National Geographic, Time*—that kept me informed and occupied.

It was the letters that kept me warm and spiritually engaged. They contained clippings, articles of interest, and stories about classmates or friends, jokes. All intended to lift me up. Mission accomplished—a really *good* little thing. And most remembered to include return envelopes with postage—a biggie in here. Paper to respond to letters was relatively easy to come by, it was envelopes and stamps that were not.

One special type of mail was usually not a good thing—legal mail. Not only was the message in legalese, but it required schlepping two flights up from my dorm to get it, and then only after signing for it in three places and opening it in front of an S&E officer to ensure it wasn't really contraband. In the beginning, it brought only bad news from my lawyers. Soon, though, I would be called for legal mail that wasn't. My father, a retired surgeon, wrote to me almost daily and posted his letters in his personalized envelopes with a caduceus as part of his letterhead. The mail room confused the caduceus—the winged staff entwined with two serpents was symbolic of the medical profession, and carried by the Greek mythological character, Hermes—with something from the legal profession. Go figure. Confusion here? The confusion and the smile it brought to me was a *good* little thing.

"TWENTY-FIVE LOW! VISITING!" screamed the floater CO in our dorm one Sunday morning. I was sitting about three feet from the entrance to his office. Floaters—transient Correctional Officers working a dorm as overtime when a regular called in sick or something—were the bane of my existence. They didn't appreciate all the time I'd invested nurturing the regular COs to get my "juice." They placed no value on my efforts to make their life easier—while gathering info or adding up chits in my personal arsenal. In this case, all that mattered was I wouldn't be spending the shift with the floater because I would be spending it with my family and friends visiting today—and I'd get to see John.

As I arrived at the entrance to visiting this morning, John was working the door along with one of the COs I knew well. John was beaming, "You have a full house again today."

"Thanks, John. Come say, 'Hi!' later," I replied. "Good morning, Officer Boeller. Any new health issues?" Not only was he a familiar and favorite visiting CO, he was also a member of my growing prison concierge practice.

"My back's great," Boeller smiled. "Since you told me about that medication, I bugged my doctor to prescribe it, and I haven't had much pain at all."

"Great."

"Doc," Boeller lowered his voice. "Wanna stay all day?"

I smiled back without answering. Another *good* little thing. A deal is a trade between the theoretical and the tangible. Theoretically, I'm supposed to go back to the dorm when visiting gets full. The tangible perk of getting to know the wants and needs of Boeller and others, is being allowed to stay in visiting all day.

"Facility A, all dorms," our regular Second Watch CO called out on another morning. "Packages."

With that announcement, about half the dorm scrambled for the door, grabbing their large empty laundry bags and heading for the gate. The laundry bags would soon hold the contents of their package—dumped into the bag unceremoniously by a disinterested CO. Before an inmate made his way into R&R—that's Reception and Release—for his package, he endured the several hour wait outside in the yard in the heat of the summer or cold in the winter before being led into the large holding cell. From there, one or two COs working in R&R would call out names, an inmate would find his package on the floor and take it up to a counter where the CO completed the ridiculously voluminous paperwork for your package and finally dump it into your bag. It's like going grocery shopping—so why all the paperwork? Oh yeah, it's the state.

Every quarter, inmates may receive a package from their family or friends purchased through an authorized vendor—a state-authorized thief. They charge exorbitant prices for relatively poor quality goods and ship up to thirty pounds to you. Aside from the rip-off of your family, they are a welcome blessing. The poor quality is a cut above anything else offered by the prison and at least there is a helluva lot better selection. Most inmates ordering packages focus on hygiene first, then personal items like clothes and next food. The food chosen depends on individual taste and the changing availability of items in the canteen on site.

At the beginning of each quarter, there is great anticipation in all dorms for the day when package pick-up will be called. This is especially true for the druggies, who sell or trade their family's and friends' hard-earned-money purchases, usually begged for under duress and with much flair and need. I dreaded that night after they called packages because all the users were major-league screwed up again—loud, obnoxious and happy—*not* a good thing. The non-druggies were just as happy, but quiet—with new warm clothes, and fully satiated with new food. Contented cows (and inmates) are happy cows.

Like everyone else, I looked forward to the new quarter. But I figured out that if you timed the delivery to coincide with the end of the quarter, or at least somewhere in the middle, there are far fewer inmates getting packages at that time, and it's less crowded during pick-up. At the start of each quarter, it's a madhouse; hundreds of inmates jockeying for position in a small area of R&R. The R&R staff's primary function is processing inmates in and out of the prison. Their secondary job is distributing packages, so they are none-to-pleased with having to work and they demonstrate their discontent by their surly attitudes. Catching them on a day with fewer packages to pass out is most definitely a *good* little thing. We all lived for our packages—thank you, my sweet. All-in-all, packages are a very *good* thing.

Some little things come in big packages. The last two years of my incarceration, CO Punkin left as my regular Second Watch dorm officer and was replaced by CO Z. Ofuati. Of Tongan descent, Ofuati was a huge man with a heart the same size. Always smiling, his demeanor is prototypical Polynesian—unless you get him mad, something not easy to do. I genuinely enjoyed talking politics and current events with him, but sports was his passion. He played college football and remained an avid sports enthusiast.

My passion for Oklahoma football gave us a commonality to the point I tried to recruit one of his high school sons to play at Oklahoma. Now "a bit larger" than his old college playing days, his girth was matched by his zest for life. It's unusual for an inmate to like a "cop," but Ofuati gave me a reason to pass by the CO's office on my way to and from work in the Program Office. I think he enjoyed my company because he could bypass the standard inmate B.S. prison talk.

About the same time, the regular Third Watch staff also changed. Our new Third Watch CO was T. J. Pace. As thin as Ofuati was not, Pace also maintained a steady, stable disposition, though a bit more jaded. I wrote this off to disinterest more than cynicism. A devout Christian, I was fortunate to be able to trade trivia and Christian book titles with him those last two years. The days when Ofuati and Pace were off could be painful. They both ran the dorm firmly and without the customary JRC inconsistency I'd come to expect. With them, I felt I could be honest and I did my best to attend to their administrative needs, as much as any inmate can do.

"Canteen! Second draw, a.m. workers only," shouted CO Pace to our dorm. I was second draw and definitely an a.m. worker. The canteen officer called each of the three draws for a week each month by Facility A, B, or C, then by a.m. or p.m. workers. I knew the canteen CO very well. Since his days as the Facility A chow hall officer, I had taken care of his clerk-type "needs." He was kind enough to reciprocate when I went to the canteen now. About my same age, we also had much in common during our formative youth years. We talked and laughed before and after I shopped. This guy, who will remain nameless, was scheduled to retire about six months after I left.

We planned on getting together—a taboo, but if he didn't care, neither did I.

I looked forward to this shout-out each month—another *good* little thing. The walk to canteen was over a half mile—not bad going empty-handed, but a trek with tens of pounds of groceries—and presented me with time to think about what I wanted to buy and greet fellow travelers on the roadway. Knowing the inmate workers at the canteen also helped. An under-the-table soda or two moved others and me to the front of the line. Another *good* little thing.

Over my fifty-one months, I moved up the ranks in the penal system from animal, to animal trainer, then trapeze artist, and, finally, to ring master—at least among the inmates—in this circus called JRC. Make no mistake, *the place* is *a circus.* Through it all, in spite of my surroundings and the circumstances of my incarceration, I was and am at peace. John was right about the little things. Appreciating them was a big change for me. The next challenge will be not forgetting that lesson.

The best of the *good* little things about prison was learning not to take things for granted.

Chapter 15: Choices, Choices?

"Damn," I exclaimed, grabbing the left side of my face as I sat at the game table in the day room.

"*Qué es* wrong with *jew moth?*" Face reacted.

"Mouth, Face, not *moth*," I was clearly irritated and not at him. "Remember the first cavity in my life they filled about a month ago?"

"No."

"Well, I do. The damn thing just came out I think," swishing my tongue around in my mouth. My tongue found a divot in my left upper molar where a filling previously resided.

"*Jew* put in a *602?*"

"Not yet," staring at Stinky. "Probably no way you can get me in fast, huh?"

"Nope, sorry," Stinky said. "But I'll tell the dentist about . . ."

"Dr. Pham?"

"Naw. She left after a few months," Stinky smiled. "None of 'em stay very long. Can't say I blame 'em. I'll let Dr. Viet know. Put in a *602* anyway."

Funny. I knew exactly what he meant.

"Mr. Pace," I said as I approached the CO's office. "may I have a *7362?*"

"You mean a *Medical 602?*"

I couldn't tell if Pace was pulling my chain. "Yeah," I laughed, as he tossed the form across the desk. Even the COs called them *602s*, walking back to the dayroom.

"*Jew* still play, no?" Face seemed hopeful.

"Sure. It doesn't hurt."

"It will," Stinky interjected. "Who's deal?"

Getting the tooth looked after was a choice I didn't want, but was now a necessity. After putting in my *602*—really a *Medical 7362*, I hoped they'd call me soon, since I put the details of my situation and also wrote in bold block letters, EMERGENCY! No such luck. Two weeks later, I was summoned to the dental area where I sat the obligatory two hours before being ushered into the dental chair—after a brief excursion for x-rays.

"Open up, please, and let me take a look." the dentist remarked without an introduction. As I opened my mouth, he began poking around with a standard metal probe into the depths of what I thought was the cavity where my filling had come out. "Wow. I haven't seen one of these in a long time." Probing some more, "This doesn't hurt?"

"I know you're there, but it doesn't hurt."

Probing deeper and harder, "Now?"

"Nope," gargling through the poorly functioning suction tube.

"OK, here's the deal," pulling out the probe and suction tube and gently closing my mouth for me. "You have a vertical fracture of your #14 molar. We'll have to pull it. I'll do it now."

"Excuse me," I protested. "How did I get a vertical fracture in a tooth that was just filled a month or so ago?"

"Don't know, but it's fractured now," Dr. Viet casually shrugged. "Gotta pull it."

I was less than pleased with going from no cavities on arrival to JRC, to one cavity a month ago, and now a vertically fractured tooth they want to pull. "Uh, I think I'd like to talk this over with my brother-in-law—he's a dentist—before we go taking out a tooth."

"Suit yourself. When you're ready, just put in a request. You know, a *602*."

"Right. A *602*. That's a *7362*, you mean?"

"I don't know what you inmates call them," Dr. Viet commented with a sense of disdain as he took off his gloves and walked away. "Just let us know when you want to proceed. It's your choice."

Yes, it was. My choice. Free will. After talking to my brother-in-law, I was more convinced than ever about waiting until release to deal with it. For all know, it might be salvageable. At least then I would have some assurance the treating dentist had my interests in mind, not the state's.

This whole concept of free will got me thinking about the scientific conflict about whether we humans have it or not. As an optimist, I believe we have free will. If we don't, aren't we simply automatons going through our pre-programmed motions?

As I sat in the penal system, I couldn't help thinking about the impact that question has on everyone in here. If we don't have free will, doesn't that mean a prisoner's behavior is predictable—or should be—and based on that prediction, there's no need for a trial or a justice system. If the chemicals in our brains are predisposed to a certain pattern of behavior, just send the accused up the river to the local hoosegow. Better yet, if they have genetic tendencies towards violence, why not just put them in prison as soon as possible—before they've committed a crime—and throw away the key? Even better, why not simply execute them? Isn't that ultimately better for society? Put them out of their misery. Or is that *our misery?* It would seem to be the logical conclusion of that theory. Oh wait, it is just a theory. Thank goodness. Hold the executioner.

"They just brought these over," Sergeant Whining sniffed, throwing a stack of 115 worksheets on my desk. "All from education. What a bunch of morons."

I couldn't let it slide this time. "Who's *they?*"

The Sergeant cocked her head and thought for a minute. "Huh. Good question," pausing, "It doesn't really matter. Just type 'em up. I want 'em back today, so they can have 'em back."

I sifted through the twelve worksheets, looking for a pattern. I knew that most of the education write-ups were pretty standard. Once I entered the first, I could copy-and-paste the others with only minor edits to personalize each one. There was another pattern I found. They all demonstrated an exercise of free will in a negative way, otherwise known as making bad choices.

Is JDCR really about punishment or rehabilitation? They would have you believe it's about rehabilitation. They claim to offer all types of vocational "training" and "education." The vocational trades—such as electrical, plumbing, carpentry, heating and air conditioning, even computer and office training—are all structured so the free staff "supervises" and the inmates do the actual work. Sounds great if the inmate knows what he's doing. What if he doesn't? The free staff is supposed to "train" the inmate in the particular profession. They offer certification in some vocational classes. In my experience, they only "train" the inmates enough to get the immediate job at hand completed, not really skilled in the trade.

The education department offers GED classes—General Equivalency Degrees and other classes at several levels, all the way up to college courses. A GED is a high school diploma equivalent. It sounds great until you realize that the primary reason they offer these classes is for money. The federal government pays for most GED classes in the United States because the largest percentages of people taking them are in prisons. When you look at actual pay scales, the only person someone with a GED is equivalent to by pay is to a high school dropout—not even close to a high school graduate. The other educational preparatory classes vary in quality based on the interest of the instructor. I met a few who were dedicated. However, the majority were just going through the minimum number of motions needed to collect their paychecks.

The problem is, all inmates are assigned a job, and many are assigned the "job" of going to school, whether they want to or not. Rather than filter out those who have no interest, the filtering is done in the classroom, left up to the individual instructors to weed out those not interested. If it were only those not interested attending, it would be better than the reality. The reality is not only are some not interested, they actually delight in disrupting the class for the ones who are there trying to learn something.

By disrupting, I mean intimidation of students and teacher, threats, and physical assaults. I think the inmates choose their behavior. It's not a biochemical cascade. The threatened instructors withdraw and *are* intimidated, many of them being females in a sea of large, gang-member males. Not only do they withdraw, their teaching is affected and burnout rapidly ensues. The instructors vent their frustrations by writing lengthy *115s* that we clerks get to type. They put those emotions to paper, writing near-novels in their disciplinary reports. I sense their irritation, aggravation, and annoyance, and can't say I blame them. I do blame the system for putting them in this situation. Wouldn't choosing—a little pre-screening selection—be better?

"Why are these *115s* so damn long?" Sergeant Whining lamented, after I brought the typed forms for her review, flipping through them, skimming the contents as she flipped. "Who wrote this crap?" Sergeant Whining looked up from her desk at me as if I had an answer to her question.

"Three different education instructors, I think," I said, half-defending the authors. "Believe it or not, I edited their originals down. The originals were much longer," staring back at her.

"Well," fumbling for a response, "good." Then lightening up a bit, "Can you believe some of the crap these guys try to pull?" Towards the end of my time, I think the good Sergeant grudgingly came to appreciate my skills, and even came to depend on them.

"Bad choices, Sergeant," I continued. "That's one of my biggest problems with this place. Bad choices and nobody seems to want to fix them."

Sergeant Whining leaned back in her chair and sighed, "On that we agree. Nobody cares. Not inmates, not officers, not the state, and damn-sure not the pansy-ass governor." Rocking as she spoke, "What am I supposed to do, huh? No, I do what every other officer does. I come to work and put on the blinders, just like a workhorse. Don't look to the left, don't look to the right. Just put in your shift hours and go home when they're over. Doc, you're lucky."

"Why's that?" I was somewhat surprised that she called me Doc. It was one of the few times I could remember not just being called "clerk."

"Because you have a brain and you're getting out of here soon. I've got a life sentence in this place," she sighed again, then smiled. "Or, at least, doin' my thirty years until I 'parole.' Retirement is all I care about now. I count the days. On any day, I can tell you exactly how many more I have left."

Maybe we weren't so different. I count, too. I decided to go out on a limb. "Do you allow yourself personal feelings about any of the inmates?"

"Hell, no!" Sergeant Whining quickly snapped. Softening, "If you do, they'll take advantage of you."

"Do you ever think about the system?"

"What d'ya mean?"

"Well," I continued, "you're a taxpayer and citizen. It's your money paying for all this. Do you think you're getting a good deal on your taxes?"

She sat for a moment. "I think I know where you're going with this—is the state getting its money's worth. The old, 'is prison for punishment or rehabilitation' thing? That question is as old as mankind. I sure as hell don't know. To work here, you have to detach yourself from those kinds of questions. I will say this, I think it's both. It depends on the individual and what they're in here for. For some, it's punishment, pure and simple—the lifers. For most of the others it ought to be about rehabilitation. You've been here long enough, though, to know that's B.S."

"But if you separate yourself from those philosophical questions, how can you be a good citizen?"

"I'm not a citizen in here," she responded. "I'm a cop. The higher-ups get to decide the rules. I enforce them, no matter what they decide."

I paused for a minute, "You're saying you don't think about the right or wrongness of those higher-ups' decisions?"

"Yep, that's what I'm saying. I just do it," answering rapidly.

"Kinda sounds like the Nazi excuse," I blurted out.

Staring at me now with great intensity, she frowned, but didn't answer. Then slowing down, she asked me, "Do you think you could execute someone if you got all philosophical? I mean a legal execution."

"No, I couldn't, but mostly because I'm against the death penalty," I replied. "And before you go thinking I'm a pinko-liberal, I wasn't against it before I came in here. After my experiences with the judicial and penal systems, I'm firmly against the death penalty now. The system is so stacked against an accused. My faith in blind and equal justice is gone."

Staring straight into her eyes, I continued, "I understand what you're saying about disconnecting your actions—like being in on an execution—from the decision to do it, the trial and all. But that's the problem with the system. No one takes responsibility, excusing their actions with the 'I'm doing my job' excuse. I'm carrying out 'their' orders, whoever 'they' are. It gets things done, but is the thing that gets done even right? Is the execution righteous? Is putting people in prison for errors in judgment appropriate? Criminalizing what really amounts to a civil mistake?"

Sitting for a long time, the Sergeant stared back at me, finally smiling. "Above my pay grade, Doc. Way above my pay grade."

It was a standard CO answer—the "I'll put my head back in the sand, thank you" response. The conversation was over.

I stood up and walked to the door "Do you want me to do anything more with the *115s?*"

"Naw. I'll handle them," she smiled. "Right now I need to take a walk."

I took that to mean think. Maybe I'd sprouted an idea?

The issue of free will is not a settled scientific issue. While I believe humans do have free will, many scientists believe it is strictly biology and chemistry. Neuroscientist Sam Harris believes we are merely "biochemical puppets," unable to choose a course of action any more than we are able to defy gravity. His colleague, Davis Eagleman, is a bit less adamant and more considerate of the societal ramifications this austere view creates. Both argue that, in effect, our choices are not choices, but that our brains are hardwired to make these decisions, mediated by biochemical reactions.

I'm more aligned with UCLA's Jeffrey Schwartz, who has very impressive PET scan evidence demonstrating that hyperactivity between two regions of the brain can be modified through a four-step therapeutic process. He studies OCD patients—those with obsessive-compulsive disorders—all of whom have this hyperactivity between the orbitofrontal cortex and the caudate nucleus of the brain. After a short course of treatment, rescanning reveals significant decreases in the hyperactivity—a fancy way of saying Dr. Schwartz has changed the way the patient makes a decision. By using his four steps, the patient is able to re-label, re-attribute, re-focus, and re-value their OCD thoughts by what Schwartz calls a *"tremendous force of will."* That's simply free will to me.

All I could think of right now was what that meant for my immediate situation and my fellow prisoners. You don't rehabilitate with indifference, apathy and disengagement. Rehabilitation requires something that a state cannot possibly be—empathetic, concerned, and compassionate. The state has no incentive to be humane, charitable, or merciful. The state's citizens do, but not the government, especially when to do so would result in more money going out than coming in. Rehabilitation is costly and risky. To embrace that concept meant fewer incarcerated persons—and less money for the state.

There are inevitable failures—and that's if those participating are screened properly. We're back to bureaucracies and bureaucrats failing by not taking risks. "No" is much easier and less perilous. No releases, no paroles, no sympathy, no benevolence or advocacy, and certainly no "there but for the grace of God go I" attitudes. Compartmentalization may be one of the steps I took to fight the enemy, but it is anathema to efficiency and competence, and contrary to the best interests of the state's citizens.

How can it possibly be "in the public interest" to send society's worst offenders to school only to teach them how to improve their criminal craft? Of course doing the opposite requires long-term thinking and planning—characteristics not often associated with government enterprise.

Since the state, and its surrogates in the penal system, is not going to make the correct choices, that left those decisions up to me. Until the day I was discharged, I was evangelical about that belief—mostly to no avail. I frequently advised others to use prison as an audition for the real world—don't do in here what you wouldn't do out there. I ran up against near-total resistance because most inmates—especially the repeat offenders—do in here exactly as they do out there, which is why they're here in the first place.

There were a few converts—Mr. Kim for one—but not many. I resolved not to let my time in prison be a defining moment in my life. That meant rededicating myself each day to making the world a better place—yeah, yeah, trite and altruistically true. In here, however, I reminded anyone who cared to listen how this was an audition for the real world, knowing full well they weren't paying attention, but hoping that maybe some part of it sank in.

Auditioning things like language skills. Since education—or the lack of it—is a primary reason many have had a rocky past and a predictably dismal future, I tried to improve day-to-day conversation by avoiding prison slang and the poor grammar of those around me. Double negatives drive me crazy along with pronouns such as "dog," "homey," and "dude."

Yeah, it sounds prudish and quixotic to think I can make a difference. I'm not that naïve. The alternative was to give into their bad habits. I was reinforcing my own desire not to change by trying to change the others, strengthening my resolve. Not using the F-word as an adjective, adverb, noun, or verb, and as every other word in a sentence was another pledge I took. I'm not as sheltered and unblemished as that sounds. How can anyone expect to get a job if every other sentence starts with *F-ing this* and *you F-ing that?* Language is important to me, not just the cursing. I was determined not to let my speech deteriorate into prison slang. Life is about choices. I *chose* not to be that way. Oh, how I wished that others realized the pragmatic reasons why it is important.

Sergeant Whining barreled through the door. "Lieutenant Croquet wants to talk to you, *on the double!*"

The Lieutenant was sitting at his desk reading a hearing report when I entered. He looked up immediately. "Look at this damn report," throwing it at me. "Bullshit mistakes. Until I leave, I only want you to do my reports. I'm tired of getting them back from the warden for corrections."

"Uh," I was taken aback. "Was *I* the one who did the report you're upset with?"

"Hell, no," he leaned forward. "I'm outta here in a few months, and I don't need the hassle. You're the only one I can trust to do my reports."

"Don't you already have your thirty years in?"

"Yeah," the Lieutenant frowned. "*I did.* I should've been gone by now, but the state bastards screwed me out of a year. That's why I'm still here. I gotta get all of my thirty years before getting out."

"I don't understand. How can they . . ."

"Hell, no!" Croquet screamed. "Nobody understands what they do in the capital. All I know is I'm gonna finish up in a couple of months."

He calmed down, "Can you just take care of me, OK?"

The Lieutenant and I had become tight before. Now, it seemed, I would be watching over him even more—as much as an inmate could. His last few months would also be my last few months. As a matter of fact, he retired just two days before my release date. Throughout those months, we laughed and swapped stories. He was a boxer in his younger days and still had the body of a prizefighter. Sometimes he'd kiddingly give me a soft punch which I knew was about as affectionate as he could allow in here. Those smacks were appreciated as a sign of respect.

The great *Hunger Strike of 2013* started out small. Several prisoners confined to isolation cells in the most maximum of maximum-security prisons in the state went on a hunger strike to protest being kept in isolation for years. While their complaints might have been righteous, their tactics were not. They reasoned that in order to make a bigger impact, getting other lower level inmates to participate in sympathy would help their cause.

Of course, being in isolation makes it difficult to spread the word, but prisons and prisoners have their lines of communication. So it came to pass that each of the thirty-three other prisons in the state were asked to join in the hunger strike, and soon thereafter, a work stoppage. Most lower level inmates decided not to join in—except for the Hispanics . . . the South-Siders—the hardcore gang member types—and the more ordinary *Paisas*. Thank goodness, I wasn't asked to participate, because the state developed a plan to confront the strikers.

The instigators of the strike were pretty much untouchable—what can you do to someone already in isolation at a maximum-security facility? Let's not forget why they are in isolation to begin with—these are the hardest of the hardcore inmates in the state, many of whom are the leaders of the gangs. Nevertheless, the underlings in other facilities were vulnerable.

In a show of brilliance, the state observed inmates not going to chow for about a week before taking any action. Of course, there is no requirement to go to chow. In fact, many hate the food to the point they eat exclusively in the dorm—preferring spreads, canteen items, and package food exclusively. Then, without notice or official documentation of who was an alleged striker, the COs began writing *115s* on all participating inmates. As Program Office clerks, we were the ones who did the write-ups—six hundred in Facility A alone. I know, because I was "asked" to compose the verbiage for the new *115* on direct order from Sergeant Whining. It read:

> On Monday, July 08, 2013, Members of the Mexican Mafia (EME) Security Threat Group requested all inmates housed within the Jefferson Department of Corrections and Rehabilitation to engage in a hunger strike (mass disturbance).
>
> On July 08, 2013, displaying allegiance to the EME, Inmate XXXXXX, X., X-XXXX, XX-XXL, took part in a mass organized hunger strike at the Jefferson Rehabilitation Center. You participated in this disturbance by refusing to eat state-issued or prepared meals.
>
> On Thursday, July 11, 2013, you missed your ninth state-issued meal, which constitutes a hunger strike. Your actions have delayed both the normal operations of the institution, and also delayed numerous Peace Officers in the performance of their duties.
>
> Inmate XXXXXX is in direct violation of JCR §3005(a}, CONDUCT, specifically, WILLFULLY DELAYING A PEACE OFFICER BY PARTICIPATING IN A HUNGER STRIKE.

How each inmate went from a hunger strike participant, to delaying a peace officer, to a member of the Mexican Mafia is beyond me.

Delaying? How? What does it take to note that someone isn't eating? They never did before. These hundreds of *115s*, and the hearings that followed, wreaked havoc that went on for several months. All affected inmates had to be served. In order to conduct the hearings, all the Lieutenants were required to work overtime, doing nothing but hunger strike hearings. Since there were so many, there were mistakes in a large percentage of them—like not paying attention to an inmate's normal days off and alleging they didn't go to work on that day, or documenting an inmate was seen eating, then writing them for not eating.

This required re-hearings and re-reviews all the way up the chain of command. What a miscarriage of "justice." Where's the proof someone is participating in a hunger strike rather than just not eating? Even worse, several *were documented* to have eaten by their dorm COs, but were still given *115s*. If found guilty, each inmate was given ninety days forfeiture of credit and varying amounts of loss of privileges and/or extra duty. Most charged inmates appealed their convictions, starting another long paper-trail process. Around and around it went. We typed all of that, too.

JDCR must have known it was coming because about a month before, all inmates were required to sign an "STG"—Security Threat Group—document, which was basically an attestation that you aren't a gang member and pledge not to get involved in any illegal activity. Should an inmate violate that attestation, it is considered an admission of being a gang member. When the hunger strike started, the charge of being a gang member was based on violation of the signed STG document and each participant was now "validated" as a gang member.

The bottom-line of this exercise in futility was to validate nearly all Hispanic inmates as gang members and to add ninety days to their terms, and not the Whites, Blacks, or Others.

And so the *Hunger Strike of 2013* and its after-effects eventually came to an end, but the toll it took lingered on.

About the same time, the state began considering inmates for early release, this because of the pressure from the Supreme Court's decision. Considering, but not actually doing anything. All of the hunger strikers were ineligible. Each chose to support their fellow inmates in higher custody, but few realized or considered the consequences of what seemed like such a trivial choice. The state also chose to overreact, in my humble opinion, not only to break the hunger strike, but as a way to label inmates gang members, whether they were or not. Keeping inmates longer means more money for the state—another misalignment of incentives. Choices matter.

"DOC!" I could hear Sergeant Zaldes from fifty feet away, through two doors. *What now?* I thought, heading to the Program Sergeant's office.

"Sergeant Zaldes, long time, no see. How have you . . ."

"Damn it, Doc. I caught Kim making illegal copies, buried with legit ones. I'm going to fire him," the Sergeant was pacing.

"Sarge, I know Kim well. He's a good clerk and there's got to be more to the story."

Zaldes sat down. "I think the damn MAC reps put him up to it. I don't care whose fault it is. I'm firing him."

"I'll bet it's a cultural thing, or he was intimidated into doing it."

"Talk to him. Find out and get back to me by tomorrow," Sergeant Zaldes was normally a decent guy. At least he was giving me a chance to intervene.

I found Mr. Kim cowering in the next office, wafting his hair back—his predictable nervous twitch, while mumbling in Korean and pacing. I sat him down to get the truth—something in short supply here. There are also always two sides to every story. As predicted, when the MAC rep asked him for copies of a church ducat, he didn't know what to do. Ducats are closely guarded, since they are a pass to many places—a passport for a prisoner to go where he shouldn't. Since Kim was still fairly new and didn't know the MAC rep well, he thought he should do what was asked.

The reason he was asked to make the copies was that inmates wanting to go to church—for whatever reason—couldn't get the necessary ducat. So the MAC rep—who knew better—decided to just get copies of the blank ducats and do them himself, all quite illegal. That's JRC §3021, FALSIFICATION OF RECORDS OR DOCUMENTS, a *115* violation and, in this case, became a major problem for Mr. Kim.

He didn't understand the specifics of why it was a violation, but I thought he realized the ethical blunder. We talked until he did understand and devised a course of action with Sgt. Zaldes. He apologized and begged for his job. Zaldes sent him away and called me.

"You were right," Zaldes smiled. "The damn rep intimidated him into doing the copies. Can you teach him? Is this guy fixable?"

"Yes sir, I think he is. He's also really computer-smart and I can adjust his ethics, smiling back. "I would really like to keep him, since he's got lots going for him, like not being a druggie or a thief. But it's your decision, of course."

The Sergeant leaned back and looked directly at me, placing his two index fingers under his chin, as if to hold it up. "Yeah, I could fire him. But I think I won't this time." He quickly sat upright, "But you let him know there won't be any more second chances. Oh, and he's your cross to bear now, too. If he screws up, I'll fire both of you."

"Thanks, Zaldes."

He chuckled, "You know I won't fire you, don't you?"

"But you could."

"Yeah," waving me out of the office, "and have all the regulars pissed off at me. I'm just the RDO Sergeant. You're the only thing keeping this office running. I'll let the regular know what happened in an e-mail. Just keep Kim out of trouble."

So ended Mr. Kim's initiation into the demimonde of Program Office clerks. Another lesson learned. Fixable? Zaldes asked. Why wasn't that question asked more often? Shouldn't that be an early definer of who to rescue? Choices? Yes, inmates and staff make them. A good choice by the Sergeant, I thought.

It was followed soon thereafter by a bad choice made by "someone" concerning hot sauce.

I've never liked my food adulterated with hot sauce of any intensity, but it is a staple in prison, probably to mask the awful quality of the food. Practically everyone in the place brings one or more bottles of various spices or seasonings to most meals. Among other condiments, the canteen sells *Sriracha* sauce in a hard plastic bottle of about twenty ounces. Sold it for decades, that is, until "someone" decided it could be used as a weapon.

Typical of the prison mentality, this was decided without any incident that even remotely identified it as a *potential* problem. Was the "weapon" the bottle or the capsaicin in the sauce? No one seemed to know.

This caused great angst and gnawing at knuckles among the inmates who might lose their most treasured condiment. The MAC reps were called in to mediate and, ultimately, cooler heads prevailed in this hot-button issue. The canteen was allowed to continue sales of *Sriracha* sauce and inmates were allowed to burn out their taste buds and stomach linings. "Someone" made a bad choice that "someone else" reversed.

It doesn't matter if something is actually true . . . as long as you *believe* it is.

"Did you hear about Jaime?" Pitr was not his usual calm self.

"No," I replied cautiously. "What now?"

"He got caught with a syringe, and they really tore up his house," Pitr grumbled. "Is he gonna go to C-status?"

"C-status? He may go to higher custody," I frowned. "Is he still here or did they take him away."

"They took him away for about an hour. He's back at his bunk now."

I knew all too well that meant S&E questioned him for an hour; and we all knew it wasn't over at all. He was on their radar now, big-time. They would be watching him for the least violation. C-status is when the UCC—a.k.a. Unit Classification Committee—puts an inmate on restricted privileges, and at JRC, that means being moved to a designated dorm where all the C-status inmates are housed. That makes it easier—supposedly—to supervise them.

Being placed on C-status is for a fixed length of time . . . the actual length determined by the UCC and, perhaps, in consultation with a *Magic 8-Ball*™ toy. If Jaime was still here, I guessed he would be placed on C-status sooner rather than later. They could also spend some time gathering more intel and sweep him up again, and then transfer him—a *114 lock-up*.

His particular violation—being caught with a syringe—is a very big deal. At the least, it is a serious *115* offense, probably a division A, meaning a forfeiture of credit that is not restorable. It's also a potential referral to the local District Attorney for felony prosecution. Another drug issue. Another bad choice.

Sometimes an inmate can effect a change in policy without "them" even knowing it. That's what I did concerning laundry sweeps. Every Sunday, each dorm is supposed to gather up and bag any extra laundry—sheets, towels, clothes—discarded by inmates going home or for whatever reason. The numbers are added up into a dorm inventory—a laundry sweep. These numbers are turned into the Program Office where a master Laundry Sweep list is created and given over to the Program Sergeant. The Program Sergeant sends it off by FAX to "them."

That's what happened each Sunday during my first year, until Sergeant Lessnut retired. He had been a real stickler for making us do the list every Sunday, "because that's policy." After his retirement in 2011, I continued to do the list each Sunday, but I could never find a Sergeant interested in taking the list. After about a month of that nonsense, I just stopped doing it on my own—to see what would happen or who would notice.

Nothing happened. Nada. Zip.

Not a word was spoken about laundry sweeps again until November 2013—more than two years later. At that time, the Facility A Captain decided to inquire about laundry sweeps, and suddenly they chose to do laundry sweeps again. They must be important; but just how important are they, if they could do without them for over two years?

"Doc!" Sergeant Whining called out to me as she rounded the corner, stacks of documents in her arms. "Take these!" handing them off.

"Where to?"

"Your office," she heaved a deep breath. "Separate them into the dorms they came from."

"No problem," I replied. "What are they?"

"602s."

"After I collate them, where should I put them?"

"Make a list of 'em—inmate name, ID, dorm, and bunk. Give me the list when you're done."

I started sorting through the mountain of at least two or three hundred 602s that really were *Form 22s*. Just organizing them was a project unto itself. Answering them was going to be even more daunting—a task I was glad I wouldn't have to do. A good twelve hours of work later, the list was complete. I took it to Sergeant Whining who looked it over, smiled, and gave me a "great job" thanks.

"What do I do with the original 602s?"

"Hot trash."

"Huh?"

"Throw them in the hot trash," she answered.

That meant they would be destroyed.

Choices. We all make choices. I guess *not answering* a *115* won't take as long as I'd thought.

The open road at sunset, My independent vision.
Grim relief and great regret,
Heart . . . in a velvet prison.
Choices curve the road of life, Head and heart collision.
Turn you loose or hold on tight,
Heart . . . in a velvet prison.

—Heart In A Velvet Prison
William F. Williams and Harding McRae

Chapter 16: *Outrageous Outrages*

The jaws of power are always open to devour
John Adams
Second President of the United States of America

I spent most days dodging the jaws of power like a cleaner-fish darting in and out of a shark's mouth. I existed in a symbiotic relationship with the sharks, I mean, staff; close, but not too close—a penal system cleaner-fish. They knew me, but not too well. There is no point in attracting the wrath of a more powerful predator or antagonizing someone who can make my life miserable. I subsisted in a mundane, routine, ordinary, commonplace, even boring, world, and the main purpose of everyone in this world was to pass time. My work was on such automatic pilot that I could outshine anyone present or past in my sleep—which actually happened when I was awakened for work in the middle of the night. I could do it and still have personal time.

Nevertheless, there were moments when I was stopped dead in my tracks by the stupidity, the foolishness, the rattle-brained absolute insanity of a situation; the kind of absurdity that causes you to fumble for a response. *Do I just shake my head and walk away, or is there something more?* Some things defy explanation yet demand one anyway. The kind of occurrence that forces you to ask yourself, *What do I do?*

What can I say? Situations like this are not exclusive to the penal system. Here, however, there are more incidents, of that I am certain.

"I need a *114-D*," Lieutenant Croquet hollered from his office as I rubbed the sleep out of my eyes. I'd been awakened in the middle of the night to come to work. Every time that happened, I jumped about three feet off the bed. The waking COs in my dorm learned I was a light sleeper and to stand back when they aroused me.

"Does it ever stop LT?" as I opened the door to Program Office and walked into his adjacent office. Croquet was working a double shift. The nights are supposed to be quiet.

"Yeah," Croquet turned his nose up and wagged his finger at me. "It stops when we retire."

"We?"

"Well, when I retire and you get the hell out of here."

I could finish a *114-D* packet in my sleep, even my recently interrupted sleep. It consisted of three yellow paper cover sheets attached to three manila folders, the last folder containing an Inmate Segregation Record and an ASU Welfare Check sheet—both one-page check box-type forms—and the multi-part *114-D* form. That is the meat of the report where the specifics of an incident are documented. Still, that only takes about a paragraph. About ten minutes later, I presented the package to the Lieutenant for his signature, glancing over at the cage in an attempt to catch a glimpse of the offending inmate. I noticed three prisoners, two in one cage and one in the other.

The Lieutenant quickly brought in two more *114-D* worksheets for the other two caged scofflaws. *Ah, the plot thickens.* These three *114s* were the result of a two-on-one assault at 11:30 p.m., earlier that night. I was thankful they called me in at 5 a.m. to type the reports rather than the customary 3 a.m. I wondered why they took so long to call. After completing the additional two *114* packets without further incident, I went back to my dorm, showered, and ate breakfast before heading back to the office for a normal day.

When I got back, Croquet was waiting at the door for me. "I need a *CSW 114* . . . now."

"On who?"

"The two suspects in the cage this morning."

"But I thought you said it was an assault?"

"Well, there's more to it," the Lieutenant cocked his head. "Turns out the three of them staged the assault—the two were just pretending to assault the third guy."

"I don't' get it. Why?"

"Why, indeed," my boss continued. "They were trying to get rolled up and sent to JIM—to the Ad Seg unit." JIM stands for Jefferson Institute for Men, the closest higher custody prison to JRC. "They were gonna transport drugs to the boys over there. This was their way of getting over there."

"Wait a minute," I was stunned. "You're telling me they volunteered to get put in solitary, in ASU—and get who knows how much time added to their sentence—just so they could transport drugs? You've got to be kidding me."

"Nope. I guess if you owe enough, you'll do anything to get out of debt."

"Anything? Including having another year added on? I'm speechless."

"Well, while you're unable to talk, I need a *CSW 114* on each of them," the LT reminded me.

CSW meant "Contraband Surveillance Watch." Potty watch.

I was incredulous. They were willing to be thrown into isolation for a couple of months just to transport contraband. Now they weren't going to get it to JIM but would still be rolled up and have even more time added if their CSW proved "fruitful."

A CSW means an inmate is placed in an observation unit for up to seventy-two hours, or until they poop three times or pass the contraband. If they don't pass anything, or don't pass something of an illegal nature, the CSW can be extended until nature takes its course. The lucky officers assigned to this fun duty sift through the excrement looking for whatever. Yeah, that makes for a couple of most pleasant officers.

I was familiar with the concept from my ER days. But this was a completely different approach. As a physician, I would examine prisoners brought into the ER suspected of ingesting contraband, in an effort to "confirm" it. That was about confirming its presence. In prison, it's about actually getting it.

In my ER experience, the "mule" ingests bags of drugs—I've seen as many as fifty bundles or so—and waits to expel it some hours later. This is a convenient way—I guess that's open to interpretation—to transport contraband a long distance, say from South America to the U.S. Condoms are frequently used and an x-ray can reveal the presence of the multiple latex products since they are visible on x-ray. In here, condoms are substituted with plain-old plastic wrap—condoms aren't easy to come by in here as they are in the real world—and the entire bundle is ingested.

Rectal packing is another option.

The real problem with either method occurs when the drugs get out of their packaging—the condom breaks or the plastic wrap opens—and the transporter is toast. More specifically, a large quantity of the illegal substance, usually cocaine or methamphetamine, quickly enters the soon-to-be-dead victim's bloodstream causing all sorts of havoc. Mayhem like intractable seizure activity, rapid heartbeat leading to ventricular fibrillation—a.k.a. no heartbeat—and various other body system disturbances ensues, any of which can lead to death in a fairly short time. Trying to force things along with cathartics is also a bad idea since it can cause the GI tract to squeeze down on the packet, and cause a rupture or result in an obstruction. Hence, the reason for potty watch as the COs called it.

What poor soul does this? What human being is so desperate that he needs to do this? Those questions got me thinking about how little I knew most of the other inmates. Looking back, it's hard to provide more than a superficial description because of what I didn't know about them. It wasn't for lack of trying. Inmates are closed-mouthed, even in their groups. What are their hopes and dreams? Do they have any? No one talks much here. Actually, they all talk—some more than others—*they just don't say anything*.

But no one opens up. It's a sign of weakness. The hopeless recklessness of their behavior is at once shocking yet unsurprising. The incentives are misaligned. What the system wants and what an individual inmate wants are often diametrically opposed to each other. The rules governing each certainly aren't aligned. I lived everyday with many of these guys, a few I was close to by prison standards, yet I really didn't know any of them. Every story develops its characters so the audience learns about the complexities and complications of their lives. *How do I describe people whose activities I find incomprehensible, and with whom I have no personal identification?* I keep reminding myself—this is a Level II prison. What worse depravities occur in the higher levels?

"Remember Jerrick?" Stinky asked one day as I came in from work.

"Not really."

"Sure you do. The young kid, tall, skinny with pimples?"

That description fit half the inmates in the prison. "You're gonna have to give me more than that."

"The one they caught on the phone crying to his family about money," Stinky persisted. "Remember? The towers monitoring the phones called down while he was still on the phone."

All phone calls are monitored and recorded—a big reason for the proliferation of cell phones. On the rare occasions when a bored guard actually listened, they sometimes overheard threats, extortions, or other prohibited behavior and called the dorm while an inmate was still on the phone. Having observed many a call, they certainly didn't care about obscenity or profanity.

"Oh, yeah, now I know who you're talking about. What's the matter?"

Jerrick had been removed from our dorm after a stay of only about a month. During that short time, he caused a lot of angst for our White dorm rep, Stinky.

He'd been sent here at the tender age of twenty, initially to the lowers, and then transferred up to "hotel" for unknown reasons. Those reasons became apparent after only a few days—he was a train wreck. Another one of the favorite prison ploys was transferring problem cases from one facility to another—and I typed up many of those transfer requests. A former Captain for whom I worked called it, "flushing the toilet."

It seems Jerrick was out celebrating his birthday and was over-served. In his drunken state, he decided to break into a girlfriend's house. You can probably figure out where that led—pretty-much instant arrest. You would think no harm-no foul, since nothing was taken or damaged.

No, the court saw it differently. His twentieth birthday celebration was followed by a twenty-first commemorated here at JRC—the first year of a four-year sentence. Since it was a 50% sentence—no violence was involved—he would only serve two years, and then be paroled.

If only it were so simple.

Young Jerrick had few life experiences prior to his incarceration to prepare him for the temptations of his *new* brethren. Jerrick had never tried heroin until he was introduced to it in another moment of boredom by his big-house-brothers.

"Why do you ask?" I'm suspicious of questions that begin with "remember so-and-so?" They rarely end well.

"Because old Jerrick's coming back," Stinky mischievously grinned.

"Here? After all the problems he created," I grimaced. "I'm glad he's your problem, Mr. White rep."

"I said he's coming back. I didn't say here."

"Huh?"

"Remember he went away? You know why, Doc?"

"Not really."

"Jerrick was a junkie and . . ."

"That much I do remember."

"Yeah well, he's gonna have a lot more junk time now," Stinky sat down on my bunk. "Back then he got moved up here from the lowers for getting caught with a gram of heroin. They moved him up to the hotel until he went out to court. That's where he went from here. Court's over now."

"I'm scared to ask how it went."

"They gave him seven years for possession with intent to distribute in a state prison," my rep buddy responded.

"Let me get this straight," I sat beside him. "A young kid screws up getting drunk celebrating his birthday and busts into his girlfriend's house . . ."

"Former girlfriend."

"OK," I continued, "*former* girlfriend's house, and the court throws the book at him—gives him four years. He gets bored and does heroin—becomes an addict. Then he gets caught supplying his habit and they add on seven more years? Geez, did anyone ask if he's salvageable?"

Stinky stood up, shook his head and walked away. What could he possibly say? I sat there contemplating the lunacy of it. A normal kid two years out of high school will now spend a total of eleven years—they forfeited his 50% reduction on the burglary—and his life is ruined. His bad choices, sure. But the state's as well. At around thirty years old, he'll come out a major league heroin addict, with no skills—other than criminal ones—totally dependent on the state. Whaddaya think his chances of recidivism are?

Jerrick is a victim of what I was told when I first got here and had confirmed through repeated observations—there are more drugs *inside* prison than *outside*. That's in spite of the millions of dollars spent on substance abuse programs, supposed counseling, and treatment. A vicious cycle? I call it insanity. It is a psychosis, a systemic schizophrenia of divergent and conflicting incentives.

Schizophrenia is characterized by a withdrawal from reality, illogical patterns of thinking, delusions, and hallucinations; it is a situation that results from the coexistence of disparate or antagonistic qualities, identities, or activities. Huh? Sounds like a mission statement of the penal system.

Real schizophrenics are a frequent find here, and their treatment—both formal and informal—is abysmal in my humble medical opinion. To be fair, society's treatment is equally appalling. Of the 213 psychiatric hospitals in the United States, the equivalent of 28% of all those hospital beds is occupied by the mentally ill in prisons at any time. In some states, it's estimated that up to 55% of the inmates carry the label of mental illness, compared to just 5% of the U.S. population.

In the 1800s, in the U.S. and Europe, psychiatric patients were institutionalized away from the rest of society in insane asylums and many inmates were also labeled as criminally insane. Beginning in the "enlightened" 1960s, the pendulum began to swing back the other way, culminating in the October 31, 1963 signing by President John F. Kennedy of national legislation that essentially emptied the government mental hospitals in favor of community mental health.

Sounds great. But it didn't work. That's because the government—federal, state and local—has never funded the programs adequately. States' governors and legislatures emptied the mental hospitals to save money and poured the patients into community-based clinics, which withered for lack of funding—and societal indifference. Our justice systems have picked up the slack, becoming the de facto mental health system, as the pendulum now swings back in the direction of government-funded mental institutions, also known as prisons.

The other issue ignored is what to do with patients/inmates/criminals who refuse their anti-psychotic medications. A tug-of-war between the medical and legal establishments continues unresolved, creating another vicious cycle. Psychiatric patients/inmates/criminals are prescribed medications by the medical community and most do well—until they refuse to take their anti-psychotics, which, the civil rights lawyers have argued successfully, is their prerogative.

Then the crazed schizophrenic—often fueled by substance abuse to boot—encounters the justice system, violating some law, ultimately entering the penal system thanks to the justice system's solution—incarceration. Not only does no one get at the root cause—mental illness—the opposite is strenuously encouraged. How can society get at that root cause without the teeth to enforce the solution? Anti-psychotic medications and their mandatory use must be enforced. Prisons have half-hearted policies for "obtaining" compliance with taking medications. Inmates find ways around those policies, aided by a custody staff that could care less whether or not someone takes their meds. Even the prisons are intimidated by the ACLU-types.

There are plenty of psychotics in prison, on that there is general agreement. In my thirty-year-plus career as an emergency physician, I have dealt with a significant number of psychotic, violent, and crazed patients—similar to the ones in the penal system. Hell, some of them are probably the same ones I saw in the ER.

There is a pending court case of a videotaped incident where guards are attempting to restrain an inmate at another prison. The question before the court is whether the public has the right to know of and view this tape. In the 1960s, Charlie Rich sang "no one knows what goes on behind closed doors," in his song, *Behind Closed Doors*. Seems to fit now, too. The argument against allowing the public to view the tape is asserted by lawyers for the affected guards. The assertion is it infringes on the privacy of the guards, who were just performing their duty.

Allowing the public the right to view the video seems reasonable to me. What's the big deal? After all, PETA sends its undercover operatives into slaughterhouses and records similar abuses of cattle, and hasn't been prevented by the courts from doing so.

The combative inmate is seen alone in a regular cell—about six by eight feet—where he has refused medications, hygiene such as showering, and eating for several days. No doubt, he has previously been coaxed and prodded to comply. The tape shows the officers, dressed in haz-mat suits, repeatedly pepper-spraying the inmate through the cell bars to the accompanying chorus of screams, pleas and desperate entreaties from the inmate. In my time as a full-time, board-certified emergency physician, I have never found the use of pepper spray necessary. But one has to take some caring time.

In the video, guards are laughing and cracking jokes as they ready their weapons. That state also has been accused of using seven times the quantity of pepper spray used by any other state. There are always two sides to every story—some times, many more sides.

I can't fathom a sensible explanation for this use. I am appalled—appalled as a prisoner, citizen, human being. What is the ethical rationale for this action?

"Lock down! Everybody on their bunks!" Pace cried out one afternoon.

Knowing him pretty well by now, as I walked by the office on the way to my bunk I asked him what was up.

"This is a bad one," shaking his head. "I've been doing this for over fifteen years and I can't believe it."

"Here? Did it happen here? Are we gonna be on bunk status a long time?"

"Probably not," Pace shrugged a bit. "Didn't happen here—it was up north. But it's bad, man. Really bad."

He summarized the incident for me. I felt more like a therapist than an inmate for the next ten minutes while he talked. A psychotic inmate in another prison, housed in a standard two-man cell precipitated a lock down for the entire state. The crazy guy's cellmate went missing around eight in the morning. The facility was searched, repeatedly, with no trace of the missing inmate. Ten . . . twenty . . . finally, thirty hours later, the COs decided to more closely inspect the cell of the missing inmate.

They found this crazy inmate lying casually on the lower bunk reading. Further inspection revealed an obstruction in the toilet preventing it from being flushed. The obstruction was the partial pelvic bone of the missing inmate. The psychotic cellmate killed him while he slept and then methodically carved him like a turkey, pulverizing the bones by crushing them, jumping on them repeatedly, and flushing the meat and bone fragments down the toilet. Only the large, hard pelvic ring prevented him from completing the disassembly.

"How did he cut him up? Didn't that take a long time?" I could barely spit out the questions.

"Tap on the walls of any old prison and you'll find a hollow spot," Pace shrugged. "Open it up and you'll usually find a weapon—a primitive knife or something. The guy found one and filleted the guy in about ten hours is all. They said there wasn't even much blood left in the cell. Unbelievable."

"Truly. Didn't they miss him during count? You guys count all the time," I asked.

"I don't know how they missed him," Pace answered, both of us knowing the bureaucracy overlooked many details. "When they opened the toilet, he had butchered the guy perfectly—steaks, even the main organs all neatly cut up. All except for one."

"Huh?"

"The guy ate his heart," Pace shivered. "They found it in his stomach. He told them and they looked down there with a scope."

"Are you kid . . ."

"Get outta here. We're on lock down. Go to your bunk," waving me out.

As I walked back to my bunk, I became nauseous.

"Look at that jackass," I heard someone comment as I walked by.

When I turned on my small TV, it became clear to me which jackass my dorm-mate referred. There on the screen was an impromptu news conference with the esteemed governor of our state, Governor Moonstone Isadore Strange. He was trapped by a slew of reporters all firing questions at him, no podium, just a narrow capital building hallway and no escape route.

"Governor, how is your effort going to comply with the Supreme Court's order to decrease the prison census?"

"This is a complex issue, requiring much study and consultation. I . . ."

"Governor, the court ordered you to develop a specific plan for compliance this week. Do you intend to comply?"

"Of course we respect the court's decision, though we strongly disagree with it. We are working on a plan—very difficult, very many details . . ."

"Will you comply with the court's deadline?" The reporter persisted.

An exasperated governor stopped in his tracks and swept the hallway with a glaring, penetrating stare. "I'm tired of your self-serving interruptions. I'll answer your questions in due time," continuing his intense look, "on my time, not yours." He slowly walked to the end of the hall and into an adjoining conference room. "Anyone want to join me?"

The gaggle of reporters hustled and jostled for the few seats.

"I have been your governor for the last four years. Now, I know you all came today expecting me to announce my gubernatorial re-election plans. Well, hold on boys and girls. Old 'Izzy' has a trick or two up his sleeve."

Did he always. Several journalists rolled their eyes, their experience and cynicism warned of impending spin. "Governor," one shouted.

"No," he waved her off. "I said on my time. So listen up, leaning an elbow on the podium. After serving two previous terms three decades ago, I ran this last time to return the state to the basics. Cut, cut, cut. It's been harder than I envisioned, but, well you know what I mean. As you may know, my paternal father, Stone Strange, and my maternal grandfather, Moon N. Beamer, were both governors *exactly* as I am . . . except in a different state. They left office broken by the job. Let me be clear. The only way I'll be broken is by the people!"

"It's the prison system that's broken, sir," a press-passer bellowed.

"You'll hear my plan for that soon enough," the governor continued as if he were the only one in the room. He had been joined on the dais by his wife. "They say, 'a rolling stone gathers no moss.' Well, when I was young I dated Kate Moss and I went on tour with the Rolling Stones," hugging his wife. "It's time for me to roll on. Upward and onward, or somewhere out there! My wife, Ishii, has given me good advice, to seize the road untaken. Sometimes I choose not to take her advice. She wants me to stay and fight it out with the courts. I've done my best and they'll just have to realize that."

The Governor paused, and a broad grin came over him. "I've decided I will run for the U.S. Senate," glancing at Ishii. "My time in the state is done. I've finished the hard part. Let someone else finish the last small crumbs. I will take the fight to a national stage. On to bigger and better things. I leave the statehouse with a smaller deficit than when I came and more revenue, thanks to higher taxes. All-in-all, not a bad few years, one I . . . and you . . . can all be proud of."

The journalists were momentarily quiet—a rarity—before bursting into a cacophony of questions. Yeah, old Izzy was something else. He'd changed the subject and most didn't even know it. Not one question on the prison overcrowding. Izzy and Ishii Strange were leaving for a larger stage. But what were they leaving behind?

What gnaws at me is why anyone doesn't see what's going on in here? What puzzles me is, they see and they just don't care. The governor's bait-and-switch routine with the press made it abundantly clear how easy the press could be distracted. They are the more likely representatives of the people, not the politicians. They are charged with asking the hard questions because they have access. Yet their memories are short and their interest shorter. I have personal experience with that.

What the governor was doing was a legally correct maneuver. But was it morally correct? Does society have a moral obligation to properly care for its discards? Does it have a responsibility to care for its criminals, mentally ill, physically incapable unfortunates? If it does, and I believe that is the case, does it likewise have an obligation to do it to the best of its abilities? Isn't it obligated to do so with high standards, by caring, interested staff, as any other fiduciary relationship should expect? If its agents—guards, counselors, medical and psychological personnel—don't measure up to those standards, does government have a duty to elevate their game under threat of termination? Who sets those standards anyway?

We throw inmates away and forget about them. Is that really in the best interest of the society or inmate? Is it not a short-sighted approach, an expeditious one, but destined to create more problems than it solves? Having seen it from both sides, I've changed what I believe. How do I get others to change?

"Doc," Sergeant Whining met me as I arrived for work. "In my office . . . now."

I didn't like the way that sounded. I dropped my things on my desk and walked next door to the Program Sergeant's Office.

"Yes, Sergeant. What's up?"

She'd taken a seat behind her desk, lightly patting her left outstretched hand with a letter. Patting more rapidly she asked, "Does this look familiar?"

"Uh, it's a letter. Why?"

"It's yours."

"OK," I was confused. "Is there a new rule against writing letters I don't know about?"

"No, you can write letters," tossing correspondence in my direction. "Is it yours?"

It was a standard size envelope, with my typed return address and a typed address to an old high school friend. I remembered mailing it about five days prior. When an inmate drops mail into an institutional mailbox, it is posted unsealed. "Yes. It's one of my letters. Why do you have it?"

"Your CO took offense to it," the Sergeant wasn't smiling.

The custody staff reads all outbound mail and seals it before it is posted. Inbound mail is screened in the mail room prior to being distributed to the dorms. If contraband or pornography is found, they forward to the Program Sergeant.

"What? I never write anything . . ."

"The address is typed. You know you're not supposed to use your computer for personal correspondence."

"My wife sends me the pre-addressed envelopes," I countered. "I write so many letters to the same people it saves on handwriting."

"And the typed letter?"

I'm sure I turned more than a bit red, "Well, that's . . ."

Whining interrupted. "I couldn't have read it if it wasn't typed."

I was really confused now.

"You know, I really don't care if you type your letters," she lightened up a bit. "You clerks gotta have a few perks, huh?"

"What's the, uh . . .the uh, issue?"

"Your First Watch dorm CO took offense to what you wrote. She's a devout Christian you know."

"She sure doesn't act like it," I pushed back. "Guess she hasn't read the 'do unto others' part of the Bible." I rarely encountered CO Barton since she worked 10 p.m. to 6 a.m., when I was asleep. But she was mean, vindictive, and downright sadistic—none of those characteristics were very much Christian as far as I was concerned.

"I don't get it, Sergeant. This letter is about . . ."

"I read it," Whining cut me off. "I know what it says. She's bothered by you using circumcision in a letter."

"Are you kidding me?" For a Christian she sure doesn't read well, I thought. "It's a discussion about the Apostle Paul's work and the conflict between the book of Acts and the letters Paul sent. The friend I was writing is a minister and a doctor. We've been delving deep into the Bible. I don't think Paul would have personally circumcised Timothy as Acts says he did. I think the Epistles contradict that because . . ."

"Doc," Sergeant Whining grinned widely. "You don't have to convince me or have a divinity discussion. I believe. You want it back?"

"Don't tell me to write a *602*," I frowned.

"Of course not. Obviously, Barton didn't read it. She just saw the word and became offended. Knee-jerk response. She came barreling up here complaining to me about you, saying I had to do something about this vile language. No thought, only reaction."

"What are you going to do?"

"Mail the letter for you," looking deviously at me. "I just wanted to watch you squirm," laughing a little. "Barton is a Christian in name only. She knows all the verses and can quote scriptures, but there's a difference between talking the talk and living it."

"There are many in here that do that," I replied. "I'm not just talking about Christianity. It starts in the capital and works its way down to here. I'm so . . ."

"Go in peace," the Sergeant waved me out. "Maybe someday we'll have that discussion. Remember, God is here even in this prison. C. S. Lewis said we are all on the road to perfection, some of us are just farther down the road than others." She paused before continuing, "Give her a break. She's not very far down the road."

As I left the Sergeant's office I was smiling as I walked. Could Sergeant Whining be a closet Christian? Quoting C. S. Lewis is not what I'd expect from a hard-nosed JDCR Sergeant. God works in strange ways, truly strange ways. *It is a game*—to be won or lost.

> *My contention is that good men (not bad men) consistently acting upon that position would act cruelly and unjustly as the greatest tyrants. They might in some respects act even worse. Of all tyrannies, a tyranny sincerely exercised for the good of its victims may be the most oppressive.*[3]

---

3 From *God in the Dock*, by C. S. Lewis (1948)

Chapter 17: *Indignities and Other Ramblings*

"It's futile."

"Why?"

"I'll bring you *Part As*."

"I don't need *Part As. Part Cs* . . . that's what I need," chasing after the supply officer as he walked down the dirty hall. "*Not Part As!*"

I'd asked Officer Crapulveda for *115 Part C* forms.

Stopping at a doorway, Crapulveda smiled. "I *know* that's what you want."

All I wanted was a package of forms. I'd run out of them in the Program Office. The supply officer's answer set off a light bulb. "What's the deal, Crapulveda?"

"I'm not going to the supply area. Besides, we're out."

"You know we can't do disciplinary reports without them. Whaddaya want me to do?"

"Don't know."

"What do I tell the Lieutenant?"

"I told you. It's futile."

"What's futile? All you have to do is go to supply and get them, problem solved."

Taking a serene pause, Crapulveda looked off down the hall and smiled more broadly. "Is the institution at a standstill?"

"No, but . . ."

"Then it's not what you *need*. Don't you mean it's what you *want*?" chuckling. "Today, you can't have what you *want*. When the institution is at a standstill, that's when you *need* them. And when it is, then you *might*," he paused for emphasis, "get your forms."

"So what do I tell Lieutenant Croquet?"

"Nice day, good morning. It doesn't matter. He'll know."

"He'll know? Know what?" I was beginning to feel like the guys at the Alamo—major league out of luck.

"Doc, how long have I been here?"

"About thirty years. I think that's what you told me," I responded. "You're retiring in a month or so."

"Correct," Crapulveda was leaning against the wall. "I told you about not worrying about getting something done today because there's always tomorrow. Always. Let me ask you a question," as he pointed down the hall at a wall. "What if the higher-ups wanted that wall painted red, but the warehouse sent over blue paint. What would you do?"

"I'd send it back and send it with the proper form for red paint."

"And what if they sent you blue paint again? And again . . . and again? See, you don't get it," the Facility A supply officer continued. "You paint the wall blue and when they come take a look at it, you comment how pretty the red wall looks."

"But it's not red."

"Right. Trying to change what they sent over is futile. I know it, the higher-ups know it and you should know it, too. That's what I said earlier. Change doesn't happen here. It's futile."

"Don't they want it red, since they're the ones that ordered it?"

"You assume they remember," Crapulveda grinned. "Or that they care what color. Who's "they" anyway?"

"But . . ."

"Have you ever wondered how I survived thirty years without blowing a gasket? It's pointless trying to change this place. You go with the flow. Like a leaf floating downstream in a river," flicking his wrist through the air. "Go with the flow, or you'll run into a boulder. I told you, I'm not going where the Part Cs are and we're out. Go with the flow," he smiled and walked slowly away. "Besides," looking at his watch, "it's time for me to eat anyway."

What I'd actually asked was a simple question about forms. The answer I received was enlightenment, Crapulveda style. I have always been a jouster at windmills, one who takes on idealistic struggles. Now he's telling me, who cares if the report doesn't get completed for lack of forms?

Me? Why do I care? This isn't my struggle.

Crapulveda? It isn't his struggle either.

The, Lieutenant? It is his struggle, but not really. Besides, he knows—or so Crapulveda says.

It's "they" who should care, and Crapulveda says "they" don't. And even he didn't know who "they" was . . . or were.

This illumination had wider implications. No wonder *602s* aren't answered. No one cares about them. They're the blue paint for a red wall. It comes back to incentives again—and their misalignment.

Why am I the only one that seems to care whether the reports are done? I'm a friggin' inmate! It's their bureaucracy—let them joust a while.

"Why do you care about getting those forms?" John asked several days later in visiting. "You're a clerk. You aren't the supply guy."

"I try to take care of my Lieutenant. I've always believed that anything worth doing is worth doing right. Take care of the guy above you and he pulls you up with him."

"Admirable. But he's not pulling you up anywhere. He couldn't even if he wanted to. And what happens when you're perfection conflicts with this place?"

"I'm not sure."

"Do you think your Lieutenant is gonna fight this fight with you? Or for you? Hell, no. Don't lose sight of your goal," John counseled.

"And what goal is that, John," I asked.

"*You're going home soon.* Learn from this experience, but don't let it dominate your life."

"How do I not let it dominate?"

"By remembering who and what you are," my prison philosopher/mentor advised. "You gotta modify your perfectionist tendencies. I'm guessing they drive your family and friends crazy anyway."

"Yeah, just a little," I blushed.

"They'll figure it out without you."

"Who's *'they'*?" I still wanted to know.

John lowered his head without saying a thing and just stared at me.

I smiled at my mentor, "Are you saying I don't need to *602* it to find out?"

John patted me on the shoulder as he left. "There are no *602s* in the real world."

"I'm not so sure about that. I may write one for the real world."

"Stay within yourself," John turned to leave. "Remember what and who is important—God, then family and friends, and everything else after that. Leave this time behind, as if it never happened. You echo the story of Issachar."[4]

Giving up the quest—the quest to right the wrongs of this life—is a tough sell to me. I've always been quixotic, frequently to my own detriment. Somehow, giving up fixing the problems of JDCR isn't in my DNA. Leaving it—yes, as if it never happened—not my style. I've come too far and thought too much about it just walk away. As an inmate, I owe it to my fellow inmates. As a taxpayer, I owe it to my fellow taxpayers.

Still, I am ambivalent. Do I really have a horse in this race?

The conflict between what is morally correct versus what is legally correct is in constant tension here. Of course, the state has a legal right to incarcerate. Does that legal right come with any moral baggage? Like trying to fix what's broken? I'm reminded of the Powell Doctrine of war, "If you break it, you own it."

While the state didn't break these guys, they certainly recognized it via the court judicial system which handed them off to the penal system. For what? Once handed over, what is the moral purpose? Doesn't the state, through the agency of the penal system, have a moral obligation to try to fix what's broken?

I say it does, but now that I've left the system, why do I care? That old jousting-at-windmills part of me just won't settle down, in spite of what John said. Every time I think it's quieted down, another example of the insanity stirs the embers and fans the flame of indignation.

---

4 Genesis 49:14-15

"Doc," a friendly Correctional Officer I knew called out at chow one night. "Do me a favor and fill this out," handing me a short one-page form.

"What's this about? "

"Aw, just fill it out," he laughed.

I looked over the ten-question form about tonight's food offerings. It was a survey about the quality, presentation, and the satisfaction with a meal in prison. *Was this a joke?*

"Are you kidding? What's this about?"

"Damn state. We have to have an inmate fill these stupid things out once a week or so," the CO answered. "I figured you'd do a good job on it."

Looking over the questions made me wonder why they were doing it. Questions about quality, preparation. I didn't know anything about half the questions. In my experience, no one else of the inmate species did either. *Why me?*

"Hey, who's this for?"

"Aw Doc, just fill it out. Don't ask me questions I can't answer."

"OK, OK," I ended my protest.

He was just doing what he'd been told, by somebody else doing what he'd been told, and so on up the chain. All this time and effort for something that no one really cared about—not inmates, not staff, and most assuredly, not the higher-ups. I'll bet that if I looked in the trash around the kitchen I'd find dozens of these surveys.

I completed it. Not in hope the food would improve. Windmills come in all sizes and this one just wasn't worth jousting over.

As I finished the survey, the MAC rep for Facility A came to me as got up to walk back to the dorm. "I need some copies for the food fundraiser."

"What fundraiser? I haven't heard about it."

"Well," the rep continued. "The warden OKd a food drive for her favorite charity next month. I need the menu copies so I can pass it out to the dorms."

"No problem," I responded. "Didn't want to give it to Mr. Kim?"

He took that joke in stride. Since Mr. Kim's run-in with Sgt. Zaldes, he hadn't copied anything—even the righteous ones.

"Give it to me and I'll do it tomorrow at work. I love the food but hate the price-gouging."

"Captive audience," the MAC guy shrugged. "Us beggars can't be choosey," handing me the flyer. "I'll pick 'em up tomorrow around noon."

Another ambivalence. The normal prison food sucked, so these food drives—where they bring in an outside vendor to sell real food at inflated prices, all for charity—were a treat all inmates envied. But not all inmates could participate. Only those with money on their books could participate, so there was a lot of jockeying around in each dorm, trading this or that for a piece of the action. My problem was a moral one, a small one. Still, do I want to sell out to the warden's charity for high prices, or maintain the high ground? My stomach trumped my head every time these fundraisers came up—about once or twice a year. I guess everyone has their price.

A ruler should fill their stomachs and empty their heads.
LAO TZU

"Mattress exchange!" Officer Ofuati screamed out to the dorm. We never knew when "they" were going to call mattress exchange, so when "they" did, there was momentary pandemonium. There was instantaneous, mad scrambling all around as inmates stripped their beds of sheets and rolled up their mattresses. "Only those on the list can go."

Scheduled for the first Wednesday of each month, but actually held about every six months, mattress exchange meant an approved inmate could carry his mattress the half mile or so to the warehouse and exchange it for a new one. Even more fortunate were the inmates who managed to get a "double mattress chrono" could pick up their second mattress. Double mattresses required the chrono from medical and were a hard item to come by. It required a prison physician to certify you needed a second mattress for various reasons, like back pain or diabetes. Even old age might get you one, old age being defined as over sixty.

Then the trek down the hill to the warehouse to stand in line and be hassled a bit before you finally got your "new" mattress. Once secured, then you had to carry the mattress back up the hill the half mile or so to one's bunk. I couldn't figure out why someone with a bad back or some other qualifying malady was required to carry an awkward, heavy mattress at least a half mile. Seems to me, if you could you didn't really need the chrono. And if you couldn't, well, what were you doing there having to lug the damn thing in the first place?

Should I joust? It is a game—to be won or lost.

"They started moving guys today," Stinky advised.

"I know," I could see the apprehension in his eyes. "Remember, I get a transfer list in my office each day. Don't worry. You're not on it."

"I just don't get it," Stinky shook his head. "They're spending all this time and effort moving inmates from one prison to another. Why? What's it solve? There's still overcrowding . . ."

"And it still doesn't deal with the inadequate medical and psychiatric care."

"Yeah, and slicing the same pie don't make it better, only cut up different."

The state began carrying out its promise of moving inmates to newly contracted private prisons a few months before I left. While it didn't affect me, everyone was on edge. You can even get comfortable in a prison. I think it's more falling into a routine you don't want disrupted.

Almost every inmate was anxious to know who was on the list—at least I knew who "they" were in this case. Since I had the list, that made me a popular guy. Popular is not quite correct; more like "in demand." Each day, a steady stream of inmates would seek me out to inquire if they were on the list. At a rate of twenty-five or so every few days, the prison I'd called home was changing. There is a constant coming and going of inmates, new ones arriving and old ones leaving. But this was different because of the volume—almost a complete turnover all at once. It was the right time for me to be leaving.

They were going to one of several privately built prisons. Privately built, but contracted by the state with the state prison guards' union to run them. That meant understaffing at JRC while many of the COs left to work at one of the new facilities. Good for them, not so much for us inmates. Tired COs are crabby COs. The same sick and mentally ill inmates were kept in the original facilities, since the new ones didn't take the ailing or the crazy. So how does that solve the Supreme Court's decision citing unconstitutionally cruel and unusual punishment as a direct result of overcrowding? Same pie, smaller pieces.

"Don't call me, don't write," Stinky was adamant. Pitr and Face nodded their heads in agreement.

"Are we going to play or talk," Pitr asked. "Once you get out, forget about us. Forget about this place."

"Why is it everyone wants me to forget about this whole experience?"

"Because it's like eating spoiled meat. It tastes bad, leaves you sick to your stomach, with a headache, vomiting, and diarrhea. You're better off pretending you never ate it."

"*Jes*. He *es* right. *Jew* don' wan' remember me?" Grabbing my shoulder, Face was firm, "*Mira aqui*," locking his eyes on mine.

"I'm looking." Through the years, as I tried to get Face to improve his English, my Spanish had improved.

"*Yo quiero* . . ."

"English . . ."

"*Jew* needs to look forward, no backward."

I reached for the deck of cards and smiled at my three companions. "Forward, I know. But I can't just walk away from all the problems. . . "

"They're not yours anymore," Pitr raised his finger.

"This place managed just fine before you got here and it will still be fine after you're gone," Stinky added.

"Glad I made no impact," feigning indignation. "You're saying don't write or call or anything?"

"You're gonna be surprised at how quickly you block all this out. I know. Remember I've paroled three times," Stinky laughed. "I didn't have to forget, 'cuz I knew I'd be back. But you . . ."

"You won't be back," Pitr finished. "So remember the lessons, the good ones, and maybe let a little light into the real world about this place."

We sat for a minute, me shuffling the cards, quiet. I was having trouble with the concept of pretending none of this happened. "Do any of you know about Plato or Aristotle?"

"*¿Quien sabe?*"

"Are they in Facility A?"

"What dorm?"

"Never mind."

As my days now numbered in the low two-digits, I was what's called a "double-digit midget," where others became more anxious, I was at peace—I embraced it because the time gave me calmness and a joy for living—even in here. Where I was a skeptic before, I became open to different approaches. The previously dominant cynicism gave way to optimism. The spiritual monasticism helped me see what was, and was not, important. Still, I am a realist. In the little time I had left, I couldn't avoid the temptation to try righting a few wrongs on my way out. Time is a measure of attitude.

One wrong was the inequity between which inmates are paid for work and those who aren't. Citizens I know grouse about inmates being paid at all. Let me assure you it is minimal. However, the prison economy depends on it. Those few dollars a month allow inmates to shop at the canteen, order packages and barter, although not exclusively since families and friends supplement too some extent, but they are important.

Jobs are assigned randomly and with no attention paid to qualifications. Some are paid positions while others are not for the same work. That creates unnecessary inmate tensions. As an example, in the Program Office, all clerks are paid eighteen cents an hour to a maximum of twenty-seven dollars a month. Those twenty-seven dollars are for 150 hours of work, and subject to having fifty-five percent withheld for restitution, when applicable.

Without the Program Office Captain's and Lieutenant's clerks, little or nothing would happen in the facility. Nevertheless, they aren't the only ones in the Program Office. There are reception clerks in the office, too, paid the same twenty-seven dollars a month for doing nothing—as long as they came to work. This is not the most egregious abuse. There are many paid-job assignments where there is no work, but inmates are still paid. And there are many other assignments where inmates work their butts off—literally for nothing because it isn't a paid position—like in the kitchen. Most of the cooks aren't paid, even though everyone has to eat.

There is also no equity among the various jobs. While the Program Office clerks are responsible for all the disciplinary actions—typing the forms, maintaining the multiple lists necessary to keep track of the goings on, payroll and staffing assignments—they are not the highest pay scale. The highest pay scale is fifty-four dollars a month which is paid to the "senior" inmates in a work area, known as the lead plumber, electrician, and other craftsmen.

Each worker is supposed to begin at the lowest level pay grade—level 5—and given a raise after ninety days of satisfactory performance. I came into my position as a level 4 position—as are all the Program Officer positions—and remained at that level throughout the four years I was at JRC. It wasn't for lack of performance but lack of interest in taking up the cause of getting a raise. I didn't work for the money—all twenty-seven dollars of it. However, I decided before leaving to take up that gauntlet on behalf of the clerks I would leave behind.

It took me over a month to find a custody staff employee willing to explore how to get "the boys" a raise. The decision was a no-brainer—it's policy in Title 15. That's why it is currently only "under consideration."

I forgot. No one cares.

Another wrong I attempted to correct is the unfairness of not being able to donate your inmate electronics. Inmates may order TVs, CD players, headphones and other electronics from approved vendors. While they are a godsend here, they are of little value in the real world. JRC in its wisdom insists inmates take them on release. That is the policy most of the time. Depending on the R&R Sergeant, that policy may change —even at the whim of a particular officer working in R&R at the time of an inmate's release. Since the poorest of inmates don't want to take them home, an underground effort ensued to find a way around the policy. One way around it was to have your property confiscated. Inmates were losing TVs right and left—and just before release imagine that.

Inmates would try to convince COs to confiscate their property the night before release, confiscate in name only. Others paid clerks to type up a chrono indicating the CD player, radio or TV had been transferred to another inmate's books. These were not legal, but several previous clerks operated a nice prison scam getting paid for them. When the inmate gets to R&R, he is ordered back to his dorm to pick up the electronics and return with them, under threat of being held longer.

In fact, the state can't do that, but the threat works. The inmate returns to R&R with the property and the state confiscates it and place it in "storage," never to be seen again.

Well, not exactly. That TV or radio finds its way back into the prison population. Who knows by which route, but no doubt someone profited from it. You gotta love capitalism—whether by inmate or staff. Instead of going through all this nonsense, I approached the Captain to find a more reasonable way an inmate could legitimately leave his electronics. This was unsuccessful, too—no luck in getting a policy change. The state throws inmates away and forgets about them. Apparently, the same can be said of their property.

Then there is Ms. Bark, the regular morning cook for Facility A. An individual more two-faced than she, I have not yet met. She can be charming—rarely—or a snake in the grass. She felt it her duty to act as custody staff in spite of being told repeatedly not to do so. A nice enough looking black woman, likely in her mid-forties, she was the embodiment of vindictive meanness.

Inmates do the actual cooking; as free staff, she supervises. She purposely scrimps on ingredients, pays little attention to the actual preparation, and pilfers large quantities of food for her personal use. This wouldn't be so bad if she treated the inmates working for her decently. Ah, were it only so. Food is a big deal to inmates and she intentionally throws out any leftovers very dramatically in front of those inmates who just cooked it. The other free staff cooks usually allowed inmates to eat the leftovers—a job perk for doing a thankless, unpaid job. These inmate-cooks work from 3:30 a.m. until 10:30 a.m. preparing the morning meals, cle aning up, washing the utensils for the facility, all under the constant shouting insults of Ms. Bark.

Besides abusing inmates and staff, theft of state property and actionable harassment, she also is an out-and-out liar. I typed a *115* report based on an incident she claims happened when an inmate sexually harassed her. The named inmate received a *115* and was also rolled up and sent to another facility—a *114-D*. I was actually there and witnessed the encounter—it simply never happened. What did happen was the inmate refused to do what she had asked—refusing an unreasonable request from her—and she retaliated. As a Christian, I can forgive her. I'm not sure the involved inmate can be as forgiving. Oh, she's a lousy cook, too. If you don't know what you're doing . . .

Time goes by, so slowly. And time can do so much . . .[5]

---
5 From *Unchained Melody*, Alex North and Hy Zaret. A popular song most remembered for the *Righteous Brothers* version. Originally written as the theme song for a 1955 movie about prison, titled *Unchained*.

Time is malleable, Einstein was right. My first three years seemed to take forever. The last year went by much faster, and the final few months were a blur. There's a lot of sitting around in prison—COs, inmates, free staff—plenty of sitting around. Employees mark time by the number of eight-hour shifts, while inmates measure it in years, months, and, finally, days and hours.

Crapulveda's many philosophical musings on time and other issues became laser-clear to me one morning during chow. As the inmates trekked through the line, Crapulveda assumed his normal position of sitting on a tabletop, supposedly watching to ensure no inmate took extra food. That he had only a few weeks left before retirement was his preoccupation. Like many COs, Crapulveda fixated on his watch or a clock most of the day. He spent much effort avoiding actual work while maintaining a very full schedule of *looking* busy. This day, he looked pale, clammy, and pasty. Within a few more seconds, he was on the floor. In minutes, he was loaded into an ambulance for transport to the hospital. He apparently was having chest pain.

I knew we would never see him again when I heard the story—not about his chest pain, but the narrative ending his JDCR career. Correctional Officer Crapulveda, as supply officer for the facility, never gave up the keys to the supply room, even when he was on vacation for a few weeks. When I heard he had called in another CO while he was lying in the emergency room awaiting the results of his test, I knew I would never see him again. Crapulveda, the anecdote goes, lying quietly on the gurney, summoned the officer to his bedside, and with a large grin handed them over—the keys. He gave up the keys—a miracle. The symbolism was clear. Crapulveda retired right there. With six weeks to go and plenty of accrued sick time and holiday time, he never entered the prison again. No more sneaking out of work, checking his watch, or looking busy when he wasn't. He was done. Time is important to correctional officers as well as inmates.

"They have the watches, we have the time."

Chapter 18: Back to the Future?

Prediction is very difficult, especially about the future

NIELS BOHR

The future ain't what it used to be

YOGI BERRA

Any fool can face a crisis;
it's the day-to-day living that wears you out

ANTON CHEKHOV

"Check."

I stared at Mr. Kim. I'd been daydreaming, certainly not paying attention to the chess game at hand.

"Check? How'd that happen?"

Surveying the board, I soon realized this game was hopeless.

"I think you've won this one," tilting over my King in defeat. I found myself drifting off into the thoughts of the future more each day, as I got closer to my release date.

"Play another? You don't seem to be paying attention," my young protégé observed.

"Naw," shaking my head. "Mr. Kim, do you know Plato and Aristotle?"

"What dorm are they in?"

"Never mind." I guess the ancient Greeks didn't make it to South Korea, either.

"What are you going to do first, when you get out?"

"Ah, Mr. Kim," I confided. "That is to be determined. I know I'm going to kiss the ground and my wife—not necessarily in that order. Finding a place to live and then a job are the big priorities."

"Will it be hard?"

"Probably. But I'm looking forward to it." I truly was. "I'm at peace with the world. Are you?"

"I don't know." Kim sat in silence.

I broke the quiet, "Since I'm leaving soon, do you have any questions about the office?" I was determined to train those left behind as best as possible, unlike the way I came into the Program Office. I had eighteen months of training invested in Mr. Kim. He was my star pupil and successor-apparent. I was flattered by the new nickname the other inmates had given him . . . "Doc Junior."

Twenty-six days before I paroled, however, and with less than twelve hours' notice, Mr. Kim was abruptly transferred to one of the governor's private prisons.

My friend, Leonard left us with 109 days to go before parole. I'm told he did parole on his day—November 4, 2013—without repair of his hernia. On that day, several of us remaining in the dorm raised a glass to him—actually a brown, plastic cup of non-alcoholic beverage of our individual choice. We wished him the best, not knowing what his future held.

"To Leonard," I held my cup high.

"To Leonard," five or six others echoed.

"To the future," I added.

Pitr interjected, smiling as always, "For all of us."

"Do you know about the conflict between the philosophies of Plato and Aristotle?"

"Enlighten me," John smiled, one day in the visiting area.

"Well, Plato advocated for the ideal when confronted with a problem. Aristotle was more real world and pragmatic. They both . . ."

"Were ancient Greeks," John interrupted. "Lived a couple of thousand years ago. What's that have to do with us? And why do you ask me?"

"Because you are my resident mentor, my philosopher-king."

"Uh," he frowned. "Are you sure about that?"

"I've got a fair amount of Plato in me—I strive for the ideal. Take the forms issue with Crapulveda, or the pay inequity. I want to right the wrongs."

"Oh, Doc," John sighed. "That's all very commendable, but they aren't your issues anymore."

"But they haven't been righted."

"Why you? Why are you the only one to fight the battle? They aren't even relevant to you now, but you still want to charge ahead."

"It's why I get out of bed," I leaned forward.

"Let me ask you something," John sat down, looking me straight in the eye. "Why are you here?"

"You know why. I've told you the story . . ."

"Not the story. The 'why' behind the story."

"Because I made a mistake?"

"Yeah. So did everyone in here," John shrugged. "Look deeper. What do we Christians call a mistake?"

"A sin."

"Correct. What is your sin, Doc? What did you do wrong? Are you correcting it?"

I paused for a moment, reflecting on the question. "I'm not sure what you mean."

"Your sin isn't what you might think it is. Your sin is arrogance, a lack of humility."

"Go on," I hesitated.

"Your need to control everything—to right the wrongs, as you say. It's a symptom of arrogance, not to mention your impatience and intolerance. You think you're the only one that can fix a problem. Do you ever let anyone else have a chance? It's one thing to be efficient. It's another to be a control freak. And judgmental? When you don't give someone a chance, or if you do, you're too impatient to let him work through the problem. You jump his case, criticizing and telling him how you'd do it. Jesus taught that we must love our brothers and sisters. How is being judgmental, intolerant, impatient, and arrogant a demonstration of your love?"

I sat there, stunned. What could I say?

"Judge not, lest you be judged," my mentor advised. "I'm being hard. Your motives are pure, but your execution isn't. Why are you here, I ask again?"

"I'm not sure what you're asking."

"You're here because God wants to get your attention," John warned. "The specifics of your case aren't important to Him. Getting you to see your character flaws is. Recognition is the first step to correcting them. Are you starting to see the light?"

I was a mixture of emotion—embarrassment, hurt, resentment, even anger. I also understood what he was saying. "Yes, John. I hear you. It's been my career—my job—to solve other people's problems. That's what doctors do."

"No kidding," John nodded with sarcasm. "While it may be necessary at work, you don't leave that control there. It infiltrates everything you do. You can't solve all the problems of the world, Doc."

"I can try—I should try, shouldn't I?"

"I tell you what. I'll make a deal with you," John smiled. "When you doctors solve all the doctor problems 100% of the time, then you come find me and we'll talk about fixing the world. Damn doctors, playing God all the time."

"Am I that bad?"

"No. It's called being human. Let your humanity through in place of that analytical-problem-solver-cold-as-ice demeanor." John put his hand on my shoulder. "Each of us needs a friend to guide us through our pains. That's what I'm here for," squeezing me lightly.

"Think about it," he said, standing up to return to his duties, "it's not about Plato and Aristotle. It's about you, your family, and friends, and God. Spend some of your free time thinking about your future. I'm sure your wife would appreciate that."

Who am I? Why do I get out of bed? What do I look forward to on release? Has my time here changed me? My family? My friends? Even my accusers?

All the questions John asked filled my head. I was perplexed, as he had cut to the essence of my incarceration. What John was asking me to do was put my time here in perspective and evaluate whether I'd changed. I knew I had changed. Had I changed for the right reasons? If I had, could I remember why in the future and live by it? This crisis of spirit had to be resolved before I left or my time here was wasted.

Lying on my bunk thinking about how John had challenged me became my preoccupation during my last few months. We live in the day, learn from the past and plan for the future. However, if I've learned anything from my prison experience, it's to be flexible. My time did make me less of a control freak—but old habits die slowly.

"You can't lead trump," Pitr frowned at our new tablemate, his frown quickly replaced by his perpetual smile.

"Oh, sorry."

"Whiskey" had arrived only a few weeks ago from the Jasco Reception center. No one knew much about him. He was young—aren't almost all of them? Quiet and lonely—who here isn't?

"*Jew* has played before, *jes?*" Face queried.

"Let me translate," I smiled. Face blushed. "My friend Face wants to know if you've played Hearts before."

"Yeah, a few times," Whiskey responded. "I learned in county.

"I *remember the day I died.*"

"No, no. Not again," Pitr groaned. "Why did Stinky have to leave? He'd shut you up."

"You died?" Whiskey was gullible . . . he hadn't heard my story.

"No," Face raised his hand, looked at me and made a slicing gesture across his throat. "*Jew don comprendé*, no understand. *El médico es loco.*"

"I*t was November 3, 2009."*

"Over four years ago?"

"Don't listen to him," Pitr shook his head—but still smiling. "He's very much alive. In fact, I've seen a big change in old Doc since he arrived.

Before he left, Stinky talked with me about my change. As a grizzled veteran of many years in the system, he said he thought he'd seen it all—all until I came along.

"Yeah, Doc," Pitr continued, "you've changed. I don't care how many times you deny it. You've changed and for the better, I think."

"*It was 3:37 p.m. In the afternoon.*"

"What?" The new kid asked.

"*Ay, el loco,*" Face exclaimed.

"Our friend here thought he had died when he was sentenced to prison," Pitr counseled our newest member. "Isn't that right, Doc? He might've come close to dying. But he didn't. Then we got hold of him, taught him a new language, and a few tricks of the trade . . ."

"I taught you guys a thing or two, as well," I added.

"Yes, you did," Pitr continued. "He learned about the green line . . ."

"What's that?" The new kid was as green as the line—just as I had been once upon a time.

"Another newbie?" Pitr laughed, looking at Face and me. "There's a separation between the inmates and the guards. Except old Doc here, managed to tippy-toe back and forth across it like no one else. Are you gonna play another card, Whiskey?"

Self-conscious, Whiskey quickly played a low club. "How'd he get away with it?"

"Don't you try it," Pitr advised. "Doc's kinda different. Somehow, he was able to gain the confidence of the cops. You can't."

"You said he *was able* to," Whiskey scrunched his forehead. "Not anymore?"

"*Mi amigo es going a la casa,*" Face beamed. "He es going home."

"I don't think I'll ever go home," Whiskey slumped down.

"That was me four years and three months ago," I patted my new acquaintance. "Prepare for getting released, starting right now. Make your time here a learning experience. Improve your skills. Read. Take classes. Do something to keep your mind not just occupied but also developing. Make this as positive an experience as you can."

"That's how he crossed over the green line," Pitr instructed. "Not many guys do that in here. They fall into bad habits . . ."

"Or renew old ones."

"Yeah," Pitr continued. "What Doc's trying to tell you is this time is a chance to turn yourself around."

"It's an audition for the real world," I added. "You can't do something out there if you can't do it in here. Do you read much?"

"Naw."

"Come see me later and we'll talk," I advised, playing a low club on my associate's card.

The hand progressed without event, as did the game. Playing Hearts passed the time, but it seemed like small-ball to me now. After the game, Pitr and I were walking back to our bunks, just the two of us. "Pitr, can I ask you a question?"

"Sure."

"How old are you?"

"Thirty-five." "And you've been here . . ."

"Since I was eighteen, seventeen years I've been in. Why?"

"You've always got a smile on your face and you're always in good spirits," I noted. "I'm curious how you've maintained that. Maybe some of it will rub off on the new guy. Can I ask why you're here?"

Still smiling, Pitr looked at me directly, studying me. "Double murder. They wanted to give me the death penalty."

I know he saw my face turn white. "The lawyers got it reduced to manslaughter."

"I'm. . . "

"Speechless? Funny thing is," still smiling, "I had nothing to do with it."

"What?"

"Part of being in a gang."

"The lawyers couldn't get the truth out?"

"Truth? Are you kidding? The judge, the D.A., everyone knew I had nothing to do with it," Pitr stared at me.

"They still went after you though?"

"There is no justice. I took the rap for someone else. That's what the youngsters do."

Later that day, Whiskey came by my bunk while I was reading. In his early twenties, he was confused and had that deer-in-the-headlights look, unsure of what to say, who to say it to, or when. I knew the feeling well.

"I'm guessing you have questions," was my lead.

He sat for a minute, not knowing if it was OK to talk. Painfully, slowly, he took a deep breath and spewed forth, "I'm scared to death," he whispered. "Everything I do, I'm scared I'm doing the wrong thing or insulting someone. I don't wanna get beat up."

In his deep green eyes, I saw the surrounding red sclera of someone only momentarily holding back the tears. He was rail-thin with light brown hair, shoulder length, clearly needing a haircut—and no tattoos. That told me he wasn't a gangbanger.

"No one's gonna beat you up. I promise. If you're respectful and don't get into debt you'll be fine. Listen to the guys in here. Observe. You're gonna see substance abuse, irresponsibility, violence, and stuff you didn't think you'd ever see. You have to decide what you want to make out of this situation. Yeah, I know it's hard and not something you'd pick. But it can be a learning experience like no other."

Tense, Whiskey blurted out a familiar fear, one I'd had many times. "I don't wanna die in here. I can't see ever getting out."

"How much time do you have?"

"Five years at 85%."

"Just like me," I observed. "Look up at the stars. You see your end as farther than one of those stars. I did, too. I kept plodding through, day by day. One day I turned around and could see tomorrow, just over the horizon. Now when I look at the stars, that's where I've been, not where I'm going. So will you."

"I can't even find the stars."

"You will," I continued. "It's a big universe. You can make this hard or easy, it's your choice. You can make this a positive experience or a negative one. Did you do anything before coming here—did you have a job?"

Now the tears began to flow as he pounded my locker like a jackhammer batters concrete. "I was in my final semester in college. I was about to graduate with a degree—in criminal justice. I was gonna be a cop." Whiskey tried in vain to hide his tears.

"I've been in your shoes," patting my bunk to get him to sit down, I put my hand on his shoulder. Funny, how there's a thin line between right and wrong, being caught and getting away with something, cop and inmate. In here, the staff isn't much different from the inmates, most just haven't been caught. No one thinks it can happen to him.

"I really was—am—a doctor. I lost my license and everything else—house, possessions . . . everything. You know what? I'm happier today than I was the day before my nightmare began. You know why? I discovered what was really important—family, friends. And above all, faith and hope. Do you believe in God?"

"I think so," Whiskey sniffed back the tears. "How could He do this to me?"

"He didn't. You did. But He's there for you if you let Him in. I'm not trying to be a preacher, but God made the rules of the universe we have to abide by. He also gave us free will. We get to choose what we do—no matter whether it's right or wrong—and we have to accept and pay the consequences. The rules are still there. When we break 'em, we pay a price. Not always at that moment, but we do pay for it in God's eyes. That's how He helps us learn. You made a wrong choice . . ."

"All I did was go to a bar to celebrate finishing school. Some prick tried to cut in while I was dancing with this girl . . ."

"You hit him?"

"Yeah. I was drinking. Too many whiskey sours."

"That was your choice," I looked Whiskey in the eyes. "Reminds me of Mr. Kim," I muttered in no particular direction.

"Who?"

"Nothing. Someone you don't know," shaking my head. "God gives each of us choices in hopes we'll follow His commands. Sometimes we do. Many times we don't. We are all sinners. Take this time to improve who you are. You think your life is . . ."

"It's ruined," Whiskey interrupted. "I wasted all that time in school . . ."

"No it's not," I insisted. "They can take the diploma away from you—and maybe only temporarily—but they can't take the knowledge or the experience. You just have to learn to apply it differently."

As he sat, I thought some of what I said was sinking in. After a moment, he raised his head, "What I need right now are my possessions—from R&R. I'm gonna write a *602*. You good at that?"

I laughed aloud, thinking of Leonard. "You don't need to write a *602*."

"But how am I gonna get my stuff?" Pounding on the locker again, "I'm so pissed off at these bastards . . ."

"Do you really think holding on to that anger will get your stuff back?"

"Well, I . . ."

"Holding on to anger is like drinking poison and expecting someone else to die—just let it go."[6] I smiled again, thinking of Leonard—how he loved that line.

"If you really want your stuff, don't write a *602*," I advised.

What ensued was a detailed discussion of why writing a *602* was not the best course of action, with a tip of the hat to Leonard.

"Wow. I had no idea about *602s*," Whiskey stood up to leave.

"Hey, Whiskey. When did you get here?"

"On New Year's Day."

"On a holiday? Geez." One truism of the penal system—the buses never stop.

"One last thing."

---

6 Felice Dunas

"Yeah?"

"Get a new nickname."

What about my future? John was right. That should be my prime concern. I was contemplating not only my future but also that of my family and friends at home. How had this affected them? I know that I am at peace with what it holds because I face it with the support of the "Big Three"—faith in God, family, and friends. I learned that material possessions don't compare to the spiritual possessions of the heart and soul.

I was also contemplating the future for my acquaintances in JRC and the future of "the system." I'd lived with these guys for a long time. Still, I felt like I didn't even know them. How can you live for years in a dorm of eighty-six men and not know much about any of them? Doesn't each have an "everyman" characteristic? After spending years with them, I've identified several "group everyman" characteristics.

Irresponsibility is high up on the list, as few take responsibility for anything. They blame everyone and everything but themselves. Most are poorly educated, but few are dumb, and not much interested in bettering themselves. To be fair, a few were, but didn't know how, and the system certainty offered little, if any, help. "The system"—both judicial and penal—is mired in the bog of bureaucracy.

These weren't my primary issues,—John was right about that. I simply couldn't stop thinking about them—they gnawed at me. On an intellectual basis, I knew I couldn't control these issues.

One thousand five hundred thirty-three days. That's what I endured—along with my wife and family, and my ever-faithful friends. Four years and three months. Had I learned 37,272 hours of humility? Or 2,236,320 minutes worth of patience? Or 134,179,200 seconds of truths? Is that time really so long in God's universe? In a universe where the closest stars are billions or trillions of miles away, time on Earth pales by comparison—a snap of the divine fingers. Moreover, how do you measure infinity? Remember to look at the stars.

"Twenty-five Low!"

The shout-out reverberated through the dorm, waking me from what had been a restless night. I stumbled to dress and headed to the CO's office.

"Now. R&R," Ofuati beamed. "Good luck," extending, his hand. We shook . . . another gesture of respect—touching.

I gathered my small plastic bag of possessions—my Bible, two books, a tube of ChapStick®, a few papers, and dress-out clothes—and headed into the light of day. As I walked down the two flights of stairs from my dorm to the front of Facility A –"the Hotel"—I couldn't help but sense a wave of melancholy washing over me. *How do you have nostalgia for any part of prison?* After one last look around, I walked across the street to Receiving and Release. It was a bright, sunny winter day. It was the future.

It was February 3, 2014. At 8:29 a.m. On a glorious morning. This day I am to be reborn.

Reborn all right.

Except it didn't happen that way—the way a novel should end.

Inmates being released are called around 8 a.m. to R&R. I watched through the dorm windows as ten or so lined up to enter. My name wasn't called. I checked with Ofuati. Yep. I was on the list. Enough of this. I had been the lead clerk—I knew who to go talk to—Davis Bendington, the CC-II.

Bendington seemed perplexed as to why I was still here, and made a call to an unknown at the other end of the phone line. Pleasantries exchanged, a few uh-huhs, and he turned to me, "All set. They'll call you before 9 a.m. If you don't get called, come back, but they assured me everything is OK."

Lying on my now-empty-and-stripped, soon-to-be-filled bunk was tough. I looked at the wall clock every one or two minutes. When 9 a.m. rolled around, I lay there another fifteen minutes to make sure—the new, patient me.

Nothing.

By 10 a.m., still nothing. Back up to Bendington, who made more calls and was perturbed himself. More reassurances. This went on every hour until 2 p.m. In the meantime, my wife and a few close friends nervously endured the same wait—having arrived at the gate around 8:30 a.m.

Finally, *finally!* I was called to R&R. Turns out JDCR owed me $135 and the reason for the delay was utterly ridiculous . . . they couldn't find someone to sign the check. Bendington's eventually located the person responsible for signing these checks, who assured him he would handle it. I guess I was lucky he wasn't out sick . . . or dead.

"They"—nameless still—could keep the lousy money as far as I was concerned. If I'd only known. *I should write a 602.*

Just let me out!

At 3:30 p.m., after the obligatory release hassles, I stepped into the light. Having hugged and kissed my wife, as I climbed into her SUV ready to head home for the first time in nearly five years, I suddenly realized that John had inadvertently overlooked one of the *four* Fs . . .

FREEDOM, FAITH, FAMILY, and FRIENDS

I will dwell in the house of the LORD forever

Harding's Photo Album

Figure 1. Dorm Entrance Hallway (looking out from the Dorm)

Through the locked gate at the end of the hallway, one enters a dorm. An inmate in "blues" is headed to the CO's office, just past the outgoing mailbox on the right. The door on the right closest to the gate leads to the dayroom. In the background on the left are two doors to the game rooms — one for Whites and Hispanics, another for Blacks and Others.

One of the two phones can be seen on the wall to the left and the door in the foreground on the left is the Counselor's office — except our Counselor never used the office. Bulletin boards and display cases behind locked glass are also visible.

Figure 2. Dorm Correctional Officer's Office

    Looking through the window of a gameroom door from just inside the entry gate to the Dorm. An inmate stands half in — half out of the CO's office. Ideally, he should have a "shadow," but who knows why he doesn't? A bulletin board and the outgoing mail box can also be seen.

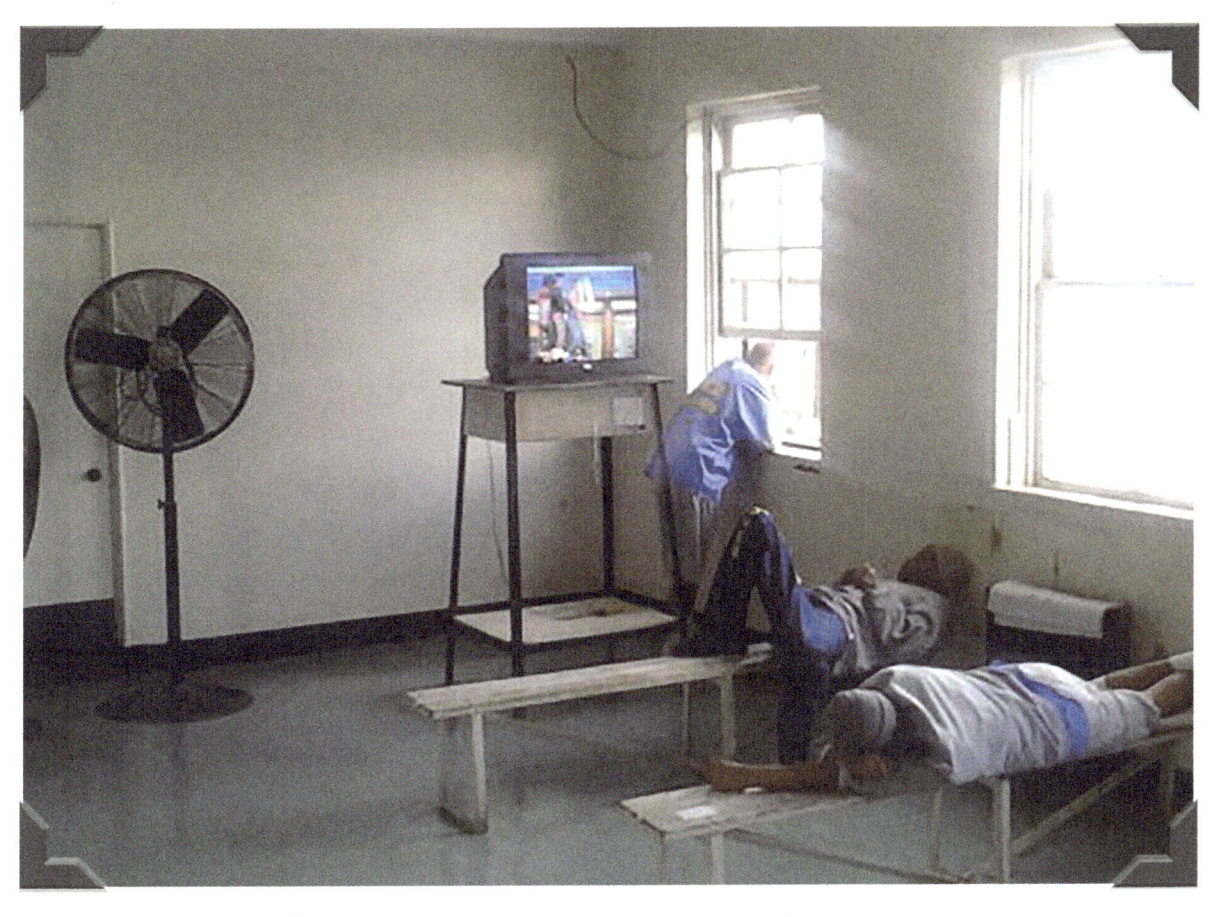

Figure 3. The Dayroom, with a View to Nowhere

    This is the TV that causes so much angst over which channel to watch on a daily basis — White, Black, Hispanic or whatever day.

    An inmate looks out the window overlooking the 'A' gate entrance to the "hotel."

    The fans are a lifesaver in the summer. Note the small, white card on the benches where inmates are lying. Those are inmates' seat "reservations" for the Friday night movie. The towel is drying over the radiator — turned on for about six months during the winter. They also doubled as great food heating stations.

    If your bunk was close to a radiator, you wanted the window open all the time. If you weren't next to a radiator, you froze from the window being open.

Figure 4. A View to a Hill

    Since the "hotel" sat atop a hill — more like a modest rise above the surrounding ground level — inmates were able to gaze out toward the real world through these grated windows.

    The windows were almost always open year — 'round. Since I was housed on the third floor, this provided a constant breeze through the dorm — great in the summer, not so in the winter.

Figure 5. Stalag JRC

This is the view from the dayroom, overlooking the gate leading to the "hotel." There is razor wire everywhere. I saw an old **Dragnet** TV episode with a scene filmed here in the 1960s. The place was without fences or razor wire. It looked better, but not by much.

The one-story buildings below form the complex known as R & R. This is where inmates enter and leave JRC and where packages are picked up. Turn to the left going out the gate, and a ½-mile long road leads to "the yard." A right turn at the yard takes you to the visiting area in the heart of the "lowers."

Figure 6. Every Prison Needs a Toilet . . .

In this view of the bathroom in my JRC dorm, we see a urinal and two toilets — note the trashcan on top of one. Virtually unbreakable stainless steel, no porcelain. Not unlike a hospital bedpan.

The trash can was a common place to hide pruno — under the trash can liner. The large, square plate behind the toilet has a metal button for flushing, but behind it, there is a mechanism which is used to delay the start of a flush cycle and can also limit the number of flushes.

Figure 7. And sinks . . .

Three sinks on one side of a short wall, three more on the back side. They are opposite the toilets seen in the last picture. Again, all stainless steel. Those rectangular, flat metal pieces above the sinks are "mirrors" – you can't see anything in them. On the edge is a large, blue hamper where discarded clothes are thrown. Each week a daily count is supposed to be taken. Why would someone throw clothes in there? Because they are going home.

Figure 8. And Showers, Community-style

    Notice the black pieces attached to the nozzles — that's rubber hose attached in order to generate a stream. Without it, the showers only spray water rather ineffectively.

    Because the water pipes are so old, the water in the showers and sinks frequently comes out rusty brown and the temperature can be hot, cold, or anywhere in between those extremes — all in the course of one shower. During one stretch, there was no hot water for months while "repairs" were being made.

    This is the same area is where I found "Tiny" in a coma. It is also the general area where "discipline" is administered.

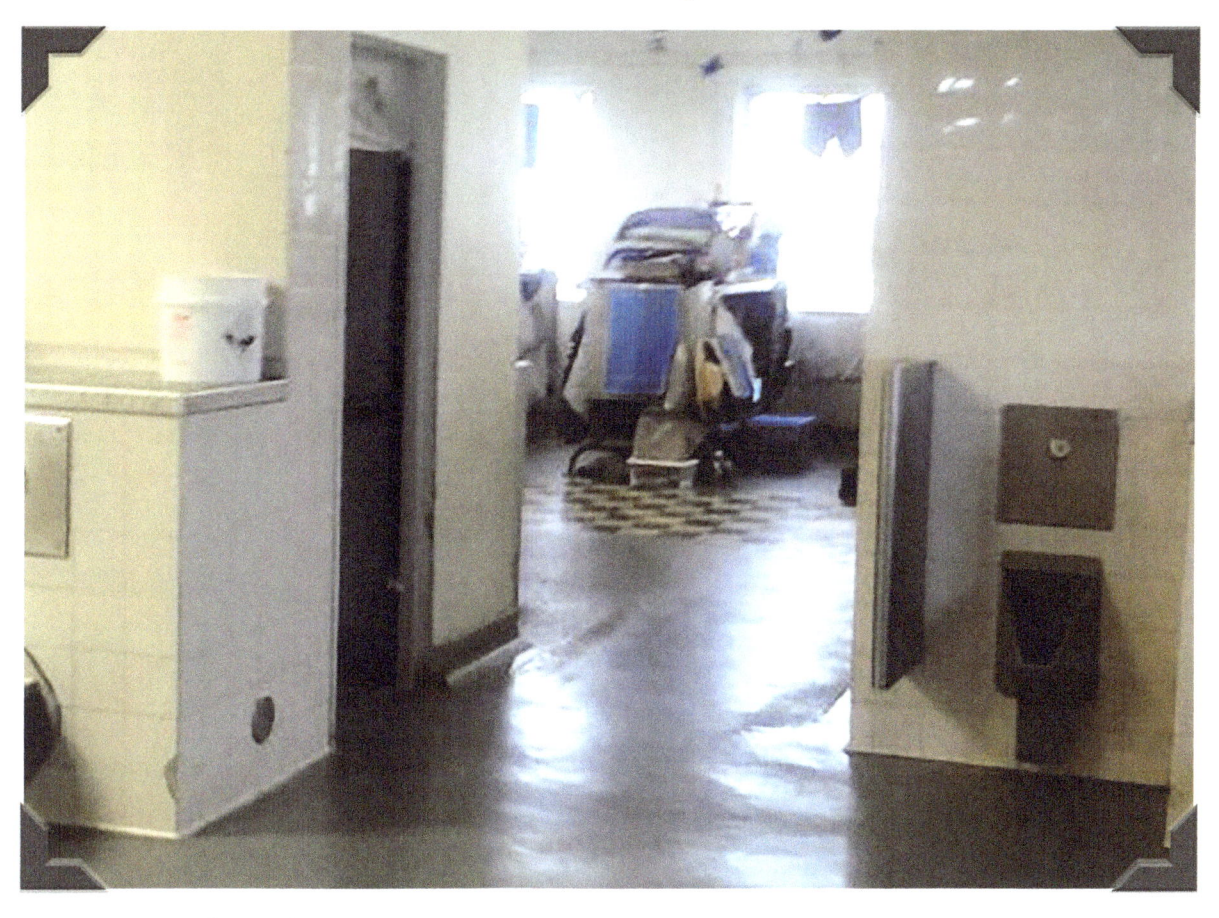

Figure 9. Scenic View of the Dorm

Looking out the bathroom into the Dorm, on the left just barely visible is the second bank of toilets. On the right is one of two urinals. The view from the Dorm in this direction isn't necessarily as scenic. The door on the left is that of the infamous "Jack Shack."

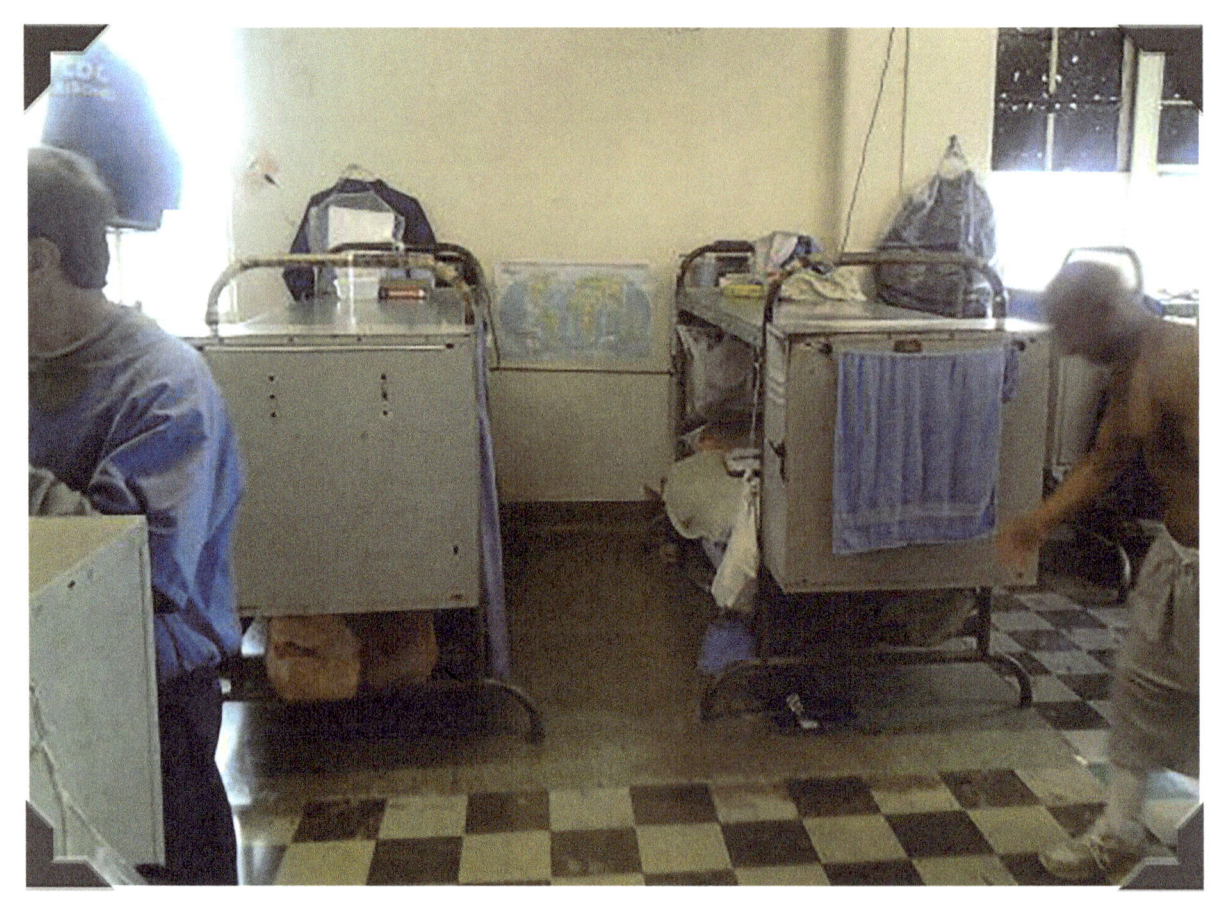

Figure 10. Double Beds, Prison — style

    The narrow space between double bunks like these is where I first met "Tiny." Two occupants to a bunk — one up, and one down, unless you get a "Cadillac." That's where the top bunk is blocked to meet the state overcrowding rules — the rules that are subject to change at any time. I was lucky enough (and had enough juice) to get a "Cadillac" my last two years.

    You can barely see the small locker at the front and back. All your possessions must fit in a single, six cubic foot locker a rule that was occasionally enforced by inspections — random and inconsistent. Since there isn't enough room, old laundry bags are repurposed into hanging spaces. Towel racks are also improvised.

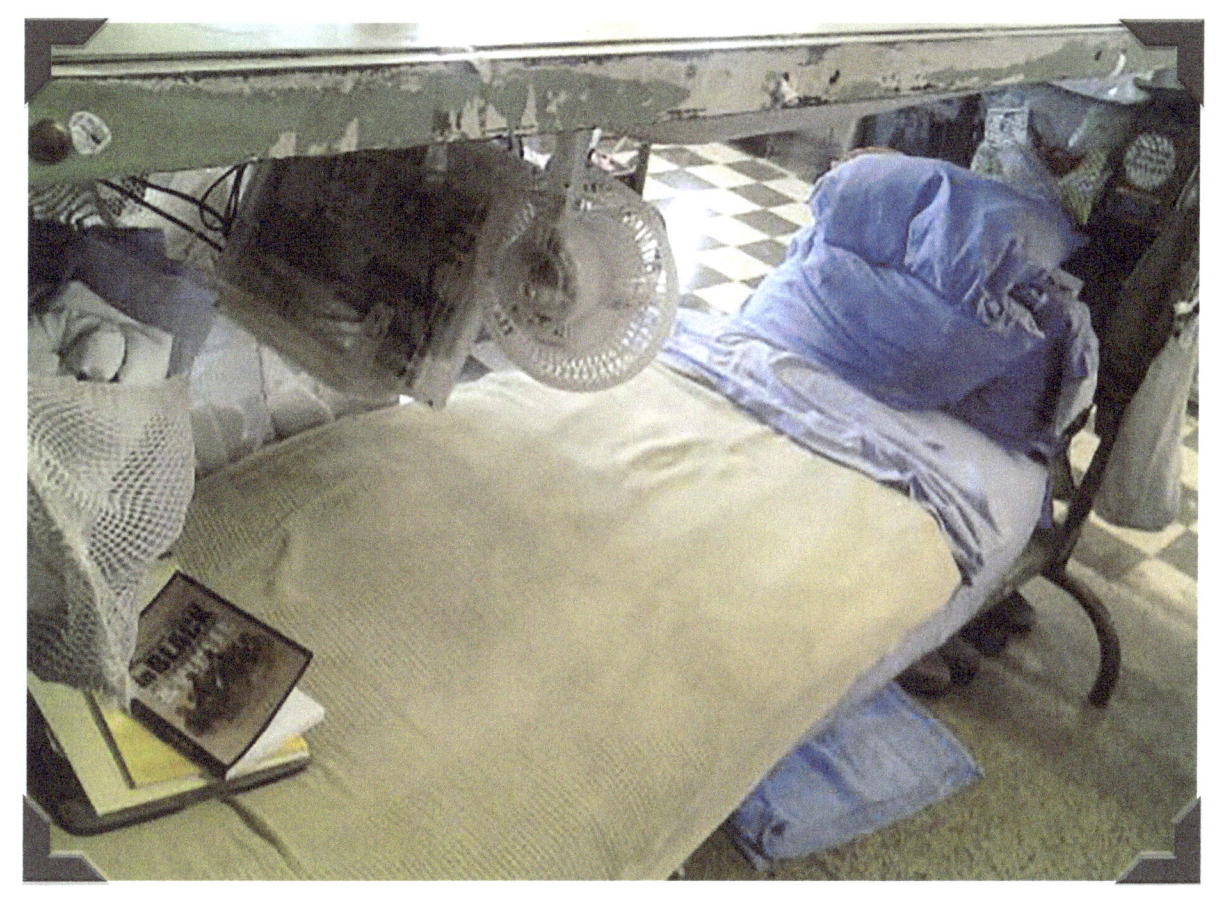

Figure 11. "Settled In"

This inmate is settled in, indicating some time has elapsed since his arrival. Notice the laundry bags hanging filled with personal things and three "pillows" — actually several coats stuffed into each of three pillowcases.

Inmates are only allowed one real pillow, so this fellow has improvised. The personal fan and 13" TV are added personal touches, ordered through a quarterly package. Notice the clear case of the TV, intended to minimize the transport or storage of contraband items.

The Dorm was originally built to house 44 inmates. It once routinely housed as many as 88. During my time at JRC thanks in part to the "Cadillac," full occupancy was never less than 76.